RING AROUND THE ROSARY
The Memoir of a Girl, a Nun, a Wife, and a Mother

Wild with imagination, yet blinded by Church formulas, her life was in chaos. She was in over her head. Attempting second, third, and fourth acts, and like playing multiple roles on a stage, the author was ideally raised by two devoted Catholic parents in her first act. She unintentionally walled herself off from life in her second act, only to run head-long into an enticing marriage for her third. Scrambling for a fourth act, this time alone with two sons, she hunted for a spiritual resurgence, one without the former constraints of powerful others, but most unfortunately, also without the seduction of the creative life her husband ignited. With sheer pluck and determination, she stayed the course until she found her way.

Ring Around the Rosary

[handwritten signature] xo

7-28-14

RING
around the
ROSARY

THE MEMOIR OF A GIRL, A NUN,
A WIFE, AND A MOTHER

GRETCHEN GROSSMAN

For my family of four

Remember always that you not only have the right to be an individual, you have the obligation to be one. —Eleanor Roosevelt

Prologue

I began writing this book after twelve years of Catholic education with my family, five years of convent life, eight years as a wife, and thirty-five years as a mother. Now I'm a grandmother.

I knew I had to get my life back together to become free within myself.

Writing was a way to unburden my jumbled thoughts, writing anything that came to mind. I made envelopes and categories: school, church, convent, marriage.

Once retired, I did substitute teaching, took trips to New York and San Francisco to see family, got together with a few friends, but outside of that, I stayed home. I did the laundry, cleaned my house, planted enough flowers, and exercised. My neighbors likely thought of me as reclusive. My envelopes filled up.

Then the writing began. Page after page. Pages and revisions. I finished my book in a couple of years. I found my first editor, Alice Peck, in New York. I emailed her, telling her what I had. She thought my story sounded compelling and wanted to read it. I shipped her my 190,000 word manuscript. Four different times over four years, she pored over my words. She cut, condensed, rearranged, questioned, probed, and extracted the heart of the story, all the while my anguished soul slowly came to terms with my past. Valerie Romack, an editor based in Chicago, also wanted a look at my book. She focused on detail and movement for five months. She wove it tighter, adding flair and personality. Valerie taught me how to recognize non-essential elements in my writing. She strengthened the story by teaching me gesture, building character, and questioning the quality and worthiness of every word, phrase, sentence, and thought. She became both my confidante and psychologist. Both editors knew me better than I knew myself. Alice then, brought the book to completion. I had no idea what editors did. They don't hold your hand. They put you to work. They push for explanation. They respect your style and your words. They teach you how to write better. I sat in front of my computer for seven years. Some of that time I took breaks and waited on responses from agents.

Now that the book is finished, should I have it published? Will I hurt my family? My friends? The Church?

Who and what is the priority here? Who will be helped if it's published? Me?

My achievement is realized, my life is now at peace. Others who, whatever their mental or physical prison, may see themselves in these pages and take heart, this is really anyone's story. Everyone has problems to solve. Could this book be your "Maria"?

Chapter 1

Every summer a carnival came to our Illinois town. It threatened more calamity than the local amusement park. Natural instinct dictated that I cling to my mother rather than wander off amid the temptations of sin and debauchery. One time though, I got jostled about in a throng of strangers' legs and lost sight of her. In and around me, girls chased and taunted boys, kicking up rusty tufts of dust. Rough-and-tumble teens glommed onto each other and bumped past me. Shrieks and shouts from rides deafened from every direction. Honky-tonk music beckoned revelers. A scantily dressed woman clung to her unshaven boyfriend in his wife-beater t-shirt, a cigarette teetering between his lips. Strong scents permeated the air. "Mother!" I wailed, near hysteria and absolutely rooted to the dirt ground.

After what seemed a long time she reappeared with my brother and sisters, the picture of comfort and beauty amid the chaos. "Honey!" she said. "Stay right here next to me and hang onto my skirt. Don't let go again."

That traveling cacophony that blew into town for a weekend then disappeared overnight, was dirty, sweaty, noisy, wild, yet tantalizing. I was puzzled as to why my otherwise sensible mother wanted to expose us kids to the seedier side of life. She bred us to crave things of good order. My hair, for example, was forever tightly braided, my clothes specially chosen and ironed for the day, reliable shoes tied on my feet, my presentation was always appropriate, all thanks to my mother's meticulous grooming skills. Carnivals represented an element of messiness and peril. If I wasn't safely tethered to her hemline, I might have been snatched from that place by a stranger. I usually threw up at carnivals.

My nature and her nurture corralled me within predetermined city blocks at home. Whether riding bikes or trudging into the neighborhood woods, all adventures were within given boundaries. I liked for things to be dependable. Even in our cavernous church with all its mystery, I still felt the safety of an established culture that honored a loving God.

But, anxiety grasped hold of me around the age of seven. Inside St. Boniface where peace reigned supreme, my eyes darted all around as I incessantly sought repetitive things to count. It satisfied some need and brought me inner calm in that place of symmetry. I counted lights, pillars, windows, statues, and all decorations. I didn't have enough digits for the amount of recurring shapes in that holy place. Over and over I reviewed: twelve stained-glass windows depicting scenes from the Bible, six colossal decorative pillars, four smaller ones that held up the choir loft, hundreds of gold-leaf fleur-de-lis that bordered everything, twenty-four sparkly clusters of glass lights that hung from the ceilings at equal intervals, dozens of red and black diamond patterns on the substantial linoleum floor, and over sixty oak pews front to back. The highly ornate altar of white and gold was flooded in lights and candles and I counted all of them. If I missed any or got interrupted I started over. Since Mass was long and I didn't understand it, I engaged my soothing habit of counting.

A grandfatherly God stared down at me from His stained-glass throne. The window pictured Him holding a large leather-bound book in His lap. His pure white hair flowed beyond His shoulders and His eyes focused solely on me. I watched the window's colored shapes momentarily project a dancing carnival mask onto people's faces, and then I turned toward the front like a good girl. Swinging one leg back and forth, the toe of my black-buckled shoe tapped the padded kneeler at the base of the pew in front of me. At specific intervals throughout the service, the congregation would rise all at once and then kneel in place. To me, the routine was like making my bed or brushing my teeth. If I didn't perform each ritual, then I probably disappointed God.

A deep breath pulled in expensive perfume scents from the surrounding women, some adorned with furs. Very devout, they knelt up straight, their hands folded delicately, and their eyes rested shut. I knew God was impressed.

Because silence was valued during worship, I matched my own behavior to its quiet. The echo of a priest reading in a language known to be dead in the world, bounced off the rafters and made the church a solemn place. I'd practice restraint in church, even suppress a sneeze, because any sudden sound would join the host of echoes battling in the air.

I wondered if God controlled the future, because I knew somebody did. And it wasn't me. From the perspective of a youngster, I'd be under the power of others forever. I was accountable for my actions at home too.

I attended that Catholic Church every Sunday from the time I was born. And then after I turned six, every single day except Saturdays for eight more years. Then back to just Sundays for four more. By the time I was seventeen I'd been in that beautiful structure over a thousand times. It was home. I knew every alcove, window, ornament, statue, spire, confessional, and pew by heart. I can still feel the curvature of the polished wood and hear the echoes of Latin music and the low hum of humble prayers. My nostrils sometimes still flare at the phantom scent of burning incense. Behind my eyelids I can still see blessed figures in the stained-glass windows and carved in the heavy marble statues, I can still taste the dissolving words of praise on my tongue.

Now, I look back at that young girl, as if she is a reflection in a mirror. I can see her, but she can't see me. I can't warn her about the choices she'll make. I followed strict discipline as a Catholic, but it caused me more chaos than I ever would have dreamed, the exact opposite of what I wanted. One day I'd reject its rules and regulations, seeking freedom from its restraints, and thrusting myself toward self-actualization, summoning inner strength and definition. With surprises at every juncture, my choices turned out to be my own private carnival.

Chapter 2

I always defined my life experiences according to those two polar opposites—the carnival and the church—my touchstones. One evil. One good. One dangerous. One safe. The first, presented itself with wild abandon. The second, with rules and regulations. Over time though, the first one started to draw me in, and the second one made me nauseous.

My faith absorbed me when I was little. I soaked in its ornate beauty. I entrusted my soul to its every command. I was young, pliable, and I knew the value of obedience. My insides glowed as brightly as a summer's day—something I learned at school. *Your body is a temple of the Holy Spirit.* My catechism—the text that explained the tenets of an ancient religion—became more complex at each grade level, insisting that I was the Church's instrument. I thought of it in a musical sense.

My father was four years old when Germans laid the cornerstone of St. Boniface back in 1900. At that time, all the nuns, priests, and everybody in the parish still spoke their native languages. It's still a charming place in contrast to modern box structures, and those attending Mass find refuge in the familiar architecture. German nuns demanded strict obedience in the school. Their authority was unquestionable. The Church was my father's safe haven through two world wars and the Great Depression. He gave it his undying allegiance ever after.

I liked being cozy in church with my family. Each Sunday morning, my sister Elizabeth read books to me while I squirmed every which way, until my mother whispered, "Sit still, honey. Echoes in church startle people." And she was right. Church was so quiet that if someone hiccupped, everybody knew it. Beautiful music, prayers, and a sermon were the only appropriate sounds. Early on, I practiced slow, restrictive movements like adults.

"Church is too long," I always said.

"Memorize a few prayers and you won't feel left out," Mother always said back, occasionally bouncing my unbraided, fresh curls off the palm of her hand.

But prayers were complicated and a lisp caused words to tangle on my tongue, and I'd go back to studying the gorgeous stained-glass window depicting God and His book.

"Is that a storybook?" I said, pointing a finger.

"Uh-huh," Mother whispered, and nodded. Soaring Gothic ceilings lured my eyes up to the pinnacle, where the curvy moldings all met at the center, too high up to hold my gaze.

"Keep your hat on," Mother said, readjusting it. If I had to sit quietly, I needed something to do. I wanted to sprawl on the floor in the middle of the aisle to satisfy my geometric curiosity and see how all those lovely lines traveled up and where they intersected.

"No turning around," she said when I peered into faces or studied profiles, girth, women's hairstyles, and creases in men's necks.

"Calm down and don't point." Like a spy on a mission, I counted each scallop of the starched, white, embroidered cloths that covered flat surfaces on every altar and along the communion railing left to right, then right to left clear across the front of the church.

"Why can't I bring my coloring book and crayons to church?"

"Not allowed." Mother patted my knees to cease their movement.

I wanted everything to line up symmetrically. If there was a statue on the right side of the church, it needed a partner on the left. I didn't want anyone to be lonely. I longed to climb up and sit next to sweet Jesus in Mother Mary's lap. I imagined that she'd wrap her arms around me gently too, and look at me with that soft smile on her lips.

My eyes continued their trek around the sanctuary. I stared at the woman in front of me. She was a distinguished lady in the Church and wore a fur around her shoulders in chilly months. I tugged on my mom's blouse sleeve.

"Why does she wear dead foxes?" There were three animals entwined in her fashionable stole. Tiny feet—each with four toenails—ears, noses, beady eyes, and swishy tails stared at me from over the lady's shoulder. Sadly I got a lot of counting done on them since her family frequently sat directly in front of ours.

I have heard Mass referred to as the last remaining high drama and pageantry besides opera, and I can see why. It brought magic into my world.

The altar boy rang the bell to signal the start of Mass—foxes cast onto the pews. People stood as the priest and altar boys entered the sanctuary and Latin prayers began. I counted everybody and everything up there too.

"Never recite their words, you aren't worthy," nuns said later when I got into grade school.

I already suspected boys had a step-up with God. In a few years, the Church would elevate the status of women by focusing on an invigorated devotion to The Blessed Virgin Mary. Jesus's mother would serve as the premier icon to all women, her humility worthy of imitation.

Father John addressed the congregation from high up in the pulpit during the sermon, his loud voice echoing like God from heaven. Because Father ran a strong parish, he'd gotten the attention of the Bishop, who elevated his rank to that of a Monsignor. Often, he seemed upset with everybody.

"Is he mad?"

"Not at you."

We have pictures of him in our family album. Young, motivated, he socialized and directed young folks in plays.

"Your father usually played the hero," Mother said, reminiscing.

Monsignor seemed lonely. Occasionally, as we grew up, he'd visit with my dad in our sunroom and share a few beers. I'm certain he finagled my radical career choice after high school. And a personal detail Mother told me about him—after he retired, he moved in with a woman from his past in a small country town—caused me to question every rule the Church enforced. She said, "He's managed Church records, schedules, and liturgies alone. He's had to surrender himself at all times to God's law, so now he deserves some relief and companionship. He isn't hurting anyone and hardly anyone knows, so it's all right." That sounded unfair. I thought God's representatives on earth had to obey a set of rules like we all did. But I heard the sensitive tone in my mother's voice and decided to be happy for him.

"Stop counting, honey," my mother said, as I craned my neck, trying to watch people approach and return from the communion railing. Sometimes, I only counted the kids. Other times, just the men or the women, or those wearing jewelry.

"Stand on your tiptoes and find your brother." I peered between heads and watched him with his pals—boys in black and white cassocks—ring bells and pour liquids from cruets. They followed the priest around as he prayed from a huge book, chanted the Catholic Liturgy in Latin, washed and dried hands, and wiped possible drops of wine from the gold chalice with a holy cloth.

"It has to be real gold. God deserves our best," nuns said.

A High Mass meant the organ and choir music prolonged the service to well over an hour. Some songs froze my body in place as I listened to them: *...qui tolis pecata mundi...dona eis requiem.* Those words were strange, but comforting. I preferred the Walt Disney songs Elizabeth and I listened to that imprinted on our brains forever: *Little bread and butterflies kiss the tulips, and the sun is like a toy balloon.* But the church music was lush and heavy to my ears.

Regardless of the mighty celebration, it was an eternity for a wiggly kid to sit very quietly, look nice, and keep numbers straight. I could hear people sigh from stifling their emotions. It took a great amount of effort to perform as grateful children of God. A spiritual medley streamed through the air, everything done in unison—several hundred voices asking for His blessings, praising His almightiness. The stillness in our church made me want to shout something, like the people in the Holy Rollers' Church around the block from our house. That place left its front doors wide open in summer and Elizabeth and I sat on the curb watching and listening, transfixed. We wanted to go inside, but two little girls stepping into a colorful church alone would have been too amazing. We leapt up and imitated them from across the street before running off. They sure did have fun in there—clapping and singing and swaying with their music. They weren't in the least bit quiet.

Church was a favorite place of mine, a good place. I was a happy Catholic and dutiful child. Holy Mother Church was my Benevolent Protector. We belonged together.

Chapter

 **3**

In 1948, I attended Riverside Public School for morning kindergarten. Kids were lively and untamed in that place. I inhaled the mahogany and modeling clay smell of that old building, and climbed the worn wooden stairs that gave and groaned as each foot took a step. I cried the first week, until I made some friends. Every five-year-old girl in my class was cute as can be, but dear Mrs. Woodward chose me to be Cinderella in her play. I suspect my hair color had something to do with it—fiery auburn that shone gold in the sun. Because Cinderella was the most beautiful and brave princess of them all, I was thrilled, but very surprised, since I was the baby of the family and unaccustomed to being center stage. Now, I'd be a star.

I knew my lines better than a scripture: *I am Cinderella, I wash and cook and scrub, I wait on sister Bella and rub and rub and rub.*

I doted upon my mean stepsisters, who sang: *Tie my shoe, hurry do, make me look so fair, so the prince will dance with me and everyone will stare.*

I'm all covered with ash and soot, from my head down to my foot, I wish I could go, I wish I could go.

I couldn't wait for my older siblings and both parents to witness that shining event, but only my mother came to my performance. I was already assured of her love. Without everyone else, I wouldn't get the attention I needed.

Together, my parents chartered a careful course for our family, one of discipline laced with charm. My dad, the breadwinner, never missed a day of work in forty years. My mother was phenomenal. It would take a thousand pages to write down every wonderful thing she did for me. She was all the things I could wish for in a mom. She was smart, good, loving, and kind, with a caring wisdom that matched her gentle voice. I had an attractive older sister, who always knew what she wanted. She spoke her mind and cut a path from here to there, like a homing pigeon flying in a straight line towards a goal. I had an older brother who enjoyed his enviable status as the other male of the household. He developed a sense of humor that made us peal with laughter at supper, especially once our dad left the table. And then there was my other sister, a year older than me. Elizabeth. Sometimes we were best friends. She never once complained aloud, "Do I have to take my kid sister with me every place I go?" Elizabeth was beautiful—huge hazel eyes, jet-black hair, and olive skin. By contrast, I had red pigtails with nearly straight bangs banked across my forehead, fair skin, and freckles, not necessarily the markings of a princess. But like my mother, Mrs. Woodward thought I was special. That was decades ago. Why do I still obsess over it? In my kindergarten photo, I had long finger curls and was dressed in a pretty gown my mother had made—blue netting and satin with little flowers sewn all over. Any prince would want to marry me. In the play, he stood to my right, my fairy godmother to my left with her wand ready to work some magic. I sat up straight and smiled big in my orange pumpkin, scanning the audience—my kingdom. Life tasted sweet and I thought that starring role forecasted my future events. I got so wrapped up in that play. In my mind, I *was* Cinderella and expected a prince to search for me with my missing shoe in hand. Like a watchful predator, I noticed boys in the neighborhood, the playgrounds, parks, stores, and movie theaters. I examined each one for princely qualities. If I deemed one worthy I crouched, eager to pounce, invading his space as he shot baskets, roamed the woods, and competed in the park for a personal best. Instead of attracting affection, I became a nuisance. I swooned over blond-haired, blue-eyed Howey, the cutest of them all, until my brother finally said, "Go play with the girls."

After kindergarten, I begged all summer to remain at public school. Even at that age, I knew I ought to stay where people thought I was special. But in the fall I began Catholic school. I changed that year. I kind of shrunk. My smile switched to wide-eyed reservation, intimidation, and sometimes a frown on my face mirrored the seriousness of parochial education.

"I'm going to miss the city bus," was my first fret each morning.

"Sit still, honey," Mother said as she finished tying fresh ribbons at the bottom of my braids. I scooted off the seat, grabbed my lunch pail, two bus tokens, and plaid school satchel—homework, rosary, with prayer book inside—and raced out the door to catch up to my siblings, who held the bus every time the driver started without me.

"Sit with your sister," Mother called out.

Being the youngest wasn't a delightful circumstance, since everybody thought they had a natural duty to tell me what to do. "Hurry up," said one sibling. "Wave goodbye," said another, "Don't run across the street," said the third. As the bus rolled by, there stood Mother in her housedress, her hair pulled away from her face by a colored headband, waving from the front steps before returning to tackle breakfast dishes. It was hard leaving her for an entire day. I didn't know how she accomplished her chores without me. Just like my siblings before me, I helped her make grape jelly, bake cookies, and roll out crust for an apple pie, with me lingering next to her waiting to lick the beaters and scrape the bowls of cookie dough. I followed her around all day and listened to Arthur Godfrey and Irna Phillip's *The Guiding Light* on the radio. "You're my best duster," she said as I flitted around the room, feathering the furniture. We took naps together. We wore matching aprons all morning— mine had a bib—and put things in the pockets: stray buttons, a small toy, a random thread the sweeper missed, or a lost hair ribbon separated from the pack.

The bus driver dropped kids off a block from school. "Shh, there's Sister, hurry," Elizabeth said, pointing out the black- robed nun, a guardian of tradition, carrying her load of home- work down the sidewalk, ready to devote herself to a new day.

Just as in kindergarten, in first grade I cried for a week.

"Don't leave me here," I said. Mother sat in the back of the classroom several days in September to reassure me that I was not being abandoned. When I turned around and saw her empty chair, I crossed my arms on the desktop, buried my head, and cried. Not one other kid acted like that. I had lost my glass slipper and nobody cared. I was without my fairy god- mother, prince, coach, and attendants. The magic was over.

In class, I learned that God sometimes got angry. Bible stories told of warnings, floods, plagues, and other dreadful disasters that happened to people if they didn't do what He said. The

Catholic discipline taught students how to avoid sin and please Him. Nuns and priests—God's voices on earth—were around every corner to ensure conformity. From first through eighth grades, all students valued and accepted the rules they set down. When nuns instructed kids, "Bow heads at any mention of Jesus's name," everybody did. When nuns said, "Always capitalize any word that references God," we all did. When they said, "Don't turn around, talk, or even whisper in church," we obeyed. Before entering a pew, each person genuflected perfectly straight without losing balance or holding on, then bent one knee to touch the floor, recited a memorized prayer, and made the Sign of the Cross—the ritual of touching right hand to forehead, chest, and each shoulder, to represent the shape of Christ's cross. It had to be elegant and precise. All prayers had to be recited together, without racing. Classes moved in rigid lines through hallways. Children were quiet all day and worked to the best of their abilities. Even when the entire student body walked downtown for a religious movie about the miracle of Fatima, we were silent. We were obedient. We did as we were told because, "Someday it will be proven," nuns said, "that good behavior produces good lives. You'll see."

No one argued with nuns. It was unthinkable. About once a year when a kid would stray from the righteous path, some goody-two-shoes would rat out the rebel, and subsequent scoldings hinted at eternal damnation and we all quivered in our seats. Breaking the rules was risky. We learned to curtail impulsive behaviors.

The mysterious long black robes of Franciscan nuns—who fashioned their dress and rules after the Twelfth Century Saint Francis of Assisi—swished down halls, through doors, and around corners like dark ghosts. Kids listened for the rattling of beads that hung at each nun's waist from a belt. Nuns were married to God and wore gold bands on their ring fingers to prove it. They didn't resemble neighborhood women I knew, yet calling them Sister gave the impression they were family. I asked about them at the supper table—*Who are their families? Where are they from? Why do they dress funny? Are they happy? Do they know everything? Are priests married to nuns? Do they ever have any fun?* My questions only brought more questions.

Catholic literature was so fantastical, yet so determined. Books described heaven as a flawless paradise, hell as a scorching wasteland, and the Garden of Eden as a luxurious garden. Something didn't sit right with me about these places. First of all, the temptation of Adam in the Garden of Eden suggested the innocence of boys. Eve tricked Adam into sin—the Original Sin. I hated her, until I realized I would have eaten that apple too. I could be easily deceived. Who knew for sure what that snake really told her? Perhaps he said she was beautiful. She must have been flattered. He probably promised her something good, something fun, unlike God with His 'Thou shalt not's'.

Sister said, "Eve was a redhead," and all the kids peered over at me. I lifted my fingers to my hair, subconsciously wanting to cover it up. If my hair was an indication of sinfulness, then I wanted to chop it all off so it wouldn't betray me.

"It's hard making new friends. I'm the only one in school with this color hair. Tell Sister to say that I was a star in kindergarten," as if that was my salvation. One special day, I got recognition, something rare among so many children.

"Mother! Sister chose my art for a contest in Milwaukee!" I burst into the kitchen with excitement. "She said my picture was beautiful. I colored Baby Jesus with curly blonde hair in a garden of big, colorful tulips. Tall green grass was all around. Mother Mary wore pale blue and sat on the ground beside Him holding a bouquet He'd picked for her." I remember everything in that picture was large, filled up the huge paper, and like a Rousseau painting, barely left room for a sky. No one else's artwork had the boldness of color or largeness of design. I felt so much better when I earned that praise. Another time I performed the entire tale of The Little Red Hen on the piano for my classmates. Music and art were my favorite things, and they surrounded me. Mother told everyone that I loved school.

I was good as gold, trying to deflect all negative attention. Gentle Sister Arianna, in her first year of teaching, only got mad at a boy who insisted on pulling my pigtails every chance he got. I loved him, in the combative way that kids show affection. I was convinced all through grade school that he was my prince, though he never saw me as his princess.

It was the paranoia of committing sin that woke me up at night. In second grade, my nightmares switched from menacing cartoons to fiery pits. I rarely approached my dad in the evening, since that was his time to unwind from a hard day's work, but one time I asked him, "Is there really a hell?" He didn't take my question seriously. But it *was* serious. I was petrified.

"Oh honey, I don't know," he said, folding his newspaper momentarily and looking at me. I went to my room, lay down on my bed, and sobbed pitifully into my pillow, as I imagined the horror of that place. I worried about my feet. I reasoned that I could duck away from flames, but I'd need good, sturdy shoes—my brown leather tie-ups would work—to climb through the caves and corridors of hell. I'd seen dreadful pictures at school in my religion book. People were in inescapable peril. They were all naked and red with black, sooty blotches on their skin—just wandering with no destination and clinging to the walls of dark, narrow pathways at the very edges of a precipice towering above a river of flames. The people were being herded by a red devil with a pointy tail and an ugly, insincere smile. It would be noisy there. Screaming and cursing and crying and crashing going on everywhere, forever. Eternity! My arms squeezed my pillow and fear put me to sleep.

My anxious habit of counting structures focused in on a new obsession— counting sins. I didn't want to commit so many that I'd end up with the devil. Though nuns said, "Angels constantly hover nearby and they'll always protect you," my experiences would call that promise into question. How could the angels guard me from God's wrath? Would they abandon me if I sinned?

Pictures in the catechism grouped them like Catholic school kids in a class portrait. They wore benevolent faces and their wings folded tidily behind them. It was comforting to know that if I was at a loss for true friends, I had my own private angel to love me. But I wondered if she had any feelings for me— any loyalty at all—or if she was just doing a job.

"They are messengers of God encircling earth in vast legions," young Sister Chelae said. We believed windy days proved their existence, and she agreed that was legitimate reasoning if it helped us with our faith. Father said angels had pure intellect with unlimited power to do God's bidding and could actually appear before worthy people. Though the catechism insisted they were spiritual, not corporeal beings, it pictured them with long, flowing blond hair and white satin robes edged in gold brocade. It was hard to switch off those visions and think of those celestial creatures as levitating energy or speeding fire and air. Sister said, "They are winged spirits who come in fleets to accompany us down the hallways, to the lunchroom, out on the playground, in class while we study, to and from school, throughout the day, and all night long."

"Your very own guardian angel taps you on the shoulder, whispers in your right ear, and guides your behavior. Satan whispers in your left ear," scary Sister Lucinda said. "Knock that devil off when he tempts you to do bad things," and she brushed her own shoulder to demonstrate. "Tell him to go away and then pray hard." My furrowed brow always proved my earnestness whenever she said, "Work, play, and pray hard." We sang a song to our angels: *Dear Guardian Angel at my side, how loving you must be, to leave your home in heaven above, to guard a child like me.*

One evening, my guardian angel betrayed me. My siblings and I, along with two neighbor girls, walked home from the downtown movies on a Sunday afternoon. I didn't want to hold anyone's hand.

"I'm telling on you," someone said, an acceptable expectation of the older kids. It was a distant threat, a mere echo in my ears.

By the time we got home though, I'd begun to panic. Instead of going up to our front porch, I tried to walk home with the neighbor girls and hide away forever.

"Gretchen!" my father called out. His voice was deeper and stronger than I'd ever heard. I let go of my escape plan, hung my head low, turned and walked back up the porch steps. I felt around for the handle to the screen door, and peered up just enough to glimpse everyone sitting on the porch staring at me. My dad stood up like a giant, "Go lie down on the couch!" he said and walked into the house ahead of me. I lay there, face-down, hoping to suffocate before he returned. Dread consumed me and I dared to peek to see where he'd gone at exactly the time he came from the bathroom. He folded his razor strap in half, the thick leather cracking together. Everything I saw was enormous—his legs, his hands, and the maroon-colored strap with coarse beige on the other side, held together with hard plastic on one end, a hook to hang it on the tile wall on the other. I squeezed my eyes shut and hid my face with both hands, my body plastered to the sofa. I started crying before he even struck. The first blow landed on my bottom like hot metal and then a stinging, cold as ice, followed. I wanted so badly to scream at him, "I'm just a little kid!"

I lifted right out of my body and hovered overhead to watch the whole thing from a distance of safety. I know there were numerous blows because I saw them from up there. I saw his arm raise, then slam down. The strap was not rigid, but fluid like a wave and held tightly by a man's sturdy hand so it wouldn't slip. I don't remember sound. I saw that young body take a beating no kid deserved. She sucked in her breath. When it was over, her legs and arms curled around like a shield. My father returned the strap to its hook for when he'd shave in the morning. There was only that one fiasco. I wouldn't have known that, of course. A few years later when Mother gave him an electric razor for Christmas, I remember feeling released. Whenever I acted a little too confident though, a little too flibbertigibbet, its memory hung around like a phantom limb, so-to-speak.

I zoomed back into my body as he joined the rest of the family on the porch. I felt so weak and scared. With tears, hiccups, and strangling breaths, I felt the throbbing pain of the blows while my body heaved up and down, trying to return air to my lungs as quietly as possible. I was angry at my father for doing this to me and I hated my angel for deserting me, if she even existed. I was still innocent by years, but I thought I was on my own then. I couldn't be the baby any more. A new life experience, perhaps it gave birth to my people-pleasing trait, gave birth to my conflict with authority, my streak of independence, and confounded me with the opposite sex. But it might have given birth to my strength as well. Like kids apparently do, I was resilient and bounced back. The incident went to where people tuck their secrets. We were a family that always kissed our parents good-bye and good night. I kind of flinched when my dad kissed me. That incident was out of character for him. He didn't mean to do that. He never lifted an angry hand toward any of us kids. If he had to hit, a swat would have made his point, but it would have still upset me. He had always given me unquestionable security and all the symbols of love and devotion. He confused the living daylights out of me that day. I wondered what happened to him, what memory visited him where he felt the need to pound on me over a small infraction. Perhaps his own childhood had been even harder than he'd admitted. He and I put that scenario away forever, under lock and key, never to see the light of day again.

I found entertainment in a fantasy world, trying, I think, to lighten things up rather than brood. I played with dolls practically into high school, no doubt pursuing a way to make that night vaporize certain images, by way of princesses and ballrooms and shiny glass slippers. But sometimes I beat those ragged dolls.

I reached a milestone at age nine by singing divine music in the church choir. It rescued me from the distraction of persistent counting, and pacified my angst. Talented musician Sister Celia said, "You'll learn Gregorian Chants and five Latin Masses by Rossini, an early composer," then she trained our ears and voices for good tone, correct pitch, perfect phrasing, and dynamics. "You must sing your best," she said, "to please

God and lift the spirits of the congregation." The hymnal's words and notations were foreign, but I revered them because, like beloved doctrines, I learned that our hymns were first sung by holy people from the early Church. They lived in our worship. I loved the antiquity of that and it deepened my faith. Talented Sister Celia nodded her head while her right hand directed our voices through difficult phrasing. I was a formidable instrument of God through sheer love of the arts. Sister taught me piano from first to eighth grade. The keys were my constant companions, always in the same place, solid, warming up to my fingers as I played them.

We sang with the great pipe organ, made in Europe and shipped over. Sister said, "God will be impressed with your hard work, so don't spoil your performance with noisy shuffling. Rather, tiptoe up the winding stairwell without a sound and position yourselves in the choir loft on the tiers around the organ." I did exactly as she asked and sang *Kyrie, Gloria, Credo, Sanctus,* and *Agnus Dei,* feeling celestial. Surrounded by corn and soybean fields, silos, red barns, brown cows and pink pigs, and amid rich and poor, our humble prayers carried throughout the church and then spiraled straight up to Our Heavenly Father, whether among the clouds or into a clear blue sky. It seems a shame not to still have those beautiful round Latin vowels, rich with Old-World European flavor, wafting through the open air of magnificent churches.

"Grab a quick breath at intervals before the end of the phrase," Sister said. "If you each stagger your breathing, it sounds like one, long, and continuous stream of melody, imitating the very nature of primitive music."

I had visions of clouds and angels floating like a Chagall painting through my mind. The reverent silence of the audience set the foundation for our songs as they exploded into the Gothic rafters, which I could study at my leisure now that I was closer to the ceiling.

"The Latin songs and prayers that you memorize, by their very nature, are worthy to be heard by God," Sister Celia said. That statement made a home deep in my mind, so that every utterance became my zealous commitment. At times, the music made my eyes water and the hairs rise on my arms. I don't think I was alone in that sensation, but Catholics were modest about outward emotional displays. I never heard another kid mention goose bumps, so I kept quiet about mine. It seemed that talking about the palpable yearning for God took away from its potency and depth.

Another treasure—one my parents gave me that year, as dictated by Church tradition—was my very own leather-bound Missal, with Gospels, Epistles, favored prayers, ceremonies, rites, rituals, and songs at the tip of my fingers. Each Missal was thick with writings honoring God. Its onionskin paper created a leafy sound and I could hear those crispy pages turning throughout the congregation during every kind of church gathering.

"You get more out of the Mass when you follow along with the priest," all Sisters said. "Use the colorful ribbons that sprout from the spine to mark your place. That way, psalms, litanies, Stations of the Cross, and every kind of holy celebration can be found quickly. Parts of Missals are written in Latin with English translations. Keep your eyes on both so you know the meaning of the words."

As I grew older, so did my Missal, like an old friend. Heavier pages depicted colorful Renaissance art—angels and various saints—which matched images of my faith. I studied those exquisite paintings that included *The Last Supper*, *The Nativity*,

The Crucifixion, and the most important saints. When the Church replaced Missals with flimsy monthly booklets void of pictures, I felt my faith diminish. "Just throw your Missals away, you won't need them anymore, the Church is changing," said the nuns. I procrastinated for several years before tossing mine into the trash. I was disillusioned and confused. Then Latin completely disappeared, and the magnificence of worship deflated even further. The Church arbitrarily ended beloved traditions. Even some sins were redefined.

The older I got the more complicated things became. My ideas of Catholicism no longer read like a bedtime story. I tried to comprehend the lines between reality and mythology. When I finally understood that animal characters in movies and books were simply creations from imaginations and not real things, I began to distrust the spiritual realm too. What if the pretty pictures in my Missal were just the illustrations from the mind of an artist to entertain me? I watched priests, nuns, and all adults for signs of hesitation, but never saw or heard any. People remained solid in their beliefs. They talked about God, The Blessed Virgin, our guardian angels, and an enormous accumulation of saints as if they lived down the street and around the corner. But in a small recess of my mind, frightening doubts began to spawn like tiny insects.

Chapter

4

"**A**merica is a young country. It's unlikely we'll be favored with *real* miracles," I learned in sixth grade from spunky Sister Marcy. Miracles were European inventions. Their stories were steeped with history, cool and wild with intrigue. Father told us about a painting that would mysteriously shed tears, another that bled from the eyes, and about holy people that carried the wounds of Jesus—the Stigmata—bleeding from their hands, feet, head, and sides. A monk from Italy was one of them. Another was an older woman, also European. Rome sent representatives on surprise visits to their homes and examined the scars. "Deceit has yet to be found," Father told our class.

"Don't think you're good enough to have the Stigmata," edgy Sister Neeta said, often disgusted with us. "Those people are profoundly holy. God favored them with His very own piercings. He must love them very much."

I wondered how people could be that good. I certainly wouldn't want to bleed from my hands, feet, head, or side, but I kept checking. Other kids did too. I felt God was missing my best efforts, not to ever bestow obvious favors on me. Wasn't He watching? I had to get His attention somehow. I started writing Him letters. For one whole year, I hid them in a rainproof pouch with a piece of yarn tied to it, secured at my end to a small wood support. I tossed it up onto the little extension of the roof outside our bathroom window. I gave God plenty of time to get back to me. I sent letter upon letter, giving Him chance after chance.

Dear God, I would like You to tell me if You really exist. I need to know. Can't You see how hard I've been trying? I love You so much! I don't need a big miracle. I just want a little sign. I found out about Santa not being real, but I think You are up in heaven. Please tell me. Please? I'll give You two weeks to answer, even three.

I climbed up on the stool, opened the window, heaved the pouch onto the overhanging roof, got down, flushed the toilet, and walked out of the bathroom like nothing peculiar happened. I checked on it for that year, improving my handwriting on each attempt and coloring some pretty pictures to go along—flowers and such. I got nothing in return. I examined the papers for tear stains. I looked for droplets of blood. My heart sank every time I opened the pocket and found my notes to Jesus untouched. I was ten years old and felt abandoned by God—my Creator.

Today, it's believed that all those stigmata people were pious frauds. Even as a kid, I suspected they made things up. I visualized them stabbing themselves at their kitchen tables at night when the shades were drawn. Though in a way, they were like me, desperate for God's love, to the extreme. Back then I was willing to go along with their stories if the Church said they were possible.

Everything about religion got validated when movies were shown to the entire student body in the gym. I watched *The Ten Commandments* and wept so hard while soldiers hurt Jesus that my body heaved and shuddered. Everybody's eyes were red that day and kids' moods turned sullen. Sister told us that all

Jesus's suffering was our fault. Guilt hit me like a sledgehammer to my belly. I questioned my every action: *this is a sin; this isn't a sin; this is only a venial sin; this could lead to mortal sin.* I tried to avoid sins all day. I renewed my fervor. I memorized school rules and God's laws out of the catechism more perfectly, but worry became my new best friend.

Hollywood made a film romanticizing Saint Joan of Arc. She was a young woman who was killed for her Christian faith. I saw her body consumed by smoke and flames as she burned at the stake. She showed no fear and didn't even cry. It was disturbing when the actress who played Saint Joan, Jean Seberg, died in mortal sin after allegedly committing suicide. It seemed cruel that her character died honoring God, but the actor's death dishonored Him enough to send her to hell for eternity.

Black and white films were dreamy with tension between a priest and nun. Father O'Malley (Bing Crosby) stared into the eyes of beautiful Sister Benedict (Ingrid Bergman) in *The Bells of St. Mary's,* I thought those two people should marry one another, though the Church forbade it. Stunning Audrey Hepburn in *The Nun's Story,* beautiful Deborah Kerr in *Heaven Knows Mr. Allison,* and whimsical Shirley McClain in *Two Mules for Sister Sara* were all nuns on the big Hollywood screen, each with masculine co-stars tempting their vows. With powerful musical scores hinting at love interest, romance seemed possible, even amid austerity. The big-screen God seemed as close to my idea of Prince Charming as I could imagine. Those nuns were so in love with Him, though they could not see Him.

On free days, I followed Elizabeth, if I could keep up, to wherever things got interesting—other kids' houses, the basement or attic, the corner store, and our clubhouse, which was an old clapboard pigeon coop in the backyard, strewn with remnant feathers and droppings. My brother and his friends posted a sign: *No Girls Allowed* and *What's the Password?* We removed the sign when he wasn't looking, went right in, and waited for him to come defend his fortress. Arguments about ownership of the secret hideout followed as both parties stood their ground with me behind, eyes wide open, and watchful.

We dressed up like little old ladies in mother's flowered housedresses, jewelry, and high heels. We addressed one another with craggy voices: *How are you feeling today? I'm going blind and hard of hearing. My arthritis is acting up again. I didn't sleep at all well. I think I'll die this afternoon.* We paraded in twos, threes, fours, or more all over backyards in the neighborhood.

We frequently sported Band-Aids pressed on skinned knees and elbows after we traipsed in teams through our favorite woods—in and around, up and down, over and under, cutting through branches with our pocketknives, looking for something to trap or cage or pocket, getting plenty dirty and knowing our mother would say, "It'll perk up your immune system." We rode our two-wheeler bikes or strapped on steel roller skates, keys dangling around our necks to tighten them when they loosened. We memorized cracks in the sidewalks all around the block. We played jacks on the hard concrete, hopscotch, telephone, jump rope, and 'Mother May I.' Most of our friends were non-Catholics, which seemed daring and frankly a little sinful.

Besides all the usual board games, there'd be canasta tournaments—a game of rummy that was all the rage—on our front porch in the summer with neighborhood kids. My oldest sister always won and the rest of us accepted that before cards even got dealt. I'd sit next to her, hoping for insight, but it never mattered. My pride took a beating every time and I'd go back into the house and pound out my frustrations on the piano keys. I got really good at that instrument. I accurately divided rhythms, matched number to notation, and counted every measure—another use for my obsessive calculation.

We had an orderly home. Mother knew how to create balance. Her energies were concentrated on family schedules, traditions, and what she called "good old common sense." She got us all out the door after a hearty breakfast, turned on the radio, straightened up the house, and planned our supper. She sighed when she saw my side of the bedroom always in upheaval. She organized family projects, outings, and weekend trips. She sewed outfits for three daughters and clothes for our dolls. She created photo albums. On her free days, she visited with neighbors and met monthly with her circle of refined women from the church. They dressed in Sunday best, studied the life of Jesus and the saints, laid delicate cloth napkins in their laps, sipped coffee, and nibbled decadent desserts served on matching porcelain china with sterling silver forks. Some gossiped. My mother was one of the listeners. She raised her eyebrows, contemplated, but never spread those stories.

My father, the spine of the family, provided deep roots of security and discipline he'd learned in his youth. Usually just a raised eyebrow and a frown curtailed our questionable behavior. He had to grow up fast and faced many difficulties that a kid shouldn't have to. "In St. Louis," he said, "my brothers helped me gather coal along railroad tracks to heat our home. I built slats along our wagon, making it taller, so it would carry more. I trapped a couple squabs every day for the family supper, and helped my mom serve her famous nickel lunch-plate specials in my dad's tavern." I thought he told us this story so we'd know he could provide for his family. No one was stronger or smarter than my dad, in my eyes. This was the part of him that I loved and admired.

After his bowling nights, he surprised us with hand-dipped vanilla ice cream from the corner drugstore. He allowed Hershey bars on pinochle night—a trick-taking card game he played with other men taking turns in one another's homes. He fixed popcorn and iced drinks for us on hot summer evenings, while we sat around the radio in pajamas on the screened-in porch and listened to *Inner Sanctum, Baby Snooks, Cinnamon Bear, Amos and Andy,* and *The Shadow. Let's Pretend* was on Saturday mornings, when Elizabeth and I listened to fairytales. He took us to drive-in movies, fixed our broken bikes, helped us polish our shoes and set them by the fireplace for Sunday morning Mass. In our garden across the street he planted vegetables, which my mother canned. He paid all the bills, all the while taking correspondence courses in engineering.

We visited historic places and relatives out of town. We rode the *S.S. Admiral* down the Mississippi, and went to ball games. On the best Saturdays, we pulled on our jeans, t-shirts, and sneakers, piled into the car and headed to Koler's Mill Hideaway along a tributary of a river in the woods. As our dad set up ten fishing poles along the bank, we dug clams from the mud with our pocketknives, then opened, scraped clean, and saved their pearly shells as treasures. We swung on Tarzan vines gnarled around old trees and yelled our heads off. By noon, we ate the caught fish and six potatoes that Mother had wrapped tightly in foil, nestled among hot coals, then covered over in a pit she had dug.

"We're going fishing on vacation. Your father needs to relax," Mother said each summer. "Keep him company in the boat," she told Elizabeth and me most evenings for several weeks. We wore life jackets, carried fishing licenses, cane poles, and slippery minnows and plump night crawlers that wrapped around our fingers as we threaded them onto hooks. We waited patiently to catch one hundred fish so we could motor the boat to shore around midnight. My Irish side tried to explain to each flopping fish that it wasn't my fault and how sorry I was, before my German side knocked it out cold to scale, behead, dress, and prepare for supper or packaging. My whole family sported lovely tans, except for me—burned, blistered, and massively freckled. I thought I was adopted.

Hot summer evenings or Sunday afternoons, we piled into the car for rides through the countryside and harmonized favorite songs: "Wait 'til the Sun Shines Nelly," "I've Been Working On The Railroad," "Moonlight Bay," and "I'm Looking Over A Four Leaf Clover" with a promise of tall sodas or an ice-cold root beer in heavy glass mugs with handles. Like in the movie *Cheaper by the Dozen,* and TV series like *Father Knows Best, Ozzie and Harriet,* and *Make Room for Daddy,* (all popular at the time), we worked, ate, played, and stuck together.

As an added bonus to our stable life, the Church provided a religious structure to curb our bad behavior. We followed all the rules, went to confession and communion, ate our catch of fish every Friday, fasted on the Holy Days, and prayed before devouring each perfectly-balanced meal. During Lent—a period of forty days where we were required to sacrifice the comforts of this world—we gave up candy, cut out desserts, and turned off the TV to pray the rosary. Among the church congregation, young people were poked, prodded, and pushed to enter religious life.

This meant giving up everything in devotion to God. Neither of my sisters would have ever considered it. My brother went to seminary, but came back home within a few months. It wasn't for him.

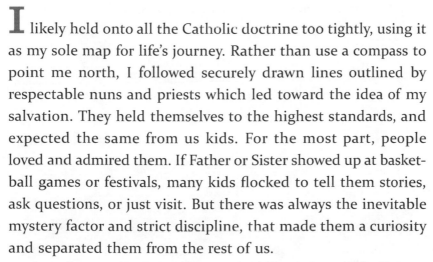

Chapter 5

I likely held onto all the Catholic doctrine too tightly, using it as my sole map for life's journey. Rather than use a compass to point me north, I followed securely drawn lines outlined by respectable nuns and priests which led toward the idea of my salvation. They held themselves to the highest standards, and expected the same from us kids. For the most part, people loved and admired them. If Father or Sister showed up at basketball games or festivals, many kids flocked to tell them stories, ask questions, or just visit. But there was always the inevitable mystery factor and strict discipline, that made them a curiosity and separated them from the rest of us.

One day, I asked my mom why she had four kids. "Priests appealed to married couples to have large families and fill up the churches," she said. "I almost stopped at three, but I'm so glad I had one more," she always added with her warmest smile, and I'd smile back at her.

Being the last born, I felt I made it into life by the skin of my teeth and I should probably be grateful to the Church for that. And to add even more weight to the matter, priests frequently reminded parents from the pulpit, "It's your Catholic duty to promote religious vocations in your children. Don't put all the emphasis on dating, marriage, and careers in the business world." I sucked in my breath, slumped in the pew, and held as still as possible—so the priest wouldn't look in my direction—then stole a glance at my father and wondered if he thought of promoting a religious vocation in me. But he never did. Neither he nor my mother ever said, "One of you kids ought to go and serve the Church."

Around fifth grade nuns started to talk directly to kids about convents and seminaries. Because monastic life was unusual, and nuns and priests were romantic figures, their lives sounded important. Like other kids, on some days an image glued to my brain of me clothed in black and white robes, converting people to Christianity somewhere in the heathen world.

"Those of you thinking about living your life devoted to Our Lord, raise your hand," Monsignor said whenever he paid a visit to the upper classes. He always looked intent on receiving a certain answer. I didn't want him to get upset, so I put my hand in the air every time he asked. Even if I was the only one, he could count on me. But that simple gesture had undertones of commitment and he stashed away that youthful promise to bring up at a later date. I hadn't earnestly wanted to become a nun. Their mystery made me feel conflicted about them. But I didn't want them to become a dying breed. Maybe too, my hand-raising was the people-pleasing, attention-seeking part of me poised for release.

Looking back now, I thought my father might not have argued were I to enter a convent. He'd been an altar boy as a kid, then for decades thereafter, nuns relied heavily on him to lead a crew of workers at every parish festival. I wanted him happy and I thought I ought to make that happen since I'd caused his worst behavior all those years ago. Without question, to me he was the world's strongest Catholic. As a good girl, programmed into perfection mode, I'd help out the nuns at every opportunity just like him. I frequently stayed after school to correct first grade workbooks for the nuns. Every Saturday for a couple years, I taught catechism right alongside of them, to young children whose parents sent them to public school. In that, I imitated my dad.

When the relentless vocation question came up, the idea of becoming a nun floated in my mind for a while and then evaporated until the next time. There was always a next time. "If you don't follow God's Will, you'll wonder for the rest of your life if you've made a mistake," was the traditionally accepted adage among Catholics.

"To become a religious is the highest state in life, almost to the level of the saints. You'll be free from the threats of hell and the gates of heaven will open widely to those who follow Our Lord," said every robed man and woman of the Church. I thought they were bragging and it felt like a bribe, but my competitive nature was occasionally tweaked. Highest state in life? Now that was a goal I could sink my teeth into. It would really make somebody forever proud.

"A young person entering the priesthood or convent brings honor to families and promises elevated status in eternity," Monsignor said to our eighth grade class as he glared at us, deflecting doubt.

Listen for God's voice calling you to serve in His vineyard, prompted advertisements in Catholic newspapers and magazines that we had to read for quizzes. Recruitment photographs showed brothers, priests, and nuns feeding the poor, teaching eager students, and caring for the sick. I always studied those pictures devoutly.

Do You Have a Vocation? Is God Calling You? Anything could be evidence, anything could be a sign that we were chosen. We needed to stay alert for those signs. The Church promoted fanciful things and drew us toward the romance of the medieval. Gothic churches—magnificent structures with steeples reaching into the sky like castles—made people look upward and elevated them beyond ordinary things. The Church chose powerful music from brilliant composers to set the mood of glorious monastic life. Beautiful art work showed how loving the religious persona was. Fantasizing a life among others devoted to Christ had the appeal of soldiering. I still have the sheet music by Daniel A. Lord, S.J. entitled "For Christ the King," a hefty, marching, rallying song popular among all Catholics. Its lyrics: *Christ lifts His hands, The King commands: His challenge, "Come and follow me,"* we sang with gusto. In eighth grade, girls were encouraged to stay after school for Vocation Club to develop interest in the convent before high school, where boys could distract us from our possible truer calling. Only a handful of us showed up to this club and edgy Sister Neeta would speak in general terms about what her convent life was like.

"Didn't you ever want to get married?" one brave girl asked her.

"I am married. Just as a husband and wife exchange vows, we promise Our Lord three vows: poverty, chastity, and obedience for the rest of our lives. This simple gold band on my finger is symbolic of our union," she said, turning it around and around with a completely earnest expression. I wondered how that worked—everyone married to the same person and that person being God.

"But," she said, "women living together in a convent is no bed of roses or bowl full of cherries," and a hush came over the group.

One spring, three nuns drove several of us eighth grade girls to their Motherhouse a few hours away, for a weekend. Some girls' lives were dedicated to God from age twelve, and we saw three of our former school friends—who weren't allowed to look our way—closed-off in a room full of a hundred miniature nuns, all focused on sewing chores. Both my mother and father scoffed at the nonsense of training their twelve-year-old daughter for the nunnery explaining to me gently that, "No matter how ideal things appeared, you're too young for a convent."

"You'll be held accountable for her lost vocation," nuns later told my mother. "You could both lose your souls." She mentioned that conversation to me while focused and grasping a potato in her hand, determinedly peeling and swiping away at it.

Middle schools emptied hormonal teenagers into high school, armed with the spiritual strength of Confirmation to ensure purity. I took that promise of abstinence more seriously than most kids, being respectful of hell and my father. No boy would lure me into sin, jeopardizing my soul. Not even a supposed prince.

Things being less rigid in high school, I consistently lost my footing, simulating various identities in a sea of new personalities. I had barely developed the social skills necessary to string two sentences together. Since I was more shy than not, I created a front, settling on being the quiet girl until I could size things up. Girls I had once called friends weren't in my classes, ate lunch with their new cliques, and casually fell in love with boys. I watched couples blossom and wondered how long I'd have to wait, knowing a boyfriend was nothing to be celebrated on the home front. Elizabeth dated from the moment she stepped into the high school. She never carried the worries I did because she didn't allow the words of the nuns and priests to consume her, I suppose.

I latched onto groups of students, listened to gossip, and hoped I belonged. I was conscious of my appearance, but wore saddle oxfords with ugly orthotics tucked inside. My school uniforms were frequently snug so that I spent 1,460 days sucking in my tummy to keep it flat. My grades were all over the place, and I worried that whispers among classmates could be about me. Typical teenage angst. I accompanied musical choral groups and created an identity for myself, making use of my talents.

"Your skirt is skintight," critical Mother Frederick said to me the one day I didn't wear my uniform. "Did your mother see you before you left home today?"

"Yes, Mother." Ursulines—who were named after the Fifth Century Saint Ursula—were referred to by that affectionate title.

"You look like you were poured into it. Don't wear it again." To my surprise and disappointment, I got no attention from a single boy that day.

I think my girlfriends might have pressured guys to invite me to an occasional dance. "Take Gretchen. You both need a date," they more than likely said, "we'll all be together so what difference does it make?"

In the gym when a boy asked, "Do you want to dance?" he seemed a little reluctant to me, and I knew by Monday I'd be completely ignored by him. One Friday night dance, I got my first kiss from a boy. He planted his lips fully on my mouth. Chills surged through my body in one nanosecond and connected every vein, artery, cell, bone marrow, and fiber as I melted into his arms. I evaluated that kiss for weeks. Excitement surged and pulsated everywhere. I was convinced it was a sin, but I carried the exhilaration around anyway and told no one, calling it up when I was alone. The feeling was fresh, wild—excitement with a hint of evil. In short order, I had to block it out completely, when I saw that boy kissing other girls. I was stranded and confused, watching him walk with them.

"How can he just drop me like that?" I asked Lisa, my new high school friend, popular with boys. "I think about him all the time and he doesn't even care."

"He says you never talk." So there it was—the talking. I rarely felt permission to voice what I really thought about things. Therefore, I didn't have much to say, didn't even know where to begin. At least without a boyfriend I wouldn't have to worry about temptations. My friends got asked out on real dates. The closest I got was when three of us girls partnered up with three boys at a drive-in movie. In the dark, mine reached over and ran his hand completely, slowly around my breast and I shot straight up in the seat, envisioning the Blessed Virgin weeping.

"What's wrong with you?" he said.

"Nothing." I stared straight into the darkness flummoxed between excitement and escape.

I knew it fell in the category of a venial sin, like they taught in Confirmation, when the bishop tapped two fingers on our cheeks as a metaphorical warning. It would lead to mortal sin if I didn't get a grip. The other four kids in the car were having a grand time, arms and legs begging for more space, their kissing endless and probably low-level sinful. With my breast still tingling with excitement, I watched in rapt fascination and didn't know how they were able to breathe. My boy got out of the car to get popcorn. Every kid in that car but me had gone to the Irish parish, where they had kissing contests on the stage behind the curtain and in the choir loft stairwell after school and on Saturdays, I heard. I was dreadfully behind in my development, but I was taught to be careful. I never mentioned the breast thing to a priest in confession, since I didn't know how to bring it up.

Just as in trying too hard to impress my father, I always tried too hard to impress a boy. "Mother, I can't get a boy to like me,"

I said in the kitchen, where our best conversations took place. She told me to focus on my grades. I didn't realize the only person I needed approval from was me.

Junior year, I set priorities to get higher grades and carry myself with more confidence. As I developed a thicker layer of emotional crust, my academic and social standing climbed. I was elected onto the Homecoming Court, and then became May Queen, a continuation of the 1954 Marian Year. The new tradition was to crown the Blessed Mother with flowers in May. A young boy and I linked arms and walked to a statue of Mary clothed in blue and white satin robes. Together we placed a crown of tulips upon her veiled head. My partner was an Austrian exchange student named Alfred. He talked about religious vocations. He said that our selection for crowning Mary was probably a sign that we both had a vocation, which would soon become our fate. I hadn't thought about that idea for four years, but he was so cute with his alluring European accent that I fully engaged conversationally with his vocation idea just to strengthen my connection with him.

Come spring, a guy asked me to a school dance. Afterwards, I pulled out a questionnaire I'd created for emergency conversation in case he approached me with sexual posturing. When Danny parked his car on a hill overlooking the lake and moved from behind the wheel over to me, I started down my list of questions: "Do you think the Russians will blow us up? Are you worried about Sputnik? Is America really the best country in the world? Are you afraid of hell?" "Do you believe in heaven?" He answered six out of ten questions before scooting back behind the wheel and turning on the ignition. I was crazy about that guy, but too afraid of those sins of the flesh—Church teachings about burdensome sex that wouldn't allow me to even visualize body parts, much less explore them.

One Saturday night, a best buddy asked me to a sleepover. I wanted answers to the secretive questions about physiology. We lay together in her bed under the covers in our baby-doll, shorty pajamas, giggling over treasured gossip like any young school girls, "Mary Ann, what exactly happens when a boy and girl get together?" I don't remember her precise words, but she got all the body parts in the right places. She's a Registered Nurse today. "It happens when you're asleep, right? I mean— you don't know it's going on. You just wake up and it's over?"

She laughed out loud, "No, they both know."

"Aren't the lights off? They don't look at each other, do they? Do they see each other's bodies? Aren't they under the covers the whole time?"

"You need to talk to your mother," she said impatiently.

"I have and she told me the same things. But I don't think I could ever do that, Mary Ann. I couldn't show a boy what I look like without any clothes." I had finally gotten brave enough to grab a hand mirror in the bathroom and peek at myself. I couldn't believe how complicated everything was. *No boy's going to see that!*

"God made us to have children. He takes care of things like that. It's not a sin, it's natural. Husbands and wives are sup- posed to do it," Mary Ann said with poise beyond her years.

In senior year, the hippest nun in the school approached several girls, fanning the embers for possible vocations. She taught P.E., wore sneakers, rolled up her habit and tucked it in to facilitate movement, laughed a lot, and was very energetic and young. Someone must have given her my name. She said I should listen for God's voice. I had a few serious dates with a boy, so she backed off. I focused on what I'd do after graduation. Classmates contacted colleges or businesses and others spoke of marriage. I decided I'd be a college girl.

On an ordinary day in early June, I rocked lazily in a chair on our front porch, visuals of campus life—collegiate libraries, new friends, and intellectual pursuits—parading through my mind. I was seventeen and enrolled at the state teacher's college, yet I was apprehensive about leaving home for the first time, worried about my adjustment, and concerned that among other young college women, a guy could overlook me. Veronica, a buddy since first grade, lived in a lakefront home her father built. When we worked on school projects or ice-skated in the bay, we always had a connection.

"Want to be roommates at college in the fall?" Veronica, also known as Ronnie, asked me.

"Good idea. It'll be fun and I won't be so scared with you there. We can help each other. Let's do it." I said.

"Did you get your acceptance letter?" she asked as she flashed hers at me in the hall, crowded with noisy kids headed to classes.

"Yes. Did you put my name down as your first dorm room choice?" I said before she disappeared from my sight.

"Of course," she said, and was gone.

I believe it would have been a perfect plan if I hadn't received a phone call after graduation.

"Is this Gretchen?" asked the voice on the other end. "This is Sister Leo, a Dominican from the local parish on the north side of town." Dominicans follow the fashion and rules of Twelfth Century Saint Dominic. "You don't know me," she said, "but a priest mentioned your name as someone who might help us chaperone some thirteen-year-old girls on a road trip this Saturday. Would you be able to come along?" The priest wasn't identified, but only Monsignor would know me well enough to mention my name. I hesitated, so she continued again, "The girls might enroll in our Catholic Academy. They'd connect better with you, being a recent graduate."

The next day, a car with nuns and girls picked me up. I'd never met any of them, but it was only a day trip, so it was fine. We drove to the next city and curiously, the three young girls who'd kept entirely to themselves in the car disappeared from sight as soon as we arrived. The nuns escorted me around their convent complex on the same city block as the school. They identified various buildings, took me into their chapel and gardens, and asked questions about my future. It was all just conversation, but wasn't I supposed to be chaperoning those girls? Where had they gone? Raised to show respect to nuns, I didn't ask. I was thoughtful and considerate. More than likely, I was shy. But those nuns executed their mission with finesse. More than a decade later, I would come to fully understand the effects of hidden agendas on vulnerable people.

As we strolled around the grounds, they told me how modern their teaching order was. They said they were considered the cheerful nuns, more lenient than most. They boasted about themselves and their lives. I was polite and complimentary. I smiled, nodded, and said things like, "Really? Uh-huh. That's wonderful, Sister."

"Have you ever considered becoming a nun?" one of them asked me out of the blue.

"Oh yes, many times, Sister," I said. Within an hour, I was eating lunch in a parlor room alone when those same nuns asked if I'd like to meet their Mother General.

"Okay," I said. Good Catholic girls answered in the affirmative when a nun made a request. I'd never met a Mother General before, but I assumed it was a fairly big deal. She was the CEO of the entire Order of Sisters, consisting of several hundred nuns. She controlled the Motherhouse, the origin of every nun in the Order since the 1800s. The Mother General's office was in the oldest building, flush with religious antiquities. The European structure gave added respect to her elevated rank.

I washed up. A Sister announced, "Mother General will see you now." I felt intimidated, having had time to work up some nerves. Two Sisters led me through one ornate parlor after another with their welcoming but formal arrangement of Oriental rugs and ornamental furnishings, until we reached what looked to be *the* most important room along a corridor of offices. Like every room, this one also had plush Victorian brocaded chairs and a sofa, but included a sizable library reaching to the ceiling and along a wall, a large window looking out on the spacious grounds, and a large desk, behind which sat a sweet-faced nun who rose and called me by name when I entered. The other nuns left me alone with her.

What followed was what my Protestant friends have told me resembled recruitment into the armed services. *Brainwashing,* they insisted. "Your future lays mysteriously ahead, my dear. The non-Catholic university you've chosen could lead you away from your religion. It may not be the correct path for you," said the Mother General, also known as Reverend Mother.

"Have you ever considered becoming a nun?" she asked like an echo of the past. What else would I say to her but, "Yes. Yes I have." I wasn't going to lie to a pink-cheeked, undoubtedly Irish, Mother General. She took my response and ran with it. It's no wonder she occupied the top rung of that community's ladder, because she brilliantly worked those old trappings from my subconscious, the ones I'd heard for years as a kid.

Moving in too close, apparently trying to grasp my soul, she asked me about my family: "Great." My church: "Great." My Catholic education: "Great." My grades: "Great." And my dating: My dating? She snagged me on that part.

"It's a sign that God is trying to speak to you on a personal level. You are meant for Him alone," she said. "I believe Our Dear Lord has chosen you for Himself."

Not surprisingly, I was flattered. Reverend Mother, this apparently remarkable woman, was impressed with me. Maybe this was the sign from God I had been waiting for. It wasn't what I had expected. Instead of the Stigmata or responses to my letters, God would favor me with a lifetime in servitude to Him. I should feel grateful and blessed at long last, having sought His love my entire life.

I was completely without rebuttal. The Reverend Mother's insistent tone implied that I had no right to resist a call from God. How I wish I'd had the courage to press my intent to go away to college. Who was I kidding? I'd never speak up for myself. I thought I was displaying my well-mannered, well-bred characteristics. At the very moment she asked her question, why hadn't I said, "You know, Reverend Mother, I once considered becoming a nun, but after a lot of thought, I've decided it isn't the life for me?" No, instead of being true to myself, a concept I never fully grasped, I went home that afternoon with a list of black and white clothing I'd wear for the rest of my life.

Chapter 6

I called my girlfriends and told them what I'd done. Lisa, who knew a lot about a lot of things, sat on my bed and tried to talk sense into me.

"You should try freshman year at college, just one year, hon. Then, if you still want to be a nun, go ahead, but give yourself a chance in the world first," she said, talking to me like I was a child, so I dug in my heels and resisted.

"But I've thought about this once before. I'll try it, and then if I don't like it I'll leave."

"I think it's a mistake. You should do it the other way around. Those nuns have talked you right out of your future. Think about it some more. It's happening too fast. You'll get in there and never get out."

"But the boys I like don't like me, Lisa. Maybe it's what I'm supposed to do," I said, quoting the Mother General, my original thoughts untapped.

"You'll find somebody in college. Don't give up because of those high school boys. You have your whole life ahead of you. They'll shut you away for good."

"But I tried to enter a convent after eighth grade and my parents put their foot down. Now maybe I can get this settled. I don't want regrets later in life."

My words and thoughts were plagiarized. I regurgitated

things I'd heard for years in Catholic education, especially the part about regrets. It was the first time I'd taken a stand on anything. Who better to do it for than God? Lisa was an only child and knew how to put herself first. I was the youngest of four and learned to work for the good of the whole—an unselfish and thoughtful person.

"What about our college plans?" Ronnie asked.

"You'll have to find another roommate," I said, shrugging my shoulders. Her face melted in an expression of disappointment. I felt terrible letting her down, but it wasn't her approval that I sought.

That night, I was in the kitchen when my dad got home from work. My mother turned to me and smiled. "Go tell your father," she said. I marched quickly and steadfastly into the living room and announced the news before he even sat down.

"That's wonderful, honey." He was very pleased with me. I went upstairs to my room and smiled at the mirror. I thought I saw the person I wanted to see staring back at me. There was a girl who made wise choices.

Mother arranged a small farewell with friends and relatives, who brought me black rosaries, little crosses, and silver medals of various saints to pray to, carry in a pocket, or wear around my neck on a chain as tokens of holiness for my newly chosen life. Overnight, I morphed back into that little Catholic girl who lay dormant—the grade school girl who loved God so much and would do anything to validate His love for her. Not once did I waver over the next three weeks.

"It's a miracle," two nuns told my mother and me at a private gathering they arranged. "God's grace has gotten through to you in the nick of time. The friendships you'll make will be long-lasting because you'll experience the same reality. Twenty other girls are entering in June." We joked about what would have happened to me had I continued my ill-fated plan to attend a state college. We joked about some of the stupid things that went on when young girls live together in a dorm.

For a while, I was the center of attention. I think I may have even been the talk of the town. Then abruptly, the phone calls stopped. Friends had moved on without me before I even left. There'd be no more careening down the street in cars. No more hamburgers, fries, or Cokes. Now, entering a brand new stage in my life, I was alone. On June 23, 1961, my family piled into our car. I didn't have much luggage. I wouldn't need possessions where I was going.

"We're picking up Monsignor on the way out of town," my dad said.

Blood drained from my face. I wondered who'd made that secret invitation and why. Had Monsignor invited himself? I was puzzled, and headed down a highway trapped in someone else's plan. Monsignor was only an occasional visitor to our home—coming over to engage in serious discussions about Church matters or carrying on debates about religious doctrine with my knowledgeable dad—and was never one to actually join our family in the close proximity of our car. Such an intimidating presence, he was a very deliberate and stern man, commanding respect. He was not noted for having a sense of humor, though it was almost funny seeing him squished in the front seat next to my mother. He acted like he belonged there, his left arm resting confidently along the back of the seat. One mile at a time and for a distance of forty, my spirit wobbled between being a shy, agreeable person to that of a rebellious, quarrelsome one, bitter that perhaps this whole thing hadn't been my idea in the first place. Perhaps my own father and the

Monsignor had had a conversation about what a great thing it would be to have one of us wonderful children be counted upon to give up an entire life to the Church. Or had my father's arm been twisted? I thought back to each time I raised my hand when Monsignor had asked the "Who wants to be a nun or a priest?" question, and he had nodded at me in return. He took me at my word. He played me like an instrument of people-pleasing music. He was the priest that arranged for the chaperoning, luring me to the Motherhouse. I put the pieces of the puzzle together quickly. My breathing quickened, my mind raced in the back seat. I felt so helpless, like a bug in a web, waiting for the arrival of the spider. But he was already here sitting directly in front of me.

I wasn't scheduled to arrive at the convent until one o'clock. The Motherhouse wasn't that far away, but my father had all of us, plus the Monsignor, on the road by eleven in the morning and broke the speed limit getting there. I could see myself in the rearview mirror, reflecting my deer-in-the-headlights stare. I pressed so hard against the back of my seat that I likely left an indentation when I exited the car.

We pulled into the convent complex, passing through two large iron gates that displayed a coat of arms and a prominent decorative "V". My father parked the car and we got out. I looked mature, a worldly young woman by contrast to where I was headed, my auburn hair like fire in the sun. I carried myself with sophistication in my smart, slender navy dress with red trim and red high heels—by all outward appearances, a co-operative girl, fully prepared for what lay ahead.

A large crowd of nuns greeted and directed people into an ancient building. Monsignor went somewhere with my family and I was directed to follow two nuns through a side door, up a maze of stairs, down long narrow hallways laden with massive dark woodwork, and into a classroom sectioned off with hanging white sheets so girls could have privacy. I heard nervous giggling the moment I slipped behind a curtain and both nuns came in and began to unzip my dress. It was unnerving. I wanted to say, "I can handle this alone." But I'd never spoken up to a nun before, or anybody. I shimmied out of my dress, slipped off my red heels, rolled down my sheer hose, and stood in only bra and panties.

One nun quickly lifted a gabardine black pleated skirt with the feel of the Middle Ages in its threading over my head, pulled it down, and fastened it. It reached to my ankles. The other nun slid my arms into a long-sleeved black blouse and buttoned me up the front. The first one threw a short black cape around my neck and hooked it under my chin. The other attached a black silky veil with a comb onto my head, covering all but my bangs. I pulled black hose over my red toes—polish borrowed from my big sister's drawer containing every red shade imaginable. I stretched hose to knees where an elastic band held them tight like the ones my Mennonite great-grandma wore. I shoved one foot and then the other into the clunky, black, squat-heeled shoes. The transformation took less than ten minutes.

"Well, those shoes will be the best thing for your feet," my podiatrist had said at my last appointment before I entered the convent. "I don't agree with your decision to become a nun, but your feet need sensible footwear."

"What do you want to go and do a dumb thing like that for?" my family doctor had said when I went by myself for the required physical. He peered over the top of his glasses with his dark Sicilian eyes and shook his head. "You're making a terrible mistake," he said as he sat facing me from across his desk. "Who put this notion into your head?" He carried on at length while I sat properly and countered with rehearsed theories.

"I have a vocation," I said. "I've never had a real boyfriend, so it's a sign," echoes of the religious propaganda still ricocheting off the walls of my apparently hollow brain. Had I remained in public school, I'd never known of such things. Both doctors treated me as if I'd lost my mind and I left their offices embarrassed, wondering why they weren't impressed. Both were Catholics. In a convent, I could reach the highest state. I'd be assured of heaven and my crown would be covered with jewels.

Had I seen myself in a full-length mirror while behind that curtain I would have abandoned those dark clothes in an instant and dashed out the door. In my navy dress, I was an easy size eight. In those appalling black pleats, I instantly ballooned to a fourteen. I was ugly and a brute. I was no Cinderella. I stood motionless, trying to adjust to the immense weight of both this outfit and my questionable choice.

They led me downstairs into a large hall bathed in too much brightness for me (the glare of sunlight streaming in through its eight enormous windows), to where parents waited for daughters at large, wood library tables with matching chairs, in the presence of clusters of nuns. Elizabeth ran up to me in a flood of tears with an insufficient handkerchief for her meltdown. She gave me a firm hug. We'd had the typical amount of arguments between siblings while growing up. I thought she'd be grateful to have the bedroom to herself. Her tears unnerved me. Catholics rarely cried. The Church's culture relegated feelings to a lesser status, useless and a sign of weakness. But Elizabeth knew when to let matters of the heart have jurisdiction. My family, plus the Monsignor, watched me approach and their faces registered alarm. I had a feeling I looked ridiculous. We sat at one of the dozens of tables and avoided eye contact. Other people in the room were certainly happy, hyper with conversation. A burst of laughter came from one group, then another. We didn't feel that way. I could have left right then, but I recognized that the Monsignor came along to prevent that. I couldn't run away from this with his eyes on me. I would lose every fragment of respect I had left.

None of us had said a word on the drive over—six of us in the car, not one single word. What would a ride home have been like if I had turned tail?

"Do you know anybody, Gretchen?" Mother asked quietly, hopefully.

"No," I said, hesitantly looking around at two dozen girls dressed like me.

"Would you like some punch and a cookie?" someone asked.

"No." I rarely turned down an invitation for a dessert, but food would only get tossed around in my churning stomach. Something wasn't right. I sat stiff, awaiting the next humiliating thing. If Monsignor hadn't been with us, one of my family members would have truly asked, "Do you really want to do this?" and with my headshake, that would have gotten us up and out. But Church hierarchy was threatening like a thunderstorm. I never argued with it. Never ever once questioned it out loud.

Panic clutched my vital organs. Elizabeth would have dragged me out of there quicker than you could say "nightmare" if I'd had the nerve to open my mouth and plead for rescue.

"They want you up there, honey," my mother said, seeing I was the only one still sitting with family. "Girls are in line. There must be a ceremony coming up."

Every newly dressed postulant was partnered according to height. My feet edged forward and I was maneuvered into place. Elizabeth, still dabbing at her moist eyes, followed me into the crowd, then hugged me more sweetly than I'd ever remembered. She was the only person standing up there with me among that religious assembly. Her anxiety penetrated me and I wanted to grab her and hold on tightly, run away with her, but the sea of nuns swept me away quickly. I was in my own flood of tears. I just caught sight of my mother watching me between all the heads and I looked deliberately at her, reality reflecting in my face and I wondered if that was all right with her. There was nothing she could do sitting there with the Monsignor. In imitation of The Blessed Virgin, few good Catholic women argued with Holy Mother Church. She was probably remembering the incident when the grade school nuns told her she'd be responsible for the loss of my vocation and loss of all our souls, if she tried to stop me. She'd been outraged by their comments then, but they likely nagged at her. Besides, I was there to try it out. She said if I didn't like it, I could just leave. But I didn't believe her. The Church had a stranglehold on me.

It was a spectacle like no other. With our new group of postulants bringing up the humble rear-end, two by two, the most important nuns led a procession of dozens upon dozens of garbed Sisters in their black veils and long ivory robes. Heavy black belts were wrapped around their waists, from which hung long rosaries that rattled—the only sound really—and nearly reached the floor. They were followed by thirty more nuns dressed completely in white, all arms hidden beneath habits, heads tilted down. We walked in silence—though our shoes now sounded like an army—from that hall where it all began, up and around tight stairwells of heavy woodwork, hardwood floors, banisters, chair rails, ceiling borders, doorways, wall and handrail carvings, past statues and crucifixes until we reached a long dark corridor that led directly into a chapel, every bit as ornamental as a Cathedral. My family was out of my sight and I was on my own. My tears felt thick and salty. They squeezed out of my eyes and ran down my cheeks and neck, soaking into the collar of my blouse. I gulped air like I was drowning. I could feel the judgment of all present. I was seconds from bursting into audible sobs. Nobody else was in that state. At seventeen years old, I was still the only one crying.

By the time our little group had gotten through the doors, everyone had knelt and was facing forward in separate stalls that ran parallel from back to front in the chapel. The new girls, twenty-one of us resembling European widows, found our way into the back pews and knelt down. Except for five nuns who were behind us and probably watching our every move, we could see everything. At the sound of a knock, every-one stood, turned toward the center, right arms uniformly ex-tended outward, holding small black books, left arm hidden beneath the habit. Chanting began after an intonation pierced the silence. Nuns would chant psalms five times a day—early in the morning, then before and after lunch and supper. Now I listened to the soothing hum of pure voices sounding as one. It lifted me slightly from the intensity of my sadness.

My face was probably a red, blotchy, swollen mess. Exhausted, I stared at my lap, trying to gain control over my impulses. *Cut and run...* Those words kept going through my head.

A merciless feeling of abandonment lurked over me, now that I was barred from all things familiar for the rest of my de-spondent life. A girl who truly was destined to love only God would have been delighted. But a girl who just wished *God* would love *her* would spend each day yearning for home. And I would count every minute.

Chapter
7

I likened myself to a prisoner spending her first day behind bars. I tried to feel my way through the fog in my brain, when the chanting suddenly finished and everyone began filing out. We followed with partners in perfect silence. A hundred of us floated through long halls and down winding stairs, and I noticed the steps and doors that led to the circular driveway outside. Through a small window I caught a glimpse of the barren asphalt, the iron gates closed. My opportunity to change my mind had passed so I moved forward with the line. The reality was too stark. I'd view this whole experience from above, like I was watching a movie hovering overhead. Rich aromas of comfort food permeated the air. *I guess I'm staying for supper.*

The room where nuns ate, the refectory, resembled an Edward Hopper painting—clean, sterile, horizontal and vertical lines. A bank of windows ran the length of a long wall. Sunlight, grass, and shrubs from outside softened the severity inside. Parallel to the walls were scores of tables already set with plates, napkins, utensils, pitchers of water, and an assortment of condiments. We stood behind our chairs waiting for the never-ending line of nuns to the end. The Mother General, along with her council of four nuns, were the last ones. She rang a small bell and a prayer began, followed by a rumble of a hundred chairs. It was as quiet as a tomb.

From the head table, nuns were in their order of number of years in the convent. Our group was the farthest away, but within sight of everything. A nun at a desk in a far corner read into a microphone about a martyr of the Church, similar to *The Lives of the Saints* I knew as a child. I valued the examples of individuals who refused to abandon their love of God under penalty of death. Written for children, no legend got any worse than "he was stoned to death" or "she was fed to the lions." But the stories I heard now were more graphic.

Soon the flames were lit, but at first they did not eat into his flesh. Since his body refused to burn, the executioner was ordered to plunge a dagger into his side. Then there came from his body, a dove and a great quantity of blood, which quenched the flames. "Adventurer Saints" by Abbe' Omer Englebert.

The only familiar face in the crowd was the Reverend Mother. I looked around for my high school chum. She had told me a week prior to expect her. Janice had auburn hair and freckles like me. I found out some months later that she'd entered, spent one night, and her boyfriend William got her out the next morning. I was so jealous that her Prince Charming came to rescue his damsel in distress. Apparently, he'd made quite a commotion until the nuns couldn't restrain him any longer— arguing loudly, rebuffing intimidation, pushing, shoving, gaining entry, and then refusing to leave. "If I had to dress in a habit and sit across from her at the table, I was getting Janice out of there," he said. Such passion! I'd been Cinderella. Where was that passion for me? My prince would be the Prince of Peace. My castle would be in heaven—later, after death. A cruel fate for a princess.

Several nuns pushed in carts. We were served platters of roast beef, mashed potatoes and gravy, salad, and green beans. Though talking and dining usually go together, strict rules kept conversation from the refectory. Passing was done using subtle hand signals. Only the voice of the reader was heard. I sat up straighter than I ever had at home.

After a dessert of fruit cobbler with ice cream, carts appeared carrying small pans of hot sudsy water and little hand-held mops with towels. Right there at the table, we washed everything and reset each place for breakfast.

The reader finished, a tiny bell sounded, and everyone stood to pray. The monotony of black and white matched perfectly with the conformity of posture and demeanor. It gratified my artistic sense of form and symmetry, until I noticed something else was happening. As the prayerful voices complemented the visual, two nuns came in from a side room and stood in front of the head table. They knelt on the cold linoleum floor, stretched out, and lay their faces down on an arm while the prayer continued. My eyes were riveted as I watched that disturbing ritual unfold. The nuns lay there for about ten seconds, I heard a knock and they got up and walked back out of the refectory. My stomach hardened like concrete.

That unsettling occurrence over, the Reverend Mother and her council filed out, followed by everyone else. Our group walked into the evening air and around the grounds. The entire compound was larger than one city block surrounded by private homes like the one I'd left that morning. I wanted desperately to run across the street, bang on a front door and ask to be let in, but we were bordered by tall, thick hedges with red roses. "Not to keep you in, but to keep people out," it was explained in lecture hall the next day.

Over a hundred nuns are assigned to the Motherhouse. The forty-five of us made up what was called the novitiate—separate quarters reserved for nuns in training. Half of us tried to become accustomed to our new black outfits, while the other half—novices, a year ahead of us—wore white and seemed comfortable. I was assigned my very own novice. My angel mother. I listened while she told me about herself. Freckled and fair-skinned like me, she was from California. I grew to like her, but she was a jabberer that late afternoon, talking on and on about the joys of convent life. I meant no disrespect, but my inability to listen was beyond any of her words that had nothing to do with me.

The eldest of the group was in charge, a nun in her sixties—the Novice Mistress. In pairs, we followed her like ducklings over to a stone grotto holding a statue of the Virgin Mary adorned with freshly picked flowers. Novices prayed, then sang some beautiful songs, devotion and holiness evident in their faces and voices. *Perhaps I could be like them*, I thought for split seconds—a flickering light in search of hope. They were young girls my own age. With bubbling joy and sincerity, they reminded me of all my earnest attempts to please God, and something about that actually reached my troubled soul.

Evening prayers brought everyone back to chapel with more chanting and ceremony, after which we wound our way down more dark halls, up more stairs, and into a community room of tables and chairs, a single crucifix on the wall. We were free to talk. Most everyone was seventeen and right out of high school, a couple of girls were in their twenties. About a third of the group was from the Academy that was part of the complex, the same one I'd been asked to chaperone those young girls around. The rest were from the city, farms, or surrounding towns. They seemed surprisingly at ease, laughing, talking. Sister Hubert, the Novice Mistress, formally introduced herself, and told us we couldn't talk again until after breakfast the next morning, "Get ready for bed, lights out at ten, and goodnight, Sisters."

She just called us Sisters. We'd only arrived a few hours earlier.

I followed into the next room, where twenty-eight cells were sectioned off with long muslin curtains. Everything was beige. Each cell measured about the size of a walk-in closet with just enough space for a thin mattress on a simple iron frame. I missed Elizabeth and I missed our bedroom. I thought if I could just get back there, I'd never leave my side of the room messy. I'd never disturb her sleep with my tossing and turning again. I'd be the perfect sister and the perfect daughter.

Someone had hung up my second outfit and laid my toiletries on top of a small dresser. I sat on the edge of the bed and reluctantly put away toothbrush, toothpaste, comb, stockings, a pair of shoes, and clothing. I could hear other girls do the same. At least I wasn't alone, though I might as well have been. I wanted to say something to the girls on either side of my curtain, ask them if they were scared too.

Shelves hidden behind fabric held one teeny mirror. I picked it up and looked in. Vacancy stared back. I waited for a revelation of some sort. I'd never seen that girl, those eyes. I was completely disconnected with whoever she was. At that very moment, in the quiet of that cell, I'd lost the lovely teen along with her future. I hadn't known this kind of desperation and I wasn't equipped to change.

Girls scurried toward showers, so I robed and slippered up, grabbed needed supplies, and followed the sound of running water to the next room. There were several stalls and sinks and

I fell in line. No eye contact, no talking, just hustling to get ready for bed in thirty minutes. It was nothing like the college dorm I could have gone to. Things would have been fun there. We'd have plenty of stories with excited chatter about boys, upcoming dances, deadlines, trips downtown, pooling resources for pizzas and soda, running the halls, rushing to classes, piling on one another's beds, squeals, silliness, crazy girl stuff.

Suddenly, two carloads of boys pulled up outside. They honked and shouted up to our fifth story novitiate. Several girls giggled and rushed to windows, waving and hanging out to see whose boyfriends were down there.

"Sisters!" the Novice Mistress shouted and turned off all the lights. It got dead quiet except for the honking, which died out as the cars sped away. I collapsed into bed and tried to stop my spinning head. My mind crazed beyond its capacity to think straight.

An older girl pierced the quiet with shouts. I assumed she was having nightmares. The lights had gone off only moments before. Maybe she just wanted attention. If that was the way to distinguish yourself in the convent, then I didn't want to. But if she wasn't faking, I didn't blame her. Her yelling unsettled me more than the silence.

Just as soon as I had fallen asleep, it seemed, I was awakened. Two nuns came through the dorm, rang a big bell, and shouted *Benedicamus Domino* (Praise the Lord). Somebody mumbled *Deo Gracias* (Thanks be to God) in response. By my definition, it wasn't even morning. My brain hadn't had enough sleep to repair itself.

Get up, get dressed, use the facilities, and then congregate in the community room. We rushed around in the same deafening silence. Everyone gathered and, like sheep, followed the Novice Mistress. We trampled down stairways, clumsy and noisy in our shoes, through hallways, and into the chapel, where nuns were already in thoughtful meditation. I felt less dizzy, but still emotionally spent. My eyes darted all over the place. I began to count everything, just as I had as a child: eight statues, ten stained-glass windows, all the pews on both sides, then all the stalls where tired nuns were fighting sleep or reading meditation books. I counted the twenty-one of us new girls in our dismal black outfits. I counted the novices, completely in white veils and robes. Then I tried counting the professed nuns, who'd professed vows for life—the ones who were older. The real nuns. I dared not turn around. The council was breathing down my neck.

Mass in the convent felt especially holy and I had a momentary rush of love for God. I hoped He was paying attention now.

After Mass and breakfast, we walked around outside again. I heard snickers and whispers from girls who'd known last night's boys—guys from the high school. That titillating talk was short-lived. Phone calls, kisses, and dates were over.

Yesterday's longings became immediate history, as we were lined up to go someplace to do something. A schedule got posted for chapel, duties, studies, meals, or recreation—one tightly followed the other. The convent took any and all of our private moments. Quiet and submissive, I followed everybody to wherever we were going.

First, we were led into the room where I had changed from street clothes into my postulant garb. It seemed way longer than twenty-four hours since I'd worn my navy dress. Each of us found a desk and sat down. Flanked by three nuns, a couple of men in suits entered, and the room took on a somber mood.

"Sisters, these men are lawyers. They've drawn up papers for you to sign stating that in the event you ever leave the convent you won't sue for monetary gain for your services to the Church," Sister Clara, the convent's historian, said after introducing herself. Those lawyers barely looked at us. I thought only nuns were allowed passed the front parlors and into the cloister.

Like a prenuptial agreement, I was pressed to sign a legal document at age seventeen. We had all entered with a dowry, not more than a couple hundred dollars. That phrase stuck with me all day...*in the event you ever leave the convent.* It teased my brain, and I tried to picture myself leaving. I couldn't. The more I consented, the longer I stayed. What I wouldn't give for an important enough reason to walk away.

The Novice Mistress began reading from her journal. It was filled with reasoning that minimized our immature thoughts of escape. Immediately after signing documents, she explained away any hesitation we might have about what we'd just committed to.

"Some girls enter the convent and only stay long enough to earn a couple years of college credit and then abandon their vocations," she said. "The convent is not in the business of giving away free education. Those women left our community, finished their degree outside, and earned a living out in the world, partly at our convent's expense. If you have it in your mind to do that, you need to fully understand why you're here."

Out in the world? She said that like it was a despicable place. Like up until now, we had spent life at the very edges of hell. Her premise gnawed at my good sense and drove a needle into the marrow of my bones.

"You have been called to serve God," she said. "You don't get paid for that. You cannot take advantage of our community. We'll take care of your needs and you, in turn, give back to us, and ultimately, to God. The papers you have signed this morning protect our Sisters from lawsuits by women who are at odds with their vocations. It means that at no future date can you ever seek compensation for time devoted to Our Lord. Don't be one of those women, Sisters. Theirs were selfish motives."

Her face was stern, her eyes piercing, and her voice was clear and strong. In compliance, I wondered who those awful girls were. I would never do such a thing. I loved God. I'd never cheat Him or my Church.

"The legal papers you signed go into the archives of our community down in Sister Clara's office. Every Sister who ever entered this convent has one on file. Serving God is the highest state in life."

I peered around at the other girls. They were totally focused and appeared to absorb every word. I wondered if she'd made that story up to guilt us into staying here. I hadn't thought we'd be treated with suspicion.

"Now we'll talk about *true* vocations," she said, turning a page of her notebook. "Sisters, if you are sitting in this room you indeed have a *true* vocation. You have been chosen by God. You're already done with the hard part. You listened to His call, tested it, and you've answered it. That you are sitting in this room today is proof that you are one of God's Chosen Few. You should not question that. Some Sisters struggle, but it's a waste of time to give in to such aimless thinking, and a sin against God. Make up your mind, as you sit here now, to put those ideas aside. It is the devil tempting you away from Our Lord."

True vocation? I'd never heard that phrase in my life. *Maybe* God was calling me. *Maybe* I'd be a nun. I'd come *to see.* I entered *to try it out.* Those were the phrases I'd grown up with. Now, I was facing a conflicting message, spoken by a Church representative, who may have a direct line to God.

"Were you to entertain such ideas," she said suspiciously gently, "you would be questioning God's Will. You would be saying to God, 'I refuse your gift. You're asking too much of me. I can't be bothered. I don't want to follow You. I'll selfishly choose my own way.' You would be rejecting God's precious grace, returning His gift sullied. Sisters, each of you sitting here has a *true* vocation. Be fishers of men, Sisters. Help more people to find Our Blessed Lord." Sister referred to her notebook momentarily, gathering her thoughts, *"Veritas!"* she said more loudly than seemed called for, as her palm hit the desk with some force.

I'd never heard that particular Latin word, but after its explanation, it imprinted on my brain in illuminated letters like those Biblical texts that monks meticulously scribe in vibrant colors and iridescent gold. I loved the finality of its meaning. Truth was absolute. I'd seen a statue of Truth depicted as female, a certain holy wisdom in her imperial scepter.

"You are here to live in Truth. To even question that is like slapping God in the face." I visualized walking by the Sea of Galilee, approaching bearded men in flowing robes wearing sandals and handling fishing nets. Boats nearby were banked along the shore. Jesus was among the group. Wisps of white clouds spread across a clear blue sky like the old pictures in our catechism.

"Look, its Gretchen. Come over here," Jesus said. "Help us with these fishing nets. I'm your Savior Jesus and you'll recognize my Apostles Peter, Andrew, John, Thomas, and James. The others are still explaining to their wives why they have to leave. Come with us. Be one of us. We need your help," He said reaching out His sacred hand. I stared at it and hesitated. I stared at those Apostles. They had such kind faces and seemed to know me. They had all stopped messing with the nets and were eager for my response. My hand slapped Jesus on the cheek. Immediately, earth opened up and I plummeted into the abyss of hell. Satan advanced, rubbing both hands with glee. Reviewing my options I pictured all twenty-one girls in black on the seashore with Jesus. Who would be the slappers? Who of us would leave our families, take His hand, and pick up those fishing nets? *I know how to fish.* My mind unraveled under the pressure.

"You have been blessed by Our Lord, Sisters," Sister Hubert said, as I snapped out of my daydream. "Many are called, but few are chosen. Look around at one another. Do that now. Notice whose company you are in." We were a fresh-faced but motley sort. Only God could love this sight. "You Sisters, are the Chosen Ones."

Could we truly have been chosen? I felt God's warmth radiate from clouds in through the classroom window and penetrate my very soul. Then, something wrestled with that notion, as I thought of Almighty God hand-picking me. That couldn't be right. It made me feel pompous. My eyes narrowed, a frown tighten my brows, and my head lowered in skepticism.

The Novice Mistress turned another page in her notebook and stared at us, speaking as one to whom all mysteries have been revealed. "You. Don't want. To stand. Before God in Eternity. Knowing you turned down. His greatest. Invitation," she said every word with such fervor that it drew in my breath. All girls in the room sat completely still. "Our Blessed Lord needs you. He asks for your help. Right here. Right now. He is calling your name. This is your invitation. This is your vocation. Your *true* vocation. Do not let God down, Sisters."

I had to please God or accept manipulation. Sister Hubert spoke on without my attention. I retreated to my own little world in search of truth—*Veritas*. I never denied my long-established tradition of approval-seeking with power figures. When Sister stated those things as absolutes, I knew in my heart that they ought to be questioned. But not by me. Who was I to object? I'm not an objector. There existed entire vocabularies, phrases of dissent, words of self-protection that I'd never brought to the surface to say who I really was, or what came to mind, or how I felt, or anything remotely personal. Even when I thought otherwise, if someone came at me with a strong opinion on any subject, I'd allow it without argument. I'd let others say their peace. I couldn't trust my instincts to remark out loud about anything appropriate to any given situation. Now, hearing this message from a representative of God, I couldn't speak up, but I definitely felt like slapping someone.

I imagined my emerging combative personality objecting aloud. There would be a collective gasp in the room, all postulants would rise from their seats and come at me, rip my clothes, pull my hair, and scratch at my face. Vengeful nuns. I decided against that course of action and went along. I kept all doubts to myself, because that's what I always did. Nobody else objected that morning. I didn't want to be singled out. That wasn't the kind of attention I wanted. I was less than an hour from home, sealed inside a fortress, threatened by platitudes, and surrounded by the enemy.

Now, I remembered edgy Sister Neeta. She had warned us about convent life in the eighth grade, during vocation club—

"not a bed of roses or bowl full of cherries," she'd said. I wondered what she'd say to me now. "I told you so," probably. I remembered how scary-crabby she was in eighth grade and wondered if that had always been her basic personality, or if she'd become that way. She was usually agitated about something, frequently scolding us, "You're headed for trouble in your lives." Two different times, she forced Brittany, a pretty girl, to sit on a tall stool in the coatroom. "Look at her! Look at the smirk on that girl's face! See it? Wipe it off right now!" edgy Sister Neeta said. Brittany tried a different pose, which annoyed Sister more.

"You're still doing it. I can see that look you're giving me. Turn the other way. Look toward the wall. Face your whole body away so I don't have to see it. Such a sassy girl! Oh!" she'd say and snap her head, fire up her eyes, stand, and slam her book hard on the desk with a *tsk-tsk* of her tongue, a handy way nuns corrected behavior when words were scarce.

I looked over at Brittany, a clever girl, popular with some of the best-looking boys. I'd known her since first grade. Her teachers had always favored her. I wondered what in the world Sister Neeta was talking about and why she held one girl accountable for her own distress. I didn't see anything wrong with Brittany. How had she gotten pitted against a nun? She maintained perfect poise throughout the tirade. I'd have gone into hysterics.

Something else about Sister Hubert's true vocation lecture bothered me five years later, when one girl was asked to leave the convent. She'd sat in that same classroom with all of us, heard the same rationale. You couldn't find a better human being. Her intoxicating laugh put us in hysterics many nights during recreation. After five years, her vocation was terminated. She had gotten a pink slip from God:

Dear Ruthie,

Our Lord no longer needs your services. Thank you for all you've done in His Name. Yours was not a true vocation. Have a nice life. Remember those legal papers were binding. Enclosed, please find a check in the amount of the dowry you entered with, two hundred and fifty dollars. Interest did not accrue.

May God bless you,

The Mother General

Chapter

8

The lectures stole my common sense. I could feel synapses disintegrate as new ones took their place. My perceptions of the world were being altered.

We gathered in the recreation room for our second half-hour of leisure time each day. There were board games laid out on the table, the same ones I'd grown up with and had so much fun playing on our front porch. I withdrew from them now, not eager to rattle the pieces of my past between my fingers. I probably couldn't get through an honest game with any competence and wasn't willing to test my skills with that group of strangers. Even though there was laughter—too much of which I'd come to think of as counterfeit—I don't believe those girls shared the sense of humor we had at home.

"You're cheating." siblings sometimes accused me.

"No, I'm not." I'd stifle a giggle.

"You can't play anymore. Game's over for you. Gretchen's cheating, Mother."

"Stop your arguing or you'll have to put boards away and come in."

"We're okay." Back to the game, I'd lose and head for the piano.

In the community room, chatter, games, and laughter competed for my attention, but I wouldn't engage. I wasn't interested in getting acquainted with anybody. I couldn't see the reason for the forced cheerfulness. I sat at the piano and began to play quietly. A girl came over.

"Hi, I'm Toni. That's really beautiful."

"I'm Gretchen. It's a recital piece. I forget most of it. Do you play?"

"Oh, yes. I love the piano."

"Here, sit down. Let me hear you for a while," I said and scooted over.

"No, you finish." My fingers found a little more of Chopin's *Polonaise*, until I felt too obvious in that small room and let the notes fade away.

"That was lovely," Toni said.

"Now it's your turn." She played a classical piece. Her touch was smooth, better trained than my own. I wanted to bombard her with a million questions about the impact this new lifestyle had on her.

"Where are you from, Toni?"

"Santa Fe, New Mexico."

"How in the world did you end up here?"

She explained that her older sister was a nun in the community. Grandparents had raised them and she wanted to be with her sister. I was moved by her story and thought of both my sisters.

"Have you ever heard of a true vocation, Toni?"

"I've never heard it explained that way, but I know we're supposed to be here."

"Aren't you here to test it out?"

"Oh no, Gretchen. I'm supposed to be a nun. And I'm so glad you're here too. This is our calling. Jesus loves us and called us here. We're very lucky to be chosen. Don't you feel special?"

"I don't know. I've never heard anything like this before. I'm not sure I believe it."

"You should accept God's grace, Gretchen. He's been watching your soul from birth and wants to keep you for Himself. That's what a good person you've been. Isn't that wonderful? You are recognized by God. He loves you more than all of His creatures."

I stared at Toni wondering if she was my guardian angel in disguise since she spoke like she knew me. I didn't like her interpretation, and felt silly even hearing it from someone my own age. She seemed so smart. What was I missing? Was I the mixed-up one? Having a true vocation would flatter me, and yet, it wouldn't comfort me.

The next night Toni and I headed back to the piano. We found some sheet music in the bench. "Do you like playing duets?" I asked.

"Oh yes. I bet we could ask Sister Hubert to find some for us."

"I have stacks at home my mother could send me. Do you know Chopsticks?" I started the downbeat and she picked up the melody. We played "Heart & Soul", and fiddled around with other duets. It was my first experience of companionship.

"So you really want to be a nun, Toni?"

"Oh yes."

"I do too. And you're going to stay?"

"Yes, I love it here."

"Me too." I managed a grin on the half of my mouth she could view from her seat beside me on the bench. "Let's play piano again tomorrow night." I'd lied to make a friend. I just needed someone to talk to.

Games always monopolized the evening. There was no opportunity to speak freely. The Novice Mistress said, "Entertaining doubts interferes with God's design for you. If someone brings it up, don't have that conversation."

It felt like I was the only one not fully committed. No one would open up. Not one girl would soften.

I was partnered with Julie for morning chores. Our first job on rotation was to mop the hardwood floors and dust the ornate furniture in a nineteenth century white frame house attached to the convent, a lovely old two-story, with a cupola way up high on top, where tiny decorative windows let in streams of sunlight. It was an historical home, built before the turn of the century. The cozy house had five small rooms and a winding stairway. Its floors slanted from age. Its tiny sofas and chairs of brocaded fabric, fancy wood tables, writers' desks, and Oriental rugs weren't dusty at all. The task hardly seemed worth our while, but we felt privileged to have landed that job. Some girls were in the kitchen peeling mountains of potatoes with a huge, noisy machine that spewed gunk into a floor drain.

Julie pointed to herself, and then to the mop. I pointed to myself, and then to the duster. We nodded in agreement. It was close quarters, like a dollhouse, and we worked quietly, trying not to bump into each other. We polished furniture that already shined, mopped where no dirt existed, and we spent an hour doing it. Warned to be careful, we paused to admire two matching horsehair chairs with high-domed seats. Together, we sat, bounced, stood, then turned back to cleaning, tickled with ourselves. Julie had impulses too. She grabbed my wrist—the contact of her skin pushed new life into my deserted sense of touch—and pointed to the circular stairs leading to the cupola up top. A rope obstructed access. She untied it, smiled big, and tiptoed up three steps, waving for me to follow. I felt like Oliver Twist, and Julie was my Artful Dodger. She had a mischievous quality.

The day before in class, she had told the Novice Mistress, "No one can see common sense either, but everyone claims to have it," when Sister asked, "How do we know that we have a soul, since it can't be seen?"

We climbed up the teeny stairs that barely held the front of each foot. I thought I'd fall, so I grabbed the handrail, visions of potato peels in my head if we got caught. After twenty or more tight, then tighter steps to the top, there really wasn't a platform to stand on. Everything just ended at the wall. To see out of the circular windows, we planted the tips of our toes onto the molding, gripped the sills with our fingertips, and then, straining under the weight of our own bodies, peered out over the city. That sight took my breath away. While trying to maintain balance, our eyes feasted on a splendid panorama of the city. We saw the tops of lush trees, homes, sidewalks, lawns, streets, and neighborhoods. Neither of us wanted to leave that perch. I envisioned spreading my arms, flying down there, then running full speed ahead. We stared longingly out at the world we'd left behind for a higher calling. Funny how this was the most elevated I had felt since I had arrived. Our toes and fingers begged for relief, so we let go and sneaked back down, deliberately stepping away from hope.

We cleaned that place every day at the exact same time, the exact same way, within the exact same sixty minutes, but I never went up the stairs with Julie again. She went by herself. If I couldn't leave the convent, then I wanted to guard against being provoked. I was happy to rotate out of that job. It was better not to tease the pain.

I felt completely disassociated from the poor unhappy girl that I was. I acted as if I wasn't really there. Had I been assigned to peel potatoes, I absolutely would have gone home. Someone knew that.

Julie and I put away the mop and dust cloths and headed back to the novitiate—the top three floors in the solid fortress of the convent where we would sleep, recreate, and study for the next two years. Along with Sister Hubert, all forty-five girls lived in that stately, red brick Motherhouse—the twenty-one of us in black and our twenty-four angel mothers in white, who'd already endured the postulant year, the training year that would correct our corrupt worldly notions and mold us into more acceptable, admirable women of the Church. A veil fully covered each novice's head, making me guess at her hair color. Freckles gave away the redheads. Not a single novice looked anything but regal to me in those flowing robes.

At recreation after lunch, I asked Julie if that view over the city made her homesick.

"Yes, but I can't think about that."

"All those houses remind me of my neighborhood. I don't think I can handle this. I just ache inside all the time. I want to go home. Are you going to stay?"

"Yes. I have a sister in here."

"So does Toni." I hadn't realized my sisters meant so much to me. I learned several girls had siblings in the convent. One had a sister enter and then leave, so she took her place. Others had aunts in there, or had bonded with particular nuns during high school. Girls from large cities shared a special connection. The

Academy girls were the most tightly knit, because they'd already spent four years of high school in residence.

Sister Hubert told us we had to leave our families behind. "You have a new family now. These are your sisters. This is your community. Jesus asked us to leave our families, pick up our cross, and follow Him." I had no one to confide in. Without knowing anyone prior to entry, I was unable to break through cliques that existed. I noticed some girls easily put a smile on the face of the Novice Mistress, while others made her scowl. When I dared to glance at her directly, she usually looked right passed me. Academy graduates—the popular girls—always sat at her game table and engaged in great rounds of Monopoly and laughter. I envied them always having her attention and speaking privately with her in the office. I wondered what they talked about. I had plenty I wanted to say but all of it was forbidden. Besides, there wasn't time to even catch my breath. The schedule was a whirlwind by design. Everyone fell into bed exhausted by the end of the day. I couldn't even feel sorry for myself. I fell asleep without opportunity to think, then woke up and was on the move.

I was giving up a lot by preparing to do God's work. I certainly expected people would be impressed with me.

"I'm going to write a letter home and see if I can convince one of my sisters to join," I told both Julie and Toni.

Chapter
9

What was wrong with me? Neither of my sisters, each in love with her nail polish and boys, would ever enter a convent to help me out of a jam. They understood the world on its own terms. I'd have to walk this road alone. My oldest sister once asked, "Do you sometimes say things you don't really mean?" *Yes! Yes!* How did she know? My words had cut in front of my thinking and were controlling my fate. But there was something left over from childhood, a nameless force that kept me in the convent. Was it sentiment toward the nuns that I'd known in my youth? Fear of damnation if I betrayed the Church? Could such an enormous God have actually handpicked me? When would I acknowledge the truth? What was the truth?

We postulants assembled in the classroom every day for religious training. It was set up like a lecture hall in that it was one-sided, premises clearly defined. No debates. Discussions were all about conceding, an arena I'd grown to depend on. I felt pressured to get onboard with the rules:

Don't do chores in a slovenly manner.

Get to chapel on time.

Wake up each morning with good attitude.

Never be late to anything.

Follow the daily schedule precisely.

No slackers anywhere.

Don't try to be an individual.

Laughter is only allowed during recreation.

Whistling is never allowed. It makes the Blessed Virgin cry.

Don't speak negatively about what you experience, or about one another.

Don't criticize what you see.

Don't question the rules.

Don't question superiors.

Learn to drink black coffee so that when you reach an older age and have to subtract calories from your diet, you won't have to start with the first beverage of the day.

Take modest portions of everything served.

Eat to live. Don't live to eat.

Don't ask for a special diet.

Guard your eyes and listen to the reading.

Use correct table manners.

Learn not to draw attention to yourself.

Blend in with the community.

Medicines are scarce and rarely allowed.

Serve as an example to others.

Seek humility with an understanding that pride waits behind it.

Don't try to be saintly.

Don't try to be more spiritual than others. That is an act of pride, as well. If you think you have that inclination, our superiors can help you transition to a more cloistered convent.

Do not complain about the size of your cell. Monasteries from the early days of the Church were void of comfort. Modern convents are allowed more luxury by comparison.

Don't attempt to scourge the body. We don't do that here. (Visions of women whipping themselves were medieval. That it was even mentioned made me wonder how intense convent life could become).

Don't be emotional about faith. Faith is an intellectual endeavor. We lift our voices in music that is pleasing to God, not dripping with emotion. (God preferred Bach to Beethoven?)

There's no such thing as depression. It's a sin and lacking in hope. Migraine headaches and disturbances of the digestive tract are manageable. Indulging yourself medically in search of physical comfort is a waste.

The list could fill a book. Their very practice would bring about behavioral and spiritual changes, moving individuals toward a greater love of God. Without opportunity to veer left or right, having no choice but to adopt the traditions and rules, I joined the culture of the convent merging my behaviors to the beat of the same drum. When my heart took the occasional rebellious syncopated tempo, that's when my insides cramped and shuttered. It was a big old tug-of-war.

I learned how to act and got good at it. The mechanically tight schedule, the practice of strict traditions, gradually, inevitably, changed who I was.

My true vocation lacked true commitment. It showed in my grades, which should have been a sign that I was unhappy. Sister stood Ruthie and me at the front of the room and announced that we'd earned the lowest test scores on a religion exam. We both slinked back to our desks, me with a dagger stuck right through my heart. Nothing like that had ever happened to me before. Sister told us that when morning bell rang, we should say: *Thy Will be done.* So I tried that. She said we should welcome humiliation. "It gives you the opportunity to suffer the same insults as your Savior. It makes you one with Him. You must treasure those times when Jesus asks more of you." I conceded to that rationale in order to comfort myself.

I searched the library for spiritual books. *Seven Story Mountain*, by Thomas Merton, put me in touch with deeper spirituality. What an unusual person. Reading his words, I wanted to love his God. I'd have to get a new mindset, dig deep, and fall in love, like Merton wrote in *Saints for Now:*

The joy of this emptiness, this weird neutrality of spirit which leaves the soul detached from the things of the earth and not yet in possession of those of Heaven, suddenly blossoms out into a pure paradise of liberty…it is a solitude of wild birds and strange trees, rocks, rivers and desert islands, lions and leaping does. These creatures are images of the joys of the spirit, aspects of interior solitude, fires that flash in the abyss of the pure heart whose loneliness becomes alive with the deep lightnings of God.

Lectures continued each morning. "In the beginning you'll follow a modified schedule. You'll rise early, but not with the professed nuns. You'll study, rotate jobs, and pray. We'll practice meditation and chant psalms," said the Novice Mistress as she passed out new books to us. The Office—Biblical psalms recited in Latin—was a daily requirement for everyone in the morning, before and after lunch, before and after supper.

"No nun is excused from prayer unless she's on her deathbed. For one who is dying, another nun is selected to recite her own *and* the dying nun's prayers." I drew myself in, lowering my eyes.

"The preferred pitch for the psalms is A," Sister said, "but our voices easily drop to G and then F. At the next intonation, voices are brought back to A, a lighter, more pleasant tone to sustain. Each consonant, vowel, and syllable must be perfectly enunciated. Diction is critical, so exaggerate consonants and vowel sounds."

So began the new regimen. One fall morning we rose at 5:30 with the entire community to chant the Office. I sang as perfectly as I could. I was devoted to God when music was involved. We were over one hundred voices, sounding as pure as angels in a Gothic chapel. Sunbeams streamed through stained-glass windows, imitating a painting.

That long Office, called the Liturgy of the Office—*matins, lauds, prime, terce, sext, nones, vespers,* and *compline,* Latin for different hours of a day—was prescribed by canon law in Rome for recitation by clergy, nuns, and even some lay people. For years, I woke up in the middle of the night mentally spouting Latin.

Rushing to chapel at that early hour was rough. One couldn't be late. With so few possessions, I didn't fuss much, but the Novice Mistress wasn't easily satisfied. After breakfast one morning, I returned to my cell and found my bed sheets piled into a big heap atop the bare mattress instead of spread and tucked in tightly as they'd been when I left. My three dresser drawers were upside-down on the bed and emptied of their contents. Underwear, toiletries, school supplies, and note-books were dumped all over. My blanket was rolled up in a wad and looked like it'd been thrown to the corner on the floor. My shelves were wiped clean, their contents mixed up in the whole mess. That insult had happened to a few others. None of the Academy girls. My mother never minded that the corners of my bedspread weren't perfectly aligned. I was a flex-ible kind of artist. I sometimes liked things askew. That intru-sion was a sucker-punch to my belly. I wanted to phone home immediately.

We were told any use of a phone was forbidden. I could see one sitting in the Novice Mistress's office on her desk, out of reach. It was as if my feet had been nailed to the hallway floor and I couldn't simply walk in, lift the receiver, and dial. I kept my eye on it for two whole years—as strong a tangible symbol of salvation as the crucifix itself. *It's selfish and sinful to argue with God's plan.* Every time I wrestled with doubts, the next lecture tricked my mind. I wanted to say, "I know what you're doing. I see what you're up to," but I was muzzled by my own inexperience.

The Novice Mistress introduced the three vows, the same ones edgy Sister Neeta had told us about back in eighth grade Vocation Club: Poverty, live frugally; Chastity, never indulge sexual matters; and Obedience, adhere to strict rules. A life-time of vows elevated nuns above other holy people on earth. "You must renounce wealth, renounce rank, renounce all things for the sake of Christ," she stated. Vows were designed to help us embrace feelings of worthlessness, bringing us closer to God, I decided. All true mystics were devoted to them.

Following rigorous study, we'd recite those vows at the end of our second novitiate year and be locked into them for three years with the Church, the community, and God. There were no legal papers for this contract, so the 'binding business' was traditional, verbal, and not debatable in any court of law. According to the Church, Catholicism held rank above civil law.

With the study and practice of vows, we'd gradually forfeit human tendencies. Convent life inferred that God valued regimen, routine, and structure—all devoid of emotion. According to the vows we'd eventually take, God wanted us poor, emotionally dead, and thoughtless. Strict adherence to rules was the way to please Him. I was fond of order and structure, but my personality poured into the mold that the Church manufactured and I was stripped of all individuality.

Each morning I paid close attention to how vows worked. At her first lecture, Sister Hubert said, "Scrutinize your possessions for excess. You only need one toothbrush and one tube of paste. Sort through everything and reduce items to bare essentials. Turn in all the rest," she said, referencing the pages of her notebook.

I didn't want to give up my stash. They were trivial items, but they were my only remaining link to home. I figured I'd simply hide stuff under my pillow, but those surprise inspections were still going on, and my bed always got stripped, my dresser always emptied. I scanned the room to read reactions. No one blinked.

"You only need one week's supply of clothing. Laundry's done on Monday and Tuesday. When you run out of something, knock on my door and ask for it," she said.

"Waste nothing. Learn to conserve. Comply with these directions now so that when you take the vow of poverty in two years, you'll have experienced its essence."

We weren't wasteful at home. My dad fixed broken things, so we wouldn't have to toss them out. He repaired appliances, locks, and watches, and did woodworking. Mother taught us to darn holes in socks, iron patches on jeans, and hand-sew rips. Shoes were rotated and polished. The throwaway society hadn't taken hold yet. We took care of our things like they were an investment. Those were the days when a toaster lasted a life-time, not a couple years if you're lucky. I already knew how to squeeze the tubes of frugality.

"To each, according to her needs," the Novice Mistress said. "A Sister who works in an office requires technical supplies. A cook shops with the bursar's checkbook. An art instructor uses special paper. Teachers order from catalogues. Musicians accumulate sheet music. Running errands dictates use of a car," she said. The point ultimately made was that nothing was ours. Everything belonged to the community.

What I eventually learned about the vow of poverty was that it had little to do with ownership and a lot to do with undernourishment of the mind. We weren't allowed to have anything that didn't drill their religious doctrines into our heads. *No offense, God, but couldn't I please have a book to read that didn't mention Jesus on every page?* Anything read, spoken, tasted, learned, seen, or thought was under the control of the Church. My poverty came from being deprived of the freedom to disagree.

The next lecture concerned our bodies and minds with regards to sex. In my interview with the Mother General, she had asked, "Are you of strong moral character?" I let her know that I was a good girl. "That's to your credit, my dear," she had said.

"What a beautiful gift you are giving to Our Blessed Lord,"

the Novice Mistress said in class. "You're taking this precious ability to love and returning it to Him unopened. You are making one of the greatest human sacrifices."

The way she put it sounded like she personally found abstinence difficult. I hadn't thought sex would be that big a deal, since something about my father's strictness curtailed that development and the Church called it exceedingly sinful, and then sterilized it, preaching that it was for procreation only. To hear a nun speak about it was totally scandalous. I stared at her intensely and wondered how far into it she'd venture, but her lecture was brief. Back in high school, we used to anticipate retreats when the priest would separate boys from girls and talk about human nature. I never learned anything, yet the hope that it would all get explained to me kept me at the edge of my seat, ears and eyes wide open for enlightenment. I was only taught that everything concerning sex was a sin. How was I to avoid temptation if I didn't know what it looked like? How could Eve have watched out for the devil in the Garden of Eden if she didn't know he was a snake?

The Novice Mistress asked, "What should you do while lying in bed at night, if immoral thoughts come to mind?"

"Say a prayer," said a girl.

"What else?"

"Try to get your mind on other things."

"What else?"

"Count sheep."

"What else?" There was a long silence.

"Turn over," I said.

"Yes," she nodded slowly, seriously. I had no idea why I said that. I thought I detected a rush to judgment by her as she directed the rest of that lecture, staring mostly at me.

"Be happy that you chose purity of soul, that you're released from the burden of the marital bed, the pain of labor in child-birth, and the despair, loneliness, and suffering that accompany marriage. In the night, if you have disturbances simply turn over, the movement will help readjust your thoughts. Turn to spiritual readings to help you handle any difficulties, Sisters."

According to everything I'd ever learned in Catholic school, a bad thought was a sin if I allowed my mind to wallow in it. What was referred to as an occasion of sin—a pop-up thought—was only natural, not sinful. If bad thoughts came to mind, I'd deliberately think, *I wonder what's for breakfast*, and daydream about waffles instead.

"Our Sisters put in a fully active day and readily fall asleep when lights go out, but realize that the solution to provocative thoughts is as easy as turning over," she said, wrapping it up. That was it. That was the extent of any discussion I heard on sex, although the rulebook specifically said, "Never enter the cell of another," and "Steer clear of particular friendships." I wondered if my hasty thirty-minute recreation conversations with Julie or Toni would be discouraged.

In bed that night, I waited for the opportunity to test out the turning over thing, so I could give God that gift as soon as possible. But I just lay there motionless, staring into the dark-ness without arousal. I became embarrassed at my own lack of knowledge.

Instead, those hormonal boys drove by again, honking un-der the windows in the dark. Not one girl snickered. The night-mare girl increased her repertoire. Apparently, nobody spoke to her about that. She kept shouting "No!" at various intervals, sometimes a gentle stream of them easier on the ear, but others like a single gunshot. I never felt sorry for her. It got on my nerves. How could she look people in the eye the next day? Hadn't she been listening to lectures? Wasn't it a sin to call so much attention to herself? I fell asleep without any stirrings.

"Chastity is a beautiful garden," Sister said. Initially, I thought about it that way, but here's what I eventually learned about the vow of chastity. It didn't work for me. I was seventeen. As a late-bloomer, I would be turning over and over and over in about one year, and eventually with little success.

Apparently, I now had the tools to sort through poverty and chastity. Obedience was the last vow to study. Though I was no stranger to good behavior, the Novice Mistress insisted we had something new to learn and she turned the page of her notebook.

"Learn to accept being treated as children," she said like it was something admirable. "Under the vow of obedience, you'll learn to become worthy to obey so great and good a God, and in doing so, will imitate the affection of children for their parents." *Children! I don't see any children.* Each of us was on the threshold of adulthood. That lecture was designed to stunt our development.

I tried to imagine my high school teachers obeying. My energetic algebra teacher Mother Frederick, approaching seventy, but brilliant with numbers and patient with me; my biology teacher Mother Marcelo, who frequently blushed in class, making us think she was normal; Mother Albertan, whose kindergarten children sang along as I played the piano; my psychology teacher, Irish Mother Colette, who taught *Prime Matter and Substantial Form* and on my essay exam of that very meaty, spiritually bloated subject, wrote "Not Exactly," and I wondered which part exactly; my literature teacher, Mother Alicia, who selected specific books for us to read that matched our person-alities—mine was *The Long Winter* by Laura Ingalls Wilder. I suppose it was chosen for me because I was often a pensive person and its author was all about engaging in thoughtfulness. That nun went away on sick leave for half the year. Rumors circulated that she'd had a breakdown. When she returned I studied her for clues, but I was unschooled in reading people's faces, so she looked great to me. Her Spanish skin was flawless, her dark brown eyes like melted chocolate. I don't think the Church allowed nuns much relaxation for fear they'd come to their senses. But that was my perspective and couldn't be relied upon. To imagine those otherwise strong individuals approach-ing a superior to ask permission made me wince. Did they have to grovel outside the classroom?

As always, The Novice Mistress anticipated our resistance. After a brief glance at her notebook she said, "This is another gift to return to God. Your sacrifice means turning over your wills, learning conformity, and obeying rules and superiors with humility in imitation of Christ." She gave us this example: "A nun had been told to go outside and water flowers but she argued that it was raining so the flowers were already getting watered. Her superior admonished her, 'Go out and water the flowers in the rain,' so she did. This story demonstrates per-fectly the vow of obedience as defined by the letter of the law. Keep it in mind when contemplating your religious life."

Where had the vows originated? The concept of making promises sounded strong, a real goal to strive toward. I never heard a single other girl utter doubts about her vocation. I at-tempted talking secretly to several, but each one would literally move away and leave me standing. I became the one to avoid, so I willed myself to conform.

Sister Hubert said the historical perspective of our founders would give us support. "In the 1800s, three women, dedicated to God, came from Ireland to this location to begin the Dominican Order, adopting *Veritas* as their motto. You'll see *Veritas* on all manner of things, representing our Sisters. The 'V' on our convent gate represents our commitment to Truth. We are teachers for Our Lord. We do not administer to the body like Orders of Hospital Sisters, who care for the sick. We value the intellect. Ours is a more elevated endeavor," she said. "Once you become a true nun, a professed nun, you'll sign your name with the letters O.P. after it, as a reminder that you belong to The Order of Preachers that Saint Dominic founded in the 1200s." Dominic de Guzman was from Spain and lived with others who imitated him. They rarely spoke. They prayed and performed penance. They fasted, avoided meat, and lived among the poor, all the while honoring and teaching about God. His story was inspirational and I wanted to get in harmony with Truth. *Veritas.* It sounded lofty. Better to focus on truth than fear.

"Our Founders designed the habit like those of Saint Dominic. They created a coat of arms significant to this region. They answered to Rome and adopted the Rules of Saint Augustine," the Novice Mistress said.

Referring to themselves as 'the cheerful nuns' prompted the notion they were a flawless group, never succumbing to the negative side of cloistered living, like a mystic. But Saint Augustine's rules from the Dark Ages, compiled into a little black book, seemed at odds with that.

I learned that Augustine, who the Church had declared a saint, lived a hedonistic life—the pursuit of pleasure being its highest good. His mother Monica, also a saint, prayed vigorously for him to change. God brought Augustine into painful awareness of his sins. Details weren't discussed, but I decided he was a thief or a murderer. To draw his passions into submission, he practiced harsh rules: strict schedule, abstinence, vigilance, and prayer to rein in his gratuitous behaviors. Besides Saint Dominic, Saint Benedict and Saint Francis practiced rules that attracted others to austerity. Multiple communities of men, and subsequently women, sprang into existence, at first small in number and then more widespread. They were a special breed of religious people, in need of lives out of the ordinary.

Armed with our very own *Rules of Saint Augustine*, we seventeen-year-old girls had classes, interpretive texts, and constant readings to foster monastic life. Initially, it was somewhat charming. Catholic discipline taught me to focus and live in the moment. Rules produced order, cleanliness regulated our living space, frugality brought the reward of simplicity, and efficiency got things done. It was an uncomplicated life physically. But like everything else, once the novelty wore off, reality slithered back in to bite me. I had all the tools to be a good nun. I was back and forth with nagging doubts. Each morning, I'd will myself back to God.

I thought about early monasticism and its origins centuries ago. I discovered that families had offered daughters and sons to the Church as payment for favors.

I theorized that some people wanted to hide themselves away because of fear. Were they fleeing for their lives and forced to create places of safety? Or were they trying to repress misunderstood natural instincts? Its funny how a practice formed out of fear, could also make me so afraid to follow it.

Chapter

10

Convent rules whittled away my personality like a pocket-knife on a stick. In trying to please others, I lost the essence of me. I changed my voice, my laugh, and the way I walked. I was a devoted instrument of denial. One day at recreation, a girl stopped me and said in front of a group, "You have sad eyes." I was embarrassed that my very own face exposed me.

"What do you mean? I've never heard that before. My eyes aren't sad."

"They look sad to me."

Windows to the soul? No one had ever approached me about how I was getting on. I was simply among the rank and file, fully committed as far as anyone was concerned.

"During Ordinary Silence you can only talk in the community room, classroom, kitchen, or outside," the Novice Mistress said. "You cannot talk on stairways, in hallways, the refectory, or dorms. When working together, if sign language doesn't get your point across, both Sisters must step to a doorway to whisper. Keep it to a minimum. Holy days are more relaxed. Brief conversations are allowed immediately before and after class but only with regards to your studies." Words piled up on my tongue and thoughts clogged my brain.

"Profound Silence, hours you prepare to receive Our Lord in Communion, begins at nine p.m. through morning Mass.

There's Ordinary Silence the rest of the day. Ours is semi-clois-tered living. Contemplatives—Trappists and Carmelites—*never* speak. Those religious individuals begin their rigid schedules before dawn. They take little time for meals or recreation. Oc-casionally, one of our sisters has transferred into those Orders. It's generally from those ranks that you'll find mystics," she said. Many saints were thought to be mystics—so close to Jesus and His suffering as to practically be one with Him. Sister warned us not to act like them.

"Sisters, don't stomp around in your shoes. There's a certain decorum becoming of a religious. You should lay the foot down on the floor quietly, with more dignity than what you've been doing. Our convent is a place of silence. Walking heavily dis-turbs reflection on the Life of Christ."

I practiced a stride that made no sound. Each movement appeared angelic and holy. After a while it came to be that one minute, no one was beside me, and the next, someone was right there, as if she'd been standing there the whole time.

"Sisters, don't crane your necks and look around. It's undig-nified. A religious person should have downcast eyes and look neither left nor right. Keep the focus on God and on the task at hand. Don't become distracted. Your veils prevent gawking."

"Arms shouldn't dangle at your side. It doesn't give a good appearance. Your stride shouldn't be distinct. Cross your hands over your breasts like the Blessed Virgin or at the waist under your cape. Refer to one another as Sister, no more first names."

The push to fully commit eventually got me. Within only a few months, I loved God so much that He was practically the only one I talked to. Mostly just, *Help me.* I'd done all of it. I walked softly and without specific gait. I never looked around. I spoke quietly, as if each word was a secret. I kept my arms crossed in front of me. I called everybody Sister. My personality was gone. I became what was expected of me. My mind became a dark place full of tangled cobwebs, like an attic that I couldn't enter out of fear of ghosts. Because I hadn't empowered myself to leave the convent, or seen that it was even an option for me, I'd follow their formula to see how it worked. The more I practiced religious fervor, the more my previous seventeen years faded like old photographs. I felt the string of time connect me to early monasticism. Something spiritual awakened in me and I finally got the sense that I was favored by God. In a moment of sudden awareness, I realized that the rigorous rules caused frustration to build up. Having no other outlet, I would turn to God. I waved my white flag to Him. That was the way to reach a spiritual life—deprivation and entrapment.

Sometimes I felt oneness with God then quickly lost it. Determined to save my soul and be assured of eternal bliss, I found more spiritual books and studied more meditations on how to imitate Christ's life. I prayed the rosary more fervently. I focused solely on God. I turned my whole life over every minute of every day in search of unsustainable joy. For one week, in desperation to reach ethereal heights, find peace, and force myself into acceptance, I knelt beside my bed with arms outstretched like Jesus on the cross. I hoped the pain would trigger a connection to His suffering—one minute, two, then one night for ten whole minutes. I abandoned that exercise because it hurt, didn't work, and just made me feel crazy. How far from reality was I spiraling?

I didn't want to become fanatical, so I decided to believe I had a *true* vocation. When negative thoughts dragged me down, I prayed for help. Anyone watching me could see that I'd become devout. Eyes perpetually downcast, quiet and pliable, I was God's instrument.

One day, a fellow postulant came up to me during recreation and out of the blue said, "You're not the only one close to God. Trying to be the holiest one doesn't mean God loves you more. God loves all of us the same." Had I become an object of ridicule? I had tried to figure things out in an honest way and that girl had decided to clobber me without cause. I had only a fragile amount of self-esteem left, but I recognized a smack-down when I heard it.

The Novice Mistress never spoke with me personally, though I followed her instructions to the letter. Other girls, Academy girls, were in her office multiple times. In two years, I'd only had three encounters with her. I decided that I must be a disappointment.

"How would you like to do some sculpting?" she asked me one day.

I was finally being recognized for my artistic talents. I followed her into the bathroom, where she handed me a small tub of grout and a trowel and showed me how to fill the worn spaces between the tiles.

"You're talking too much during sewing duty, it's been reported. You're dismissed from that task."

It wasn't me. It was the nightmare girl. A complete injustice. Who had it in for me and why? But I didn't argue with my superior, but instead seized the moment as one of those opportunities to be humble in imitation of the accused Christ. I wondered if we were imitating the right traits of Jesus.

I tried to get my bearings. I tried to remember who I was. I was a good pianist. I was Cinderella in kindergarten and bandleader in second grade with a baton and a gold cape—not a red one like everyone else's. I was artistic and creative. I read books. I *could* earn top grades. I had an assortment of friends and a nice family. I drove a stick shift. I knew how to paint the garage and to pull weeds in such a way as to stunt their growth. I held the ladder steady while my dad switched storm windows and I retrieved whatever tools he needed when he repaired things. I washed windows without leaving streaks, using newspaper and near-scalding vinegar water. I navigated the neighborhood woods with all the kids. I made complete pizzas from a box. I ironed whatever was in the clothesbasket on Tuesday's, leaving almost no wrinkles. I watched my mother select balanced meals at the grocer's every Saturday morning. I helped in the kitchen every evening. I mashed potatoes, fried chicken, flipped burgers, made iced tea or lemonade, threw salads together, lined up the dressings, and set the table. We siblings took turns doing dishes so I learned teamwork. I was the champion bath-room cleaner and always my mother's best duster. I knew to sit immobile in the boat as fish nibbled and finally took the bait.

"Now!" my father would holler. And I'd thrill as I pulled in a crappie, blue gill, or perch.

"That's a keeper," he'd say after measuring it for legal size with his wide hand-span before tossing it in a net. I loved making my dad smile. At the end of those three weeks, he was wonder-fully relaxed. I cleaned fish and eventually learned to fillet. Not well. Fried crappie with ketchup, cornbread, and lemonade—food of the gods, in my eyes. My family didn't think I was too shabby. I was a Main Street girl. I was thoughtful. I was kind. I was good. I was your normally flawed human being. I thought I was smart. But I wasn't happy. I kept forbidden memories alive, stored in boxes in the attic of my mind. The lectures tried to burn them away. I had to stay. I didn't know why, but I had to stay. I made myself. Stay.

The Novice Mistress irked me one day, when a Christmas card I was assigned to make didn't suit her. The design on the card was her idea—that of the old chapel tower, since torn down and replaced with a modern, gray-stoned behemoth. The original tower could be seen from many high points around the city and was well loved. But the lines that I drew of that spire were not straight and eraser marks had feathered the paper slightly. I had apparently shown it to her one too many times. She was tired of the bother, tired of the crooked lines, tired of me. That woman, who had barely ever spoken to me, grabbed my shoulders, turned me around, and with both her hands, shoved me stumbling down the hall. I became bitter and threw the card out. Anger turned into resentment. The better way to practice imitation of Christ would have been to speak up, using my own good mind. It took me weeks to recover. I nursed my anger until another lecture ravaged its strength.

"When you pass any older nun, just nod. As your Novice Mistress, I'm the only one you're allowed to interact with." I was immediately suspicious of that separation. Might older nuns warn us, speak of unhappiness or mistakes they wished they'd never made? If one of them had talked to me even once, I would have opened up to her. Older nuns looked grandmotherly to me. They had spent their entire lives talking mostly to Jesus and would probably have loved the new company. When I passed them in hallways, some smiled. But I thought I saw a hint of something else. Trying to please God day in and day out, exhaustion comes to mind. And possibly, regret. We were curious about every Sister in the community, wanting to know their secrets about how they managed. There was one we couldn't figure out.

"What's her job?" we asked. Middle-aged, she appeared perfectly normal, but very guarded. We could never catch her eye.

With a hushed voice, our Novice Mistress said that nun had asked permission to visit a doctor who said nothing was wrong with her, so Mother General declared her healthy. But her face was stoic. She seemed lonely, without a friend in the world. I wondered how she could bear such agony. To me, she had either become one of those very holy people—needing to transfer to a stricter cloister—or she was in despair.

"Mother General believes all illness is in the head," Sister Hubert said. "Medication and doctors are a drain on the community. And because that's her opinion, it's true."

So I learned it was dangerous to show signs of weakness. My mother said that in my great-grandmother's Mennonite community, entire towns would turn their backs on a person for certain things, putting them in total isolation. It could drive a sane person mad. I worried about that nun whenever I saw her. I resolved again to completely hide my true feelings from everyone so I'd never suffer that pain.

One Sunday, Sister Hubert announced, "Mail call!" I grabbed my letters, the biggest pile—weeks of accumulation—and disappeared into my cell for privacy. I heard from high school friends, neighbors, cousins, aunts, uncles, both sisters, my mother, and even my dad, who never wrote to anybody. I knew my mother had orchestrated this outpouring. *"Please write Gretchen, she's alone in there."*

As I removed the rubber bands and scattered the envelopes on my bed to see who hadn't forgotten I still existed, I saw that every letter had been opened. *Someone has read my letters!* I stared in disbelief. *Wasn't this America? Wasn't it against the law to open someone else's mail?* I was livid. The convent wanted to make sure no one on the outside was knocking down their solid protective wall. I knew the Novice Mistress would say, "Take it to God" if I complained. Which I wouldn't.

I read my mother's letters first. I wanted her to say, "Honey, come home. We all miss you." She never attended a parochial school. Never experienced indoctrination from early years. She didn't understand what motivated me into such a mess. My father's letter said how proud he was. It was an honor to hear from him. But his letter carried good penmanship, proper syntax, and correct punctuation, like he was writing to a nun. I knew he had slaved in earnest over that letter probably for an hour. He'd brought us up to know how important hard work was. German nuns and priests from his youth drove that into his head for many years. It was not news to me that he thought a convent was a sensible place for a daughter. I raced through letters from siblings and friends. Not one person begged me to leave. I questioned the depth of all my relationships, especially family members. I wanted somebody to read my mind. I wanted a school friend to pull up in a car. I'd sneak down fifty steps and out a back door. I pictured that happening, tracing the route over and over in my mind. I knew exactly which way I'd go. It wouldn't take five minutes. A car could pull along the rose hedge. I'd shimmy right through those thorny bushes and be gone into the night, stopping with my pals for a Coke, then heading straight home.

I wondered if I'd gotten every letter mailed to me. Unbelievably, some girls whispered they had not. The Novice Mistress held onto one girl's letters from home because her mother was so upset with her choice. Sister Hubert didn't want the postulant to be tortured with a mother's barrage of pleadings. That's what the girl told me. Maybe my mother had pleaded for me to leave and the Novice Mistress hid that letter too. Maybe a boy had written to me.

We could only answer three letters. Each one had to be left unsealed so the Novice Mistress could delete things in red. She'd edit our second, sometimes third and fourth attempts. At an outbreak of chicken pox, for example, not one letter got out with a whisper of that illness. It would have been easier for her to just dictate everything. I toyed with the idea of writing in code or ingeniously designing a slit in the envelope to hide a secret message. I reluctantly handed in my letters every time knowing they didn't tell the whole story.

I read my stash over and over, sure that I'd missed something. Perhaps I'd read them too fast. Maybe I should read between the lines.

"You had a real boyfriend?" I asked Julie.

"Yes."

"How serious were you?"

"Oh, very serious."

"Was he as serious as you?"

"Oh, yes. We planned to marry. He tried to talk me out of coming here up to the day I entered."

"Then how can you do this? Mother General said my poor dating history was a sign God wanted me for Himself. If you had a boyfriend, then what was your sign?"

"I know I have a vocation."

"So you actually believe that giving your life to God is greater than marriage?"

"Yes."

"I'm not that happy here. Some days I want to go home. Don't you ever feel like that?"

"We're not supposed to question God's Will. We have to guard against temptation. I've started praying to the devil."

"You pray to the devil?"

"When I think God is refusing me, then I test which one will answer my prayers. God or the devil."

"What in the world are you praying for?"

"It's private."

"Is your boyfriend writing you letters?"

"I'm sure he is, but Sister Hubert doesn't give me his."

"That's terrible. You mean he writes, and Sister just keeps them?"

"Yes. I know it's true. It's better this way."

"How do you know he's writing?"

"I know."

"Did someone tell you? Did your mother tell you? Did Sister tell you?"

"We can't talk like this." I didn't understand. I went to the chapel, stared straight ahead and bit my tongue so I wouldn't cry.

Chapter
11

Repeatedly instructed to break the ties that bound us to our *former* family, I secretly clung to thoughts of my mother, who faithfully wrote to me. "Saving your letters is a distraction from your goal to fully commit to Our Lord," Sister said in her next lecture. On a day when I was reeling from my battle of wills, I threw away my letters in an effort to stop the pain. To sever ties. To finally commit. When new letters arrived I thought about them differently. I held them ever so slightly away and to the side, giving them a defensive read.

"Your sisters bought new cars—a white Mustang and an orange Volkswagen Beetle. Your brother is still in the army."

Mother wrote about my dad's responsibilities. She eventually wrote about my sisters' weddings. I hardly acknowledged them. I'd become a good student of obedience. I started to think of my family as wasting their lives on nonsense. I was the one doing important things. I lost interest in what they did. In getting rid of my pain, I'd gotten rid of them.

Mother wrote about the latest crazes like pet rocks, mini and midi-skirts, knitted TV slippers, sweaters, scarves, mittens—all the rage—Mary Poppins, and the Flintstones. All those things seemed frivolous. I was critical of my own mother. What a different me I'd become.

I prayed for courage. That's what I was told to do. I was supposed to be strong. I tried to mask the anger, which I felt, but couldn't identify. I never told my mother what was happening to me because I didn't know. Personal thoughts were selfish. The second they'd prick my heart I'd deny them access. I was unrecognizable in my letters. I set pen to paper with the impulse to write, "Mother, I'm unhappy. I've made a mistake. I want to come home." Instead, "Dear Mother, I love God so much," materialized out of nowhere on that stationery. The Novice Mistress never corrected my letters. She taught me, and I taught my mother to write without substance.

I had no time to sort things out anyway, because the convent had us quickly up and doing. Always a diversion. Always a duty. Always distractions to make us forget that our lives were forfeited.

"Don't walk around the novitiate looking unhappy. Resist the temptations of Satan," we were taught. "Find joy in your love of God. Reflect the outward appearance of your soul, as one who has been chosen."

"You can't expect to be happy as a nun," one girl, who'd spoken privately to the Novice Mistress, quoted to me. That idea troubled me, and then I remembered the nuns of my youth weren't particularly happy. We'd only heard one of them ever laugh out loud.

One uplifting thing in the novitiate was that I always landed good jobs. Ruthie, the fun-loving girl from the farm, eventually dismissed from the convent for reasons I never figured out, always worked the potato machine or mopped the basement floors.

"There's a job rotation posted monthly," Sister said. "Everything is accounted for. You're assigned where needed. Take it to God. Find Our Lord in your work."

We washed mountains of dishes and industrial-sized pots and pans in forty minutes, organizing for the next meal. In silence, we rushed to finish early. So we could go outside and catch some fresh air before chapel. Some of us prepared food or assisted the cook on the infirmary floor, where nuns who were very ill or very old got exceptional care.

There was no buildup of dirt, grime, or dust at all. Walls and ceilings were scrubbed down seasonally so that everything smelled sterile. Ladders, buckets, mops, and cleaning rags were pulled out daily. Nuns operated at one hundred percent capacity. Every job required certain skills, and all talents were scrutinized. From the Mother General to the cook, nurses, bursar, bookkeepers, musicians, and teachers—everyone got plugged into a cooperative slot.

Four of us trained on the chapel organ. I sped down flights of stairs, lengthy hallways, and slid onto the organ bench. I practiced as much as the scheduling allowed, accompanying the community by spring. *I could play music for a lifetime.* I envisioned myself on great organs playing robust processionals, *pomposo* fanfares, and *allegro* toccatas. Magnificent music would emanate from my fingertips, my footwork, my touch, my talent. I would lift the hearts and minds of people, taking them closer to God. *Thank You for the music.*

A more tedious task—the laundry—took nearly two days. It wasn't obvious to observers that a nun's habit totally came apart. Long, heavy, sweat-absorbing robes, yards of linen and muslin from a hundred nuns—many more during holidays when scores of them returned to the Motherhouse for retreat— were disassembled, washed, ironed, re-sewn, then returned to each one's cell every week. I stitched and delivered, then practiced the organ in-between.

In perfect silence, nuns transferred clothing from enormous washers to enormous dryers and ironed on giant hot presses. Those jobs were heavy and collectively burdensome. I never heard a complaint or saw anyone out of sorts. Rather, I saw joy. Each woman appeared true to her commitment in fulfillment of God's invitation to serve. It made me believe that no one buckled under the colossal weight of the lifestyle. Like them, I tried to stir up my love for God every moment. The mere practice of the effort brought me closer to my goal, calmed my nerves, and dissolved the adversity of fight. Years of indoctrination, suppression of feelings, and people-pleasing practices drew me away from everything I knew to be safe and comfortable. Religious intrusion directly conflicted with American citizenship—the right to seek happiness, which was apparently a fruitless concept.

I managed their disciplined life. I embraced the Church. I did what they told me to. I set my sights on God. To say that I was lonely would be a sin, but not a lie.

"Sisters, don't become the kind of nun that sticks with only one companion. I'm referring to particular friendships as defined in *The Rules of Saint Augustine*," the Novice Mistress said. "During recreation, be sociable and learn to get along with everyone. Don't gravitate to a select few or a single person. Make God your only Constant Companion."

All of us noticed one particular nun who always whispered with a single partner while strolling around the grounds during recreation. Her excessive coziness was mentioned in class and Sister Hubert talked about her.

"She's a very religious individual. You do see her frequently with only one person at a time and occasionally they're holding hands. If her eccentricity makes you uncomfortable, know that she is profoundly holy." I was jealous of that nun's exceptionalism.

Referring to a nun who'd been left behind her class, I asked Toni, "Why was Sister Natali kept in the novitiate an extra year?" "There's got to be a reason. Nobody talks about that. Is there a secret? She's usually alone except for lectures, and she's in the office a lot."

"She might be one that the convent wants to keep an eye on. Maybe she exhibits suspicious traits or odd behaviors." *Suspicious traits? Odd behaviors?*

"You and I spend recreation together. Could we be under some scrutiny? Has that ever been mentioned to you? Maybe we should try to circulate more."

Everyone made an effort to know other girls, but it was no use. People gravitated back to whomever they felt most comfortable with. Of twenty-one girls, I got to know only two. The others were simply there every day. But I'd soon realize true vocations took precedence over true friendships.

Several of my high school friends had entered an Ursuline community in another city. I heard that on their entry day, their street clothes were wrapped in newspaper and handed back to their parents. "Your daughters are dead to you now," they were told. They were back home in a week. I imagined their recreation conversations: *"Psst. Let's get out of here."* They had one another to lean on.

The Mother General moved women around to various missions—parishes in the state with churches, schools, rectories for priests, and convents for nuns—like pawns on a chessboard. Friendships died before they were secured. Saint Augustine's rules ran directly counter to Aristotle's belief that man's greatest exercise was friendship. In the convent, our greatest exercise was to avoid it.

Winter promised the richness of beautiful music. Our choir instructor, breathtakingly beautiful Sister Rebecca, made us sound like angels. Some voices soared so high that I would not have been surprised if an apparition of heavenly bodies materialized. I wanted the windows opened to release our music out into the world. The very second the music stopped, chains recurled around my ankles.

My family arrived one afternoon for a visit. We hugged and I shared suitable stories.

"Sisters, share nothing with regards to our lives. Don't complain to your families or tell them anything that would expose the cloister of our convent. Pray to Our Lord for strength," the Novice Mistress warned before each visit.

I talked nonstop, about studies and schedules, and who was who, afraid to pause, and I never arrived at a relaxed, quiet moment. Mother, Father, and both sisters listened as I blathered away. Eventually, only my folks came to visit. My sisters probably thought I was crazy.

At the Christmas visit, my mother had made me two aprons of her own design, with tiny flowered prints. The Novice Mistress said, "Put them in the attic. They'll be given as gifts to the convent's benefactors."

"My mother made these for me," I said. She reemphasized her words and held out a key. I stomped up two flights of steps. My mother had just left. I missed her so much, but only my feet acknowledged it.

I'd never been in that secret room. I pulled a chain and a single bare light bulb came on, forcing me to squint. I saw boxes with names on them. I found one for me and lifted the lid. There were my navy dress, red heels, lacy bra, frilly slip, hose, and jewelry. My hand smoothed the linen fabric. So pretty.

My dress wouldn't fit me now. The cook, tender-hearted Sister Beatrice, knew how to satisfy the need for comfort, my pleated skirt was tighter than the first day I put it on. I abandoned my mother's aprons and my dress, pulled the chain, and closed the door, which locked behind me. I headed to chapel. *Why must I give up my mother?*

She had also brought me a box of her famous chocolate rum balls. I didn't tell anyone about them. From under my mattress, I rationed them out each day. I kept my cell in perfect condition until I'd eaten the last one.

Exactly one year from the day we'd entered, we were to be married to Christ in a ceremony that included a single-file walk down the chapel aisle dressed in white.

"Sisters, don't shave off your hair to fit under the veil. A short trim will do. We are still women," Sister Hubert said. A couple girls, not me, shaved their heads completely.

"I don't feel ready to be dressed like a nun," someone said in class.

"That's a common concern. Once you wear the holy robes, you'll assume the spiritual and mental attitude of a nun. It's more than a symbol. It actually promotes the behaviors you desire. Grace comes with the habit."

We were about to adopt new names. The Mother General made the final decision, though we could submit three choices. She made up a name for me. Sister Greta. Every time I saw it written or heard it spoken, I thought of Greta Garbo, a Hollywood star during my mother's youth. She lived in New York and became reclusive, hiding under disguises when venturing out. Miss Garbo's seclusion and my life behind a wall matched perfectly.

One day before the ceremony, the Novice Mistress presented

us with an assortment of cords, each with a series of knots, spread on her desk—chastity belts. We'd never seen nor heard of them.

"Tie the chastity belt loosely around your waist next to your bare skin," she said. "When undressing, it's a reminder that your body belongs to Christ, your Husband, your Lover."

Calling God my lover made me squirm. Some things were just too odd. Like the wedding garments unearthed from some ancient closet. Silky white skirts, long-sleeved white blouses, and netting to be used as veils hung limply on wire hangers. Piles of white shoes thrown into two boxes lay beneath. We stood quietly for a minute, then some scrambled to get the best ones. My mind moved forward to the moment my sisters would catch sight of me dressed, not just unfashionably, but ridiculously out of sync with their world.

"This part of tomorrow's ceremony will only last ten minutes," Sister Hubert said as she watched me finally make my way through to get what was left over. The shoes were too small. The skirt was unflattering.

Marking the start of our second year in the convent, the day arrived when we walked single file down the aisle all dressed in white. Our families, a hundred nuns, a multitude of priests, several Monsignors, with the Bishop officiating. We'd be given away to God by an army of Church Hierarchy as the choir, organ, and bells all celebrated.

"What is your desire?" the Bishop asked.

"To become Brides of Christ," we said in unison. We left chapel, changed into new white habits and veils, returned, stood together in the sanctuary, and the Bishop addressed us by our new names.

"Gretchen, hence forward you shall be called Sister Mary Greta."

Outside, under the sun and among the trees on the lush lawns, we gathered for beverages, sandwiches, and visiting. My family, lots of relatives and friends came. I hadn't expected the big crowd. I saw my reality in their expressions. My body and my truth were hidden under yards of white muslin, my cheeks squeezed out from the tight headdress, face garish and pink, freckles popped out, and a smile plastered on my overwhelmed face. Denial is a strange and uncomfortable existence.

A long hot summer stretched ahead. Besides regular prayers, daily Mass, and chanting the Office, I now recited the fifteen-decade rosary.

"Sisters, now that you've removed all doubts about your vocation, keep conversations limited to your studies. Deeper, personal relationship belongs to your Bridegroom," the Novice Mistress said. Friendships dried right up.

What we learned the first year got intensified the second. The disturbing ritual I saw at my first day—nuns lying prostrate in the chapel—was introduced. If I dropped a spoon, accidentally bumped a table, spilled something, or created a noise while serving meals in the refectory, it interfered with the spiritual reading and was a fault. Running late or allowing a door to slam were faults. A convent was a perpetual quiet zone. Faults were different from sins. They were fumbles with penalties designed to keep us humble.

Once while I swept, my broom handle hit a small overhead pedestal holding a statue which fell and shattered when it hit the ground. I gathered up the pieces and showed them to the Novice Mistress. She was quite alarmed. Major fault. For three successive nights I had to kneel and prostrate in the refectory in front of the council. I'd have bought them ten statues if I'd had any money. It was an offensive humiliation. I almost threw up.

We carried small notebooks and pens to jot down faults:

Walking improperly, causing heads to turn.

Getting distracted by something.

Taking a bite while on kitchen duty.

Losing something.

Falling asleep during meditation.

Dropping a book.

Losing your grip on the kneeler.

Tearing clothing.

Each week, we brought our list into the community room for Chapter. The Chapter of Faults—a ritual from early monasticism—required us to sit in two rows of chairs facing one another in the recreation room. The Novice Mistress was at the end peering down at us. Silence was imposed. Eyes focused on laps. We stood, prayed, then sat and waited.

Each in turn faced the Novice Mistress, read from her notebook of faults, knelt down on the floor, and prostrated until the Novice Mistress knocked on her prayer book—a signal to stand and return to a chair. When all faults and prostrations finished, we stood, prayed, and left to collect another week's worth. Everyone became careful not to let doors slam, to walk quietly, and monitor movements.

The prostration had a name. *Venia.* It means "forgivable sin," and stems from venial sin. We practiced that complicated ritual so as not to feel foolish, or awkward, or fall over, like learning a new dance in high school, only not any fun. It was a contorted series of moves that protected the white habit and made sure a nun looked graceful, although laying still as a carcass on the floor wasn't pretty. Waiting until the superior knocked on her Office Book wasn't attractive. Doing the whole thing in reverse to get up wasn't lovely. Some Sisters welcomed the humiliation. If any of my high school friends had witnessed it, they'd have grabbed me out of there. *I wonder if they're still writing.*

Twenty years later, television would relate stories of families rescuing loved ones from unusual cults—defined as cults because they were unfamiliar to this country—to get them into immediate counseling and undo the brainwashing. I knew cults lifted some of their protocols right out of the monastic handbook. The only difference between my experience and theirs was the long established Church with its enormous power and license to behave without interference. Catholics accepted that back then.

I remember describing the Venia to my friend, Gina, some years later.

"Gretchen, do you realize how sick that is?"

Her reaction was reaffirming. I was ashamed for allowing myself to be treated so badly, but that place had a way of wrapping a blindfold around impressionable youths. What was initially disturbing to me became acceptable behavior, desirable even. It had not been apparent at the time how insidiously and slowly it devoured me.

"Sisters," the Novice Mistress continued her indoctrination. "Some of you may feel you're no longer Catholic, that your new life doesn't resemble the Church you were raised in. Our convent takes its every directive from Rome."

I no longer thought about leaving. That notion vanished. I

got swept up in the schedule and before I knew it, days turned into weeks, weeks into months, and months into years.

The Venia continued to haunt me. No other girl minded putting her face to the stale tile floor for forgiveness for being human. I couldn't warn the twenty-eight new recruits to run while they still had a chance. Our class was now the oldest in the novitiate. Our angel mothers had moved on to their missions. Three novitiate walls exposed bare corkboards.

"Where is your initiative?" the Novice Mistress demanded of me and pounded her fist on her desk. "Our bulletin boards have been empty for weeks!"

It was autumn, so I envisioned a Native American theme. I'd been taught to honor the tribes that respected our earth. My spirit was stronger than my religion. Happy hunting grounds held more passion for me than mansions among the clouds. I had admired brave Pocahontas and Sacajawea in my history books. I saw Native Americans dance in powwows in the north woods, rhythmic drums pulsating with every beat of the heart. I accessed images, stories, and poems I knew as a kid. "Indian Children," by Annette Wynne:

> *Where we walk to school each day,*
> *Indian children used to play....*

And the beautiful "Song of Hiawatha" by Henry Wadsworth Longfellow:

> *By the shores of Gitchie Gumee,*
> *By the shining Big-Sea Water,*
> *Stood the wigwam of Nokomis,*
> *Daughter of the Moon, Nokomis.*

Where art was concerned, I still knew to follow my instincts. No sketching needed, just straight-out cutting. Scissors in hand, I cut here. I cut there. In a trance, I sat alone in my cell. Bed, floor, and me, got covered with bits of paper. Soon, I was pinning autumn foliage along one side of the cork and a canopy over the top. Cuttings plumped into fullness, reaching out and off the board. I created the form of a lone, dark figure with wild, colorful feathers jutting from his head then wrapping around his arms, embellishing his wrists, ankles, and legs. His nearly naked body, profiled in dance, circled a flaming wood-pile and gave the illusion of movement and sound. One leg, bent at the knee, angled high in the air, the other stretched from sacred ground, his back arched forward and his muscles clenching hands that grasped shakers and beads. Gently curving lines of smoke from tips of long tongues of fire wove through the leafy forest, disappearing into the evening sky.

That silhouette bragged of my passion. I heard his guttural chant. I felt his pounding rhythm in my heart. He showed all the intensity I wasn't allowed to. The artwork is now safe in a treasure box in my home, though it is faded and slightly ripped.

If given time and materials, I could have decorated every bulletin board in the convent. My imagination was still alive. I waited for comments, but none came. I thought my bold artwork probably provoked controversy.

Another visiting Sunday arrived. The love I'd felt for my family had evolved into keeping them at arm's length. I talked about my studies, schedule, and the timetable of my progress through the novitiate.

Earlier that morning, a young girl named Sally secretly decided she wanted to leave. She had drawn attention to herself by looking unhappy and angry. The Novice Mistress was rattled. She failed to change the girl's mind behind closed doors. She directed two of us to take Sally into the attic and grill her. I sat staring in amazement while the other novice reasoned, pushed and prodded. It was obvious Sally's decision was firm. She didn't argue, but instead sat in rigid defiance.

"She doesn't want to stay," I went and told the Novice Mistress incidentally.

Sister Hubert was furious. Rather than call off the effort, I was dismissed with a wave and a humph, and someone else was sent in to break her down. Minutes before the visitors came, I heard Sally caved under stronger pressure. But two hours after visitors left, we learned she actually had slipped out with her parents the moment they arrived. Her name was never mentioned again.

I was surprised by my lack of confrontation with Sally. I'd just sat there listening. I had no words to coerce her. No secrets with which to enlighten her. Rather, I was in awe and disbelief witnessing her strength. I wondered what that said about me. I had no idea. But a little itch told me something deliberately put me there. And what would I do with that advantage? I put it among my hidden secrets where common sense was stirring unseen, unacknowledged. Just building.

That evening, our Novice Mistress performed the Venia in the refectory. I was horrified. That woman was older than my mother and there she was on the floor. I don't know what pummeled me more, the Venia or Sally.

Chapter 12

Ultimately, it was Sally that got to me. How had she escaped? I was so angry at her. How dare she know what she want. How dare she stand her ground. How dare she muster her courage. I had shared chores with her and witnessed the impenetrable wall she maintained in order to keep her guard up—talking to no one, eyes never straying like she had no peripheral vision, body language warning me away.

I spent a year as a postulant, a year as a novice, marking the end of the novitiate. Beginning my third year at age nineteen, I'd be a real nun. Time to commit to the community, promise vows for three years, and assume the habit of a professed. Another ceremony.

"Sisters, what is your desire?" the Bishop asked.

"To be accepted into the Dominican Community and to take temporary vows for three years," we said in unison.

We followed one another into the sanctuary. The Bishop handed each of us new habits and veils. We left, changed, then returned as professed nuns. We hadn't signed a contract, but there were witnesses and spoken promises. We prostrated, covering the sanctuary floor, a black blanket of female bodies lying face-down and still. A total desertion of all worldly things. My family watched me. I never asked what they were thinking.

"Sisters, you will never be more pleasing to God than you'll be at that moment. You should have three wishes prepared. God is more likely than ever to hear your prayers as you lay prostrate before Him," Sister Hubert said in class the day before our Profession.

I envisioned God up in heaven saying, "Come to me, my beloved." No, actually, I didn't think of God that much. A little movie started in my head interfering with my concentration as I lay on the sanctuary floor. Visions rushed by split seconds at a time. I saw clouds shaped like animals, I saw fields of corn, and I saw people from my past. I saw my family, all my relatives, my home on Main Street, the backyard, bikes and trikes and roller skates, our swing set, our weeping willow, our sandbox, sidewalks, the woods, the lake, our fishing boat. I saw Monopoly pieces, decks of cards, our front porch, the piano, each high school friend, the football field, school dances, and my first kiss. Then, there were the neighbor ladies, church ladies, quilting grandmothers, lovely Hollywood nuns. I recognized the church I grew up in, the enormous windows, the communion railing, the fashionable women in their wildlife fashion, the poorer folks who prayed with such fervor, and the stained-glass God with His book. I remembered my bedroom, my dad's flower garden, my mom's hands, downtown department stores, Hershey bars and bowls of popcorn, movies, my navy dress and red high heels. My life was flashing before my eyes.

I was dying.

The ceremony nearly over, I wished for health, happiness, and, for the life of me I couldn't remember my third wish, the one suggested by Sister Hubert. (Three years later, I remembered. I'd forgotten to ask God to make me a nun for life). The ceremony ended. We got up and left the chapel in a procession, always one behind the other.

Because ours was a teaching Order of nuns, that summer we prepared to teach in the fall by practicing on summer school kids. We studied manuals, memorized finger plays and songs, designed bulletin boards, and invented playground games.

In August, I moved to my first mission in a Chicago parish. That convent was a modern, lifeless yellow brick building—I preferred red. Every sound reverberated off the walls. There were no rugs anywhere, but instead, hard linoleum floors, steel fixtures, and deadbolts on heavy doors—none of the Old World architecture that captivated my imagination.

At nineteen years of age, I taught fifty first-graders, six piano students, accompanied the high school girls' choir, did household tasks, and took a college math class. I was also expected to provide relief for the parish organist, feisty Sister Angelica. The Monsignor had such control over her that she couldn't leave for summer break. His temper tantrums were notorious. Only Sister Angelica knew his musical pauses, rhythms, dynamics, and pace. Stories of his rants reached all the way to the Motherhouse, 150 miles away. In a rush of stark reality, I realized that all my organ lessons, my piano lessons, my youthful musical experiences, were now directly related to the Monsignor.

The first morning, I sat on the organ bench while Sister Angelica squatted behind the choir loft railing and stared intensely into my eyes. Monsignor immediately saw through the ruse and stopped the Mass. Over his loudspeaker, he demanded, "Get that Sister off the bench."

"Stay put," Sister Angelica said.

"Sister, get her off the bench." he said louder.

"Don't move," she said.

"Sister, I won't resume Mass until she's off the bench."

I looked at Sister Angelica, who remained rooted to the floor. Through the mirror I watched Monsignor fidget with things on the altar. He folded a small cloth, fiddled with a ribbon, adjusted a candle, then turned completely around, squared himself against the altar for support, and stared straight up into the choir loft.

"Get off the bench!"

Suddenly, Sister Angelica sprang alive, her two hands positioned themselves over the keyboard, her elbow nudged me off, her feet planted where mine had been, and his Mass was back to normal.

"Dear God," I said aloud.

Sister Angelica declared Monsignor could be weaned off of her one interval of Mass at a time. That exact scenario went on for a week and then abruptly stopped. I had failed as the replacement organist. Sister Angelica said my piano students weren't challenged. I had too big a workload with a choir, students, and classes.

Nuns in that suburban house became aloof. Failure on any level was intolerable in a place that sought perfection. I attempted to participate and be friendly during recreation, but people wouldn't respond.

One evening, someone hid my papers during evening recreation. After searching at length I eventually found them under the couch. "Maybe you shouldn't mix work with pleasure," one of them taunted me. Then if they ate at all, the tables of hungry nuns picked at the lasagna I prepared for supper.

"Too spicy," someone said. It was my mother's recipe. It was delicious.

My watch broke that year and my superior said, "Stand and hold it." Then she walked away. It took several seconds before I realized the humiliation was intentional. Clever Sister Marcela, still teaching in her seventies, said, "When I was a young nun, had someone given me a quarter, I'd have gotten on the bus and gone home." I never saw a bus and a quarter wouldn't get me home, but her words spoke volumes. I went into the superior's office, laid my watch on her desk, then left without speaking. I never asked for another thing.

I caused myself plenty of trouble that year when I ripped my habit on the spokes of a bicycle wheel earlier and was grounded. The backyard was off-limits for me when there were picnics. I could watch everyone from the kitchen on the other side of the glass door. No one spoke to me. I was ignored like a contaminant. The thought occurred to me that I could bang my head against my cell wall a bunch of times and get relief that way.

I wondered how nuns could be so cruel. There were cantankerous ones and others who appeared kind-hearted. I recalled instances from childhood. Young Sister Chelae, once a favorite of mine, threw my workbook at me in fourth grade, sideswiping my cheek. Another time she attacked me personally.

"Who put your hair up in those ponytails?" she asked, not at all quietly.

"My mother."

"Do you think you look good like that?"

My face turned crimson red with shame and heat. Its two tails swung out from both sides of my head like parentheses.

"You look like you're six years old. Don't wear them to school anymore."

When I told my mother, who frequently tried different styles on me—her little Dutch girl—she fixed my hair like that the rest of the week.

"Does Sister have hair?" I asked her.

"Probably," she said with a shrug and a sigh, leaning against the kitchen counter and shaking her head.

That happened a long time ago, but there I was, face-to-face with some of those same uncharitable behaviors. I realized that it could be me someday.

Then there was obsessive Sister Edwin, who secured a corner of the basement for herself. Every Saturday she sorted through her collection of empty boxes, rearranging and nesting them according to size.

"You never know when you'll need just the right box," she said, tucking one inside the other, inside the other, inside the other. Some nuns snickered at that. I wanted to wrap my arms around her but I knew that was inappropriate. I always went out of my way to treat her with respect and kindness after that.

There were other strange things that happened that year. Melanie, a high school choirgirl, repeatedly gave me folded notes written on theme paper to slip to the assistant priest.

"Don't tell on me," she said.

I minded my own business and passed them on, marking the pleasure of the priest. By then, I was fed up with trying to conform. I no longer cared what other people were doing in their lives. Melanie's letters might have been cries for help, but I knew better. I rather liked the intrigue.

"Keep your distance from the custodian," we were warned earlier in the year. "He crosses the boundary of the cloister with his talk."

The custodian blessed the holy water. I watched him pour gallons into fonts—the bowls in each vestibule where the faithful cross themselves before entering God's home—and then he made the sign of the Cross over it.

"It wouldn't get done if I didn't do it," the custodian said.

He and I sometimes talked and laughed. It almost felt like freedom.

"What do you want to be a nun for?" he asked while mopping my classroom floor one afternoon.

"I'm not staying," I said. I'd said those words out loud. I heard my voice casually say *I'm not staying*, as if I'd just spoken about the weather. The janitor was the friendliest person I met that year. Sometimes his son would sweep the floors. He had a major speech disorder, but I hung on his every word. I'd ask him to repeat and repeat and repeat, to make a connection and to hear an outside voice.

To keep fifty six-year-olds quiet, I taught them about God, their guardian angels, the devil, saints, and The Blessed Virgin for the first half of the year, imitating the nuns of my youth. I scared them with the same stories I'd grown up with and they sat stiff in their seats, staring at me like I was lying. The second half of the year I couldn't teach religion to small children any more. I read them Bible stories instead. That's when the first half hour of the day became thrilling. I loved the excitement of teaching them to read, write, and work numbers. I corrected every single paper, of every single student, every single day. I knew exactly where each one needed help and kept a close eye on them.

We watched President Kennedy's funeral and The Beatles', the only two times television was allowed in five years. The Beatles' invasion was a mystery since I only saw them once. But watching girls scream in delirium whipped me back to the legitimate emotional life of a teen, which I still was. Regardless of the sorrow felt by every American, Kennedy's assassination allowed me to cry real tears in the convent. I put that sorrow upon my sorrow. Two deaths.

The convent prepared us for the inevitable question that people of the parish would likely ask about our college degrees. "Sisters, you have many degrees. The degree of the body temperature, degrees of communication, degrees of intellect, degrees of this, degrees of that. Why of course you have degrees. Parishioners don't need to know you haven't graduated," said the nun who prepared us for anything that might come up on our new missions.

"You look awfully young," one parent said, "like you're still in high school. How old are you anyway?"

"It's the freckles," I said. "They can be deceiving."

"Have you finished college? Do you even have a degree?"

"Yes," I fibbed.

Veritas.

I told a deliberate lie as instructed, but not as big a lie as the one that I'd been telling myself. I was tortured, miserable, lonely, and desperate to find someone to trust. I felt abandoned by God. So I abandoned God. An assistant priest came for confessions. I opened up to him with potent words that matched my truth.

"Father, I hate it here," I whispered to the stranger through the grille.

I felt like a phoenix rising from the ashes. Lightning didn't strike. No one yanked me from the confessional. He didn't argue and he wasn't shocked.

"Why aren't you happy?"

"I don't like it here. I don't like these people. I'm not supposed to be in here. I'm not supposed to be a nun. I want to quit and go home," I said kneeling in the dark on the hard board of a kneeler.

"How long have you felt like this?"

"Three years."

"Have you shared this with anyone?"

"No, Father. I don't get along with anybody."

"Why is that?"

"I don't know."

"Are you under vows? How old are you?"

"I'm twenty now. I have two more years of vows."

He paused, and then asked, "Do you like anything about the life?"

"I like the teaching."

I had expected beauty in the convent. There was very little in the way of art or music. The yards of fabric, folded, tucked, and draped over my body had become a nuisance. People were not who they appeared to be. Everything I knew about this life before I lived it had been dramatized.

That priest gave me a code name, so that he could identify and counsel me further.

"Call yourself Martha next time." I wondered if he was a confidante to other nuns in the house.

I walked out of the confessional and joined nuns in the chapel pews. They all exchanged looks and then followed me with their eyes, since I'd stayed in the confessional longer than appropriate, which further fueled my isolation. So I quit attempting to engage. I sat out recreation barely listening to conversation.

Without explanation or forewarning the Motherhouse sent a nun to straighten me out. The same one who'd asked me to chaperone those high school girls, directed me into the front parlor and shut the door.

"Jesus loves you. Pray to be worthy of your vows. Fulfill God's plan by giving yourself completely to Him," she said. "To seek Him is to find Him. The nuns in the house perceive your lack of commitment."

She talked at some length. Her voice fluctuated between cutting and slicing. I knew I'd never be a true Bride of Christ like she was. Outwardly she was young, pretty, smart, and committed. That's what people saw. But that's not who she was to me. My eyes glazed over. I realized nothing she said had anything to do with me. Anger had exhausted me. Sarcasm had captured my private thoughts. My personality divided into more fronts than I could identify. Denial of my true feelings had pushed me to the edges of despair. Rather than taking up the cross with renewed zeal, as had been the mentor's intention, I decided to start listening to someone I'd barely paid attention to, a more trustworthy person. Me.

My third year in the convent ended. I left that awful mission and returned to the Motherhouse. Familiar faces were no comfort. Those girls I'd lived with for two years in the novitiate didn't talk to me. Toni however, suffered a similar type of ridicule at her mission, in a house with only three nuns, who weren't appreciative of her quiet nature. Whereas I had the classroom as my refuge, she hated the teaching part of that life.

"These women are cruel, Toni. Nuns are supposed to be good. If this is what lives devoted to God are like, I want out. I can't take this anymore."

"God is testing your commitment," she said. "You have to remain strong. You are a good person. Can't you see that Jesus is asking more of you because He loves you more? You are very dear to Him. You must fly to Him. He wants you to share in His suffering. He knows you're strong. He knows you're special. He knows your soul has an insatiable thirst for Him."

And with that, I quit talking to everyone.

Chapter
13

I began my fourth year as a nun. I was alone, surrounded by hundreds. When I first entered the convent, I thought, above all else, that at least I'd be safe. I no longer believed that. Thankfully, a retreat was imposed on the convent. For two weeks, talking was limited to every third day for an hour. Perfect for my mental state.

That summer at the Motherhouse, I took a course taught by a Dominican Father, entitled, "The Seven Proofs for the Existence of God." Initially intriguing, it turned out to be a useless exercise for me—pure intellect without benefit of heart. Too complex. Too chiseled. Too flawlessly defined. I didn't like that glaring exposure of my apparent intellectual limitations, which I now view as pure common sense and clarity.

Probably based on scholarly works of Saint Augustine, the course was for those who enjoyed the entanglement of intransigent logic—a confusion of words, outlines, debates, and doctrines—that went on for weeks. As the scholarly priest and lowly students argued like legislators in class, I let my head drop, stretched my arms across the desk, took a big breath, shrank into my seat, and tried to become as insignificant in that classroom as I apparently was to the Church. I memorized syllogisms, whose logic was tangled in intricacies that I couldn't comprehend. I strung words and phrases together from study notes. After cramming for weeks, I took the exam.

Truly, that class had no connection to God. For me, the proofs were simpler: people's strength in the face of defeat, the sick being healed, babies being born, the poor and destitute given hope, a hummingbird in a garden, animals being rescued, the temperate violin solo in a symphony orchestra moving an audience member to wipe away tears, works of art enchanting the eye, butterflies alighting on dew-covered blossoms, an old person's gnarled hands still working with vigor, complete strangers reaching a common goal together, and regular people fully aware or not fully aware, of their value. That's where God exists. There lay my proof.

When I received an average grade for that class, I felt average—mediocre to the convent-God. If He hadn't endowed me with an aptitude to understand proof of His very existence, how could I be called upon to give Him my whole life? I was sick to death of praying. I decided to be selfish and take care of my own pressing needs. I set my own priorities. I followed the schedule but didn't show up for recreation. I was my own best friend. I had my own *Veritas*.

I walked soulfully into the chapel, sat in the back pew. I stared straight ahead at nothing. I was a tortured and empty shell of a person. Sadness consumed me. A good long time I stewed with my troubles, face fallen, looking at my lap, an empty mind, nothing but disappointment, nothing but grief. Then like always, about to get up, about to leave and go do something, about to say *Thy will be done* again, about to recite another memorized tool, about to just go back and do the same old thing, try harder to conform, like I learned in the novitiate, be a good girl, suddenly, a surge of anger boiled in my gut and my body wouldn't move. Something churned and churned and churned forcing me to stay put and pay attention. It felt like sobs might come to the surface. I'd had this turmoil before. I recognized it from my childhood. Sobs that came to me like messengers, the ones that might cause me to cry uncontrollably, the very same ones I fought to suppress the first day I entered. The ones I fought so hard to control. I knew these sobs. I *knew* them. These sobs were my friends. These sobs were my soul. They were the real me. They were my common sense grabbing ahold of me and shaking my body so hard I'd have to listen. Like some kind of panic attack that worked its own magic without my assistance, putting my mind, body, and spirit back together like humpty dumpty, after they'd been separated into broken pieces for too long. These sobs were spilling over the edges in a flood of emotion that no individual could ignore or push away with prayers, rules or regulations. This time I paid attention. This time I felt the hurt. This time it's on me. I'm the one in charge. This is my truth. Words spewed from my heart that had a life all their own: *I want nothing to do with this life. I can't find any peace. I don't have any friends. Nothing is working. Nothing is right. You don't listen, God. You don't answer and you don't listen. Are you even there? Is there even a God? I need to fix this. I need to do something. I can't wait any longer. I know what this is. I know what's going on. I know what to do. I do. I have it in me. I'm my mother's daughter. I am strong like her. I came from a strong family. I know it's against the rules, and I know I could lose my soul, I could end up in hell, but I don't even care. I don't believe that stuff anymore. Even if it's true, I can't take this anymore. I have had enough. I am not supposed to be here!* I stood and exited the chapel without genuflecting, without holy water. I just got up and left. I pounded down hallways and stairs to a place in the convent where I wasn't allowed, determined to make an appointment with the Mother General, an unheard of and brazen move. Sister Clara stared, shifted, lifted her brow, but silenced her judgment and wrote my name down for two o'clock the next afternoon. My insides were about to burst. I thought my nerves would explode into pieces. I thought I might burn up. The next day I entered the same office where I'd been recruited three years earlier. I wasn't shy anymore. I sat right down and spoke right up.

"I don't want to stay. I don't like being a nun."

"Is the vow of chastity giving you problems?" Mother General asked.

"No." It wasn't her business and I wondered where that peculiar conversation would go. "I don't like any of the vows. None of them make sense to me. I feel resentful all the time." Take away natural instincts and they become cravings.

"You're bound to your vows for two more years," she said. "I could draw up papers for dispensation and forward them to Rome, but the Holy Father is a very busy man. It would take two years to finalize them. And there's always the chance the dispensation would be denied. Whatever the outcome, it would still take two years. By that time you'll have the luxury to reconsider, your three-year vows would be satisfied, and you could make a decision from a more worthy position."

"But I don't like it here."

"Every week, I get phone calls from women who were once in this very convent and beg to return." I could tell she was trying to manipulate me. "Life on the outside is very hard for them. The adjustment is severe. They are distraught when they talk to me. They tell me leaving was a mistake. Some women call weekly, begging me to reconsider. It feels cruel to deny them, but there's no chance of reentry until several years have passed, as many as ten. Even then, I never promise. People who leave the convent obviously don't know their own minds and are thought by the Church to be weak and unstable, having disregarded God's Will for them," she said. "Walking away from your vocation will invite trouble into your life."

"But I *am* troubled. I'm so unhappy." I squeezed the ends of my chair's armrests and pressed my body forward. I felt as if I'd burst out of my skin. She didn't comprehend what was happening here.

"My dear, happiness is not a credible aspiration for a nun. You have an artist's temperament, a fiery personality, and that is why you find restrictive life so difficult." I'd only spoken to her a single time in my life. How could she judge me? "If you push this decision, you'll be sorry for breaking your vows. Your soul could be in jeopardy. It would be difficult for your family. Having a daughter reject the religious life would bring dishonor on them, particularly one who left without fulfilling her vows. You'd be discredited by the Church and that would hurt your parents." Could my family's reputation really be damaged if I left this torment? I pictured the look in my father's eyes if I came home a failure. I reconsidered my decision for the sake of my parents.

"Be strong in your vocation. Our Lord needs you. You've been an asset to this community and a credit to yourself. I am certain your conflicts will resolve themselves over the next two years."

I rose from my chair and left the office. I was so upset. I hated everybody and everything. Like a caged animal, I wanted to lash out with teeth bared. I wasn't even allowed to engage my own mind without intrusion. I chose to harbor the comfort of my rage. Just like Sally, the girl who left while I was in the novitiate, who kept everyone at arm's length in an effort to stand her ground, my personality changed from nice to not-any-more.

Summer classes absorbed my time. An opportunity to spend a day on beachfront property nursed my hopes. At the lake, we walked through woods, found cabins, stripped naked, and shimmied into swimsuits. Fellow nuns scattered away from me. Word was out about my discontent.

Thirty years later, one Sister shared that I looked like a broken human being that summer. Well, I practically was. My spirit was tattered. My mind lay dormant. I was alone. No one had to convince me that the Catholic Church had stunted my growth and broken my spirit. I barely knew who I was. But I pulled strength from my core, from my upbringing, from my DNA, my family, and my ancestors.

I didn't recognize women without their habits. I wondered if any were lesbians. I couldn't help it. That just popped into my head because the convent seemed obsessed, always talking about particular friendships. "Never enter the cell of another" was in the rules. They moved Sisters from place to place to prevent friendships. Rumors of select nuns raised eyebrows. I don't know what happened to Sister Natali—the Sister who was being watched, who was prevented from taking vows with her class. After a while, I surmised what it meant, but without visuals. I never allowed visuals.

My eyes wandered to a group of three women walking together. Others sat on towels further away on the sprawling grass. Some took a boat ride. A circle of ten engaged easy conversation. Nuns sang popular songs, accompanied by two Sisters playing guitars. Dozens more were in a lodge where there was eating, a gathering around a large fireplace, and food preparation in the kitchen.

The sandy beach stretched along a protected inlet of the lake, bordered on all sides by trees and shrubs. Boats whizzed by with regular folks skiing behind. Sailboats slanted lazily on the water. Out there—freedom.

My mother had mailed my swimsuit from home. I felt so fine pulling it on again. I'd lost weight and my body was smooth. That silly, stringy chastity belt had gotten tossed out after my first crisis as a Bride of Christ. On a day, when I had gotten so fed up with everything and hated everybody, the only thing I could think to do was fling that ridiculous rope into the trash. And I never asked for a new one. It was tied around my body like the Church was tied around my life. I found my own grassy area, spread open my towel, and stretched out all four limbs. The sun warming my body was luxurious. Deep breaths released my troubled mind. I began to envision myself forever stripped of the habit. As I lay there alone, my internal camera moved up, up, up to watch a life form—me—a part of the living matter of existence. One of the pulsating creatures that breathed oxygen into itself. I felt relaxed. I was sensuous and I didn't turn over to quiet sinful thoughts. Rather, I allowed the stirrings to ebb and flow. Oh, happy sexuality. Where have you been hiding? How lovely. How delightful. How rich. How would I ever be able to stop this yearning? I dared to think of putting myself back where a man might fall in love with me. Now that I was older, could I navigate the world maturely? That day created a springboard that launched me toward an optimistic future.

I was in an altered state after that beach day. A speck of hope, the tiniest most fragile spark of passion and truth, had been aroused. I spent the rest of the summer sweating under the weight of the habit that hid my individuality, suppressed my personality, and prevented my actuality.

Within a couple weeks, I received a new assignment for the fall. Like the lowly pawn that I was, I got moved back to the city and across town from the Motherhouse. The next mission had a new superior, with perfection as her objective. She had easy friendships with some of the nuns and even members of the parish, though she cautioned everyone else in the house, "Be brief in your conversations with lay people."

Just as the Novice Mistress and my previous superior, she never spoke to me either. I concluded that she'd been made aware of my unhappiness and requests to leave. She was very devoted to Our Lord. I could see it in her demeanor and hear it in her words. I knew I was a threat. I was a different person.

I was drawn to the older nuns in the house. Though many seemed generous in spirit, each one reminded me of a grand-mother who'd denied herself the pleasure of a private life, warm home, and loving offspring. I listened and watched them care-fully. I thought I recognized loneliness and disappointment seeping out from beneath their habits after decades of forfei-ture and restriction. That must have been the reason for not being able to converse with them during our novitiate years. They might say, "If I had it to do over, I wouldn't."

Old memories of antagonistic nuns repeatedly slammed into my brain. Kids passed around rumors when I was a kid about one who hit piano students' hands with a ruler. I didn't believe it until I witnessed her cruelty firsthand. Suzanne, a favorite friend of mine, had apparently let her eyes wander rather than fixate them on her music book during singing class. Suddenly, a loud crack stunned everyone. What just happened?

I turned around to see Suzanne's cheek a brilliant red and her eyes glistening. Every kid gasped. Suzanne held it together, while cruel Sister Fortuna warned us what could happen if any more eyes moved off those musical notes. I wanted to leap up and strangle that nun, who stood only three feet away.

She'd been assigned to our parish temporarily, taking the place of talented Sister Celia who was ill. She tried to turn us kids against that popular nun we'd known since we were seven.

"All you kids think Sister Celia is so great. That's all I ever hear. *Sister Celia is wonderful. We miss Sister Celia.* She's never coming back to this school. I'm the new music director. I'm here permanently." Nobody liked that idea. I'd never heard anyone, least of all a nun, speak so disparagingly.

When Suzanne took that abuse, I sneaked a peek at our classroom teacher, spunky Sister Marcy. Her body bristled, her face turned beet-red, her arms rigid at her sides, hands balled into fists, and she stared daggers over at cruel Sister Fortuna, two rows of desks away. I expected all hell to break loose. Sister Fortuna demanded we sing. As she moved away from Suzanne, we managed some wimpy attempts, eyes glued to the page, priorities jumbled. Once music class ended, that angry nun left our room and never returned. We all sighed and whispered in relief.

"That won't ever happen again boys and girls," Sister Marcy said.

Suzanne was the bravest person I knew. I would've crumpled to the floor, and my recovery would have been questionable.

That nun got removed from our parish. She wasn't even a good musician. She made plenty of mistakes on the organ at Mass, where she played too loudly, too abruptly, and without joy.

Sister Celia returned and that was a miracle if I ever saw one.

Thinking back on those nuns of my youth made me wonder about my eventual personality. Though all nuns were strict, we understood they were keeping us from sin. It must have been exhausting for them and on some days they probably wondered why they even bothered. They were hard-working women devoted to educating us. Every kid had a favorite. They impressed us with their knowledge, got us to memorize prayers, one for every kind of difficult situation. If I could choose something good to come of my experience as a nun, I would want to become somebody's favorite. But it seemed to me I would become one of the mean ones.

At my second mission, nuns were friendlier. I was invited to walk through the neighborhood during recreation with two of them. We spoke with parishioners out sprinkling lawns, watched students ride bikes and skateboards, and admired gardens. I was relieved when they dismissed the superior's harshness saying, "We're intelligent women. There's no need for her control. We are part of this parish. These are our families. We're with them every day. It's silly for her to think she can direct our every move." They were able to engage their own minds even behind walls. Their independent behavior was a breath of fresh air.

I was twenty at the time. I had a girls' choir, taught second grade, played the organ for Masses, funerals, and one wedding. I was enrolled in a psychology class, but was unfocused and failed that class on purpose. I wasn't interested in studying how the mind worked. I only wanted my own back.

Again, I shared private thoughts about my unhappiness with a parish priest, but this one refused to listen to me.

"God needs you," was about all he said. After that, he literally backed away down the hallway each time he saw me approaching. I decided I didn't need him.

Elegant Sister Rita, the kindergarten teacher, let me get it all out. Whatever I needed to say, she let me. On one of her home visits, her brother challenged her, "If I could prove to you that God doesn't exist," he'd said, "your whole life would be a lie, wouldn't it?"

"What did you say to him?"

"I told him he was absolutely right. And he is right, you know, Sister Greta. My life might very well be a waste. If God doesn't exist, I've done all this for nothing. But I'd have taught kids regardless. I'll continue as a nun." Rather than argue, she faced her youth-inspired choices with honest assessment.

Gorgeous Sister Alexis shared that it was her final year. "My vows are up in May and I'm going home." The next year, she secretly phoned and spoke about her adjustment to a couple of us. "It's really a shock," she told me. "You'd better think seriously about what you're planning and make sure it's what you want. It's really hard out here. I don't fit in. Some people hold it against me. You'd find it difficult. I wouldn't do it if I were you."

"Are you coming back in?"

"No."

That next summer, at the end of my fourth year, I made an appointment with Mother Georgia, the newly elected Mother General. She was rumored to be a thoughtful individual and nuns whispered of a gentler, more understanding future under her leadership.

"You can't break your vows," she said straight away, tossing out my hope for discussion." And dispensation is out of the question. The Church considers such selfishness worthy of scandal. Sisters devote their lives to God and their Church without question. Why do you try so hard to be any different?" she asked as she stood up to signal my dismissal.

I left her office feeling ridiculed, humiliated, and cut to shreds. She wasn't at all what they'd said. She wouldn't listen. She wanted me gone from her sight. I was a sinner. I was less than she. Why didn't I just snatch the veil off my head, toss it on the ground, and stomp all over it right then and there? I was still infected with my people-pleasing disease—a trait so loathsome that once I realized it and finally escaped its affliction, bold words and strong actions would forever redefine me. My seething pain had turned me into someone I didn't recognize any more. I had been a creative child, the well-loved daughter of two wonderful people. One youngster among four siblings, all of whom I wanted to see again. What had become of me? I pushed away any attempts from others to even have the simplest conversations. My eyes, my face, must have looked more resolute. It was adjusting to the new front of honestly I felt within.

It was the era of Rome's Vatican II and the Papacy of Pope John XXIII, the fresh-air pope. He said the Church had grown stale and antiquated. "He's ruining the Church," my father said. Pope John said it needed to change with the times. The Church had come under criticism from other religions. Pope John pushed for the Church to modernize. Modern religious writers suggested eliminating long held customs, like allowing meat on Fridays, women discarding head coverings in church, English replacing Latin Mass, priests and altars facing their congregation, eliminating communion railings that separated sanctuary from people, hearing confessions of entire congregations rather than individually, guitars replacing organs, and some statues, images, and paintings disappearing because Eastern religions accused Catholics of being Iconoclast by adoring statues. School kids would no longer be threatened with sin, and all catechisms got discarded. Radical spiritual writers provoked shocking ideas and some of them made their way into the convent and right to our dining room table for spiritual reading. One priest wrote, "Your faith is enriched and deepened only if you have allowed yourself to truly doubt the existence of God. Otherwise yours remains a juvenile level of faith." Our superior was horrified by that book and all copies of it disappeared from the convent overnight. After so many years of spiritual tyranny, I appreciated a priest who acknowledged that we all harbor occasional doubts. I respected his perspective and took on his invitation, toying with God's existence for the pure exercise of deepening my faith. What came from that was a realization that it could actually be true. Deliberately letting go of hope caused me to think differently about the nature of the universe. If I were an accident of fate, not a thought born out of an Eternal Light, I'd live differently. I entertained notions of a lonely planet in our galaxy spinning through infinite space, free of all religions, and governed by science. Doctrines, dogmas, sins, and thoughts of heaven and hell faded. If there was no God, then why was I wasting away in a convent?

Pope John was old, but he had a youthful and progressive mind. Things continued to change in the Church. He must have been very spiritual. If his philosophy helped empty monasteries and convents of unhappy people, I think it was a good thing. Shouldn't the Catholic Church be satisfied with The Ten Commandments and The Golden Rule? Simply offer its members the beauty of the music, the traditions of prayer and liturgy, the prestigious ceremonies, and the intriguing mythology?

Personally, I loved the myths and legends involving angels and saints. Joseph Campbell gave credit to the spiritual treasures of mythology in *The Power of Myth,* when he said Buddhists, Native Americans, and Catholics were its preservationists.

With new friends at my second mission, including parents and lay-teachers, I was happier, and focused on the importance of teaching youngsters to read. Every day I created an environment that helped children learn. I loved my job. My students thrived. During Christmas holiday, when the convent was nearly empty of nuns, three of us were invited to see the decorations in one parish family's home. We drank liquored eggnog and I became silly and adorably happy.

Jan, a teacher, happily married and wished that I could be too, gave me a poetry book as a gift—*Chosen specifically for its size as it can be slipped without notice into your meditation book,* she wrote on the inside cover.

"I thought this would be more comforting than stories about the sufferings of Jesus," she said. I finally told her I was leaving the convent.

"Really? When?" She laughed, practically clapping her hands and jumping up and down.

"In a year."

"That long? Can't you just leave whenever you want?"

"No," I said like the brainwashed person I still was. "I can't simply break my vows. The Church has restrictions and a timetable. I promised vows for three years. I have to fulfill that."

"You know that's nonsense, Sister Greta, don't you? You realize you can just walk away?" Her words blistered my senses.

"Jan, I took vows. I can't just leave."

Chapter

14

In early mornings—when I wasn't meditating on pleasures and fantasies from the night before, shifting in my seat to calm the sensations like the ones on the beachfront a year ago, and while other nuns likely contemplated Jesus's suffering—I read Jan's little red paperback book of rhythms and rhymes. Like Henry Van Dyke's "America for Me," I wanted to renew my citizenship where hope was a right. Like Langston Hughes's "hold fast to dreams, for if dreams die, life is a broken-winged bird that cannot fly," I wanted to spread my own wings and fly freely. Christopher Morley's "animal crackers, and cocoa to drink, that is the finest of suppers, I think," brought my mother to mind. A nursery rhyme: "As I walked by myself, And talked to myself, Myself said unto me, Look to thyself, Take care of thyself, No one cares more than thee." One particular poem by Dorothy Walter Baruch got stuck in my head for good reason: "Around and round and up and down, around and round and up and down, on the merry-go-round I rode around, around and round and round." It spoke to the repetitive and cyclical nature of the convent and my brain.

Jan was a lover of beautiful things, an artist who worked in oils. Why couldn't I reason like her? I'd taught youngsters with better thinking skills than mine. Church doctrine had controlled my thoughts for years and I finally knew it.

I'd been focused on school, and then my leap toward freedom got fueled by a single event. Out of the blue, the entire community of nuns was given permission to see *The Sound of Music*. I had heard vague descriptions of its plot, but didn't know what to expect. I thought it would be like *The Nun's Story* with Audrey Hepburn. Remembering that movie's impact on me, I wasn't eager to see another film on monastic life through the sentimental eyes of Hollywood. But I went because we were allowed to.

I sat in the theater and passively, routinely, watched the movie unfold. Then something clicked. Feelings welled up again. Halfway through the story I saw myself as Maria. There she was on the screen showing me the steps out of the convent doors. Leaving wasn't a sin. No one dragged her back in. She was not only happy, she prospered on the other side of the wall. I wondered why we were allowed to see that film.

I identified with Maria. I wanted to be Gretchen again. I resented all that "Sister" stuff. I already had two sisters. Real ones. Who loved me. And I missed them. I could stop going endlessly to Mass, praying the rosary, and chanting The Office. I could starve the exhausting pretense of contentment. Live honestly. The mysterious habit no longer satisfied my need for dress-up. I could see my mom whenever I wanted. My dad too. The separation had been unfair. What I'd been taught was all wrong. I was waking up. My imagination caught fire. Things were connecting in my brain. Complete thoughts. Reasoning. Critical thinking. The iron bars of my imprisoned mind were dissolving right there in that cushy theater seat with arm rests. The flow of fresh ideas made me delirious. At long last I was generating courage at the very moment I needed it. I envisioned myself walking away. Hollywood helped get me in. It could damn well get me out.

As we left the theater, nuns criticized Maria. I sat quietly in the car. My breathing changed. Emotions churned. I was coming alive.

Back at the convent, I walked across the cold linoleum floor. I glanced toward the work area. *Oh, lovely typewriter, rescue me.* I'd been in the convent five years and was expected to write a formal letter to the Mother General to request permission to take final vows. I grabbed a sheet of paper, an envelope, sat down, put paper in the roller, adjusted both margins, and clicked down.

Dear Mother General,

I am writing to let you know that I will not be renewing my vows in June. I have decided to leave the religious life. I am making this choice after lengthy consideration and cannot be persuaded from my decision.

Sincerely,

Sister Greta

I pulled the paper from the typewriter and rolled in the envelope. I typed the return address in the corner, the address of the Motherhouse in the middle, took the envelope out, and folded the letter with the care that a sculptor gives her most prized work. My fingers stroked the paper. Its surface sandy but soft. I tucked it safely into the envelope. My breath raced. My heart pounded. My movements were deliberate and my mind secure. I walked slowly and confidently into the office where the superior sat reading. I placed the unsealed envelope on her desk. She kept her eyes fixed on me. I turned and walked out, feeling her gaze on my back.

I climbed the stairs in slow motion to the second floor, went to my cell, undressed, and put on my bathrobe. Down the hall I stepped into the shower. My face completely relaxed, wanted to smile. I turned on the faucet and felt luxurious and alive. Water streamed over my naked body. I inhaled the steam, filling my lungs with deep memories.

I toweled dry and returned to my cell. In my nightgown I sat at my desk. I picked up a stray paper. I wadded it up and tossed it into the wastebasket. That was incredibly thrilling. I sat and stared for a minute. I pulled out a stack of paperwork. At first I discarded one sheet at a time, and then, I stuffed all of them in the trash. I sat some more and took a deep breath. I reached over and grabbed some late-in-the-year school work, religious pamphlets, a couple books, accumulations of this and that, and all together jammed them into the basket filling it up. Each purge brought increments of relief. I made a trip to the outside trash. When I came back I opened all my drawers. Without considering anything, I threw out holy cards, medals, stationery, letters, handkerchiefs, black stockings, pens, pencils, erasers, paper clips, and stickers. I cleared out everything. Except for my three habits, veils, Office Book, Rules of Saint Augustine, large and small rosary, and enough clothing for one more month, my cell was empty. I sat listening. Nothing came crashing down. I figured my letter had been read, perhaps a phone call made, maybe some nuns in the house had found out. But no one knocked at my door. It was a lovely, peaceful night for me. I sprawled on my bed. My head needed that pillow. My chest rose and fell, rose and fell slowly. Then more slowly. Sleep came easily without bother or fuss.

The next day I felt the eyes of Holy Mother Church upon me. No one spoke to me, but it didn't matter anymore. I probably could have left immediately and without argument since now I felt I had the upper hand, but I needed to explain my decision to my parents.

Late Sunday afternoon the kitchen was free. I looked over at the phone on the wall. Funny I'd programmed myself from noticing it before now. I froze for a moment. My tummy rumbled. Then the phone summoned me forward. I laid my hand on its receiver. I hesitated. I listened. No one was around. Slowly and quietly I lifted the receiver with my left hand, then dialed with my right. A simple gesture. It rang. A nostalgic sound from my past. If my parents answered I'd have to, say something. *Be home. Please be home.* They were approaching sixty years old. Probably my mother would be fine, but my father, whose smile could melt any human heart, might feel let down. Still, I knew I was loved. Mother answered and she was pleased to hear from me.

"Why, Gretchen! Let me get your father on the phone."

"Hi, honey. How are you?" they both said.

"Hi. I'm fine. I'm good. I have a few more weeks left of school," I said, buying time. "I've put things away for the year. I'm in the kitchen right now. We just finished supper. Everybody's busy."

"We've never gotten to talk on the phone. Is this something new?"

"No, it's just me." I said, still keeping my voice low. "I wanted to call and talk to you. We were allowed to see *The Sound of Music* yesterday." I mentioned the plot. They'd heard of it. "I'm homesick."

"Don't get too homesick," my father said. My heart dropped to the floor.

"But I can't help it. I'm really homesick."

"What do you mean?" Mother asked.

"I'm just homesick. And I might be having a nervous breakdown." I put that notion out there because between my upset father versus my own well-being, there was no contest.

"We don't have nervous breakdowns in our family, honey," Mother said. I hoped she would take the conversation to the next level. I repeated the same thing—movie, homesick, very homesick. After some awkward silence, hesitant talk, and a little stammering, they told me to take care of myself and we hung up. That's as far as I got.

I stared out the window. If this wasn't a nervous breakdown, then why did I feel like Alice tumbling down a bottomless pit? Dorothy caught in a tumultuous tornado? I was experiencing too much emotional turbulence. My chest tightened again. Surely they understood what I was getting at. But after years of compliance, I was suddenly mutinous? I'm sure they were stunned. If I couldn't go back home, my freedom would be retracted before it could be achieved.

The next day I put a sealed letter on the superior's desk, telling my parents that I would be leaving the convent in June, and I hoped I could return home. I wondered if the superior would mail it.

Mother's letter arrived by return mail. Unopened. First one ever. She used to address her letters with, "Darling." This time she wrote, "Flibberty." She'd called me by that endearing name since I was small. She knew the real me. "What's your dress and shoe size? I'm getting your room ready. Everyone is thrilled."

My torture was over. Five years of trouble began to dissolve throughout my body. My forehead relaxed. My shoulders. My jaw unclenched. My breathing slowed. Over and over I forced halting breaths, all the while overwhelmed by a swirling brain that lacked the capacity to stop its astonishment. My eyes burned from brimming tears. My throat swelled from a rush of something. I went up to my cell, sat down and held onto the bed. The fight was ending. The anger I'd carried toward everyone in that community was draining out of me. Relief and sadness fought for attention. I was going home. My vows would be satisfied on June 23rd, the same date I entered. A month away.

The community was stunned that nuns were abandoning their ranks. Pope John's fresh air had opened the doors and windows wide. I learned four of my classmates were also leaving, including the nightmare girl. A religious exodus in the Church began. I had no idea others felt the same as me since that conversation was never allowed. Thank God the future of the convent was in jeopardy. I was hardly surprised when nuns ignored me at a Sunday picnic. I sat down at a table with my plate of food. Everyone got up and moved. For several hours of holiday celebration I was shunned. "These modern girls don't have the discipline we had. They can't take the rigors of what this life entails," I overheard a conversation that was intended for me. It was a lovely day otherwise. The sky was clear. There was a mild breeze. The Universe wasn't angry with me.

Monsignor from my hometown startled me with a visit to my classroom one afternoon, after students had left for the day. What did he know? He never would have shown up out of the blue. Someone must have alerted him about my decision. It had the same feel of conspiracy that surrounded my entry five years earlier. Would he attempt to change my mind? What would I do if he pressured me? But wait—I had this.

"How are you?" he asked.

"I'm fine. How are *you*?"

"Good," he said, coming right into my empty classroom, sitting in a front desk, folding his hands just like kids do. I sat at my own teacher's desk. This was my classroom. The one place I felt like an adult. He was only a visitor.

"I've had great students. I feel good about the year. I think they're ready to move on."

I mentioned no future plans. He must have sensed my resolve. I didn't gush, I didn't fawn. I spoke from a place of calm. Neither of us brought up the real reason for his visit. I talked about the parish, the pastor, and the group of nuns, until he finally left. I stared out the window and saw him walk to his car and drive away. I noticed the continued steadiness of my breathing. His intrusion was a test of my strength, and I had proved myself.

Sister Hubert, my former Novice Mistress, asked me to the Motherhouse across town in an attempt to get to me. She seemed so nice. We were in a room not ten feet from the Mother General's office, where I'd been recruited. I could still feel its encompassing shadow.

"Move your chair closer," she said. "Cross your arms on my desk so you can relax and get leverage. Take a deep breath, and tell me how you're getting along. Do you think you've made the right decision?"

"Yes, I'm sure, this life is too hard for me," I said without a full disclosure of the emotional blow I'd suffered.

"I could counsel you further if you'd like. You could visit every Saturday morning through the rest of May." That was such misplaced and misdirected sympathy. For five years, I could have used some help. It annoyed me that she thought I was in the least bit interested now.

"I don't need it. I know I'm doing the right thing, I haven't been happy for a long time. I tried to leave after my third year, but Mother General wouldn't allow it. I tried a second time and was disappointed again. My decision is firm." Words of confidence emerged as they should have years earlier.

Her face changed from hope to disappointment. I perceived a hint of disapproval. "What will you do when you leave? Where will you go?"

"I'm moving back home and returning to school," I said, recalling those selfish women she'd spoken of who exploited the community to get their degrees.

"Does your family agree with your decision?"

"Oh yes. Definitely." I stared straight into her eyes.

"And your father?" She made her disbelief clear with that question.

"Yes." My mother had set the tone—*everyone is thrilled,* she'd written. Even if he wasn't thrilled, my father would come to realize that now I was equipped with strength of will that matched his own. The rest of my family would bring him along.

"Not all of our Sisters are welcomed home. You're one of the lucky ones," she said, ending our conversation.

I'd lived under Sister Hubert's direction for two years and had never gotten to know the woman who everyone characterized as wonderful. I saw her delicate side only when she tended her large collection of purple, pink, and white violets in a tiny room, each sitting in rows on tables, bathed with sunlight streaming through the windows. She knew the condition of each plant on a daily basis, turning one, watering another, plucking a leaf that had turned brown. Now she was finally taking an interest in me. Too late. I was done. As far as I was concerned, there was nothing left to discuss. It felt cruel to speak so bluntly, but it's all I had. I thanked her and walked out of the Motherhouse for the last time.

Chapter
15

June 23, 1966 was a beautiful day. I hadn't taken an honest breath in five whole years. I was going back into the world. What had changed since I was locked away? Various religious sects attempted to find ways of appreciating each other and ending their competition for souls. There was a word for it. Ecumenism. In the world at large, the first Earth Day was on the horizon. The Bay of Pigs had come and gone. I'd never heard of it. Elvis left the army about the same time I left the convent. The *Flying Nun* TV series would become popular, but I couldn't watch it. The sexual revolution was about to begin, and I nearly missed it.

I stared into the mirror to apply light make-up, eyeliner, mascara, and lipstick. I hadn't forgotten how to do it, like riding a bike. My mother had sent my hair rollers, so I had springy auburn curls. I'd barely slept all night, trying to nestle my head in the pillow for the last time in a bed that was not my own. My eyes had a shy warmth and a small smile hesitated across my mouth the next morning when I studied my reflection and tried to remember that girl from five years ago.

A car turned into the drive below my window and I hurried over to look. I saw my mom and dad through the window blinds. I held my breath, as if that would make the moment last longer. I watched as they parked, opened their doors, and walked up the sidewalk.

The doorbell rang. I heard footsteps, and then voices echoed in the barren convent. My heart pounded with the excitement of a teenager, which I still was in many ways. I'd spent critical years confined in a closed society, while my peers had finished college, were mothers, or held down jobs. It was a setback, but also a move forward for me. I didn't care. I just wanted out.

My mother had also sent a new summer dress—yellow and white checks—a half-slip, hose, a stylish bra to lift my spirits, a gold necklace, colorful earrings, and a delicate bracelet. Fashionable white summer shoes adorned my feet and I could see my toes through the cutouts. I felt lovely. The dress was so light and breezy. New energy was awakening my feminine self. My level of happiness couldn't be measured. Like one who had fulfilled a prison term, my impending liberty was overwhelming. Flashes of paranoia teased my mind, fearing it was just a fantasy.

On the bed lay my three black and white habits, my long fifteen-decade rosary, the *Rules of Saint Augustine*, and the Office prayer book. I wasn't allowed to keep mementos, and I wasn't tempted.

At the foot of my bed were both pairs of sensible shoes, whose black leather was now cracked and softened. Oddly, I hesitated leaving them behind since they'd walked me through my turmoil, and reminded me of my great-grandma, the Mennonite turned Baptist. She happily left her community in the late 1800s, traveled by train with her two small children from Lancaster, Pennsylvania across four states, and escaped an abusive home. She offered me strength when I needed to redirect my life toward greater peace. When I questioned my religion, I thought of her.

I refreshed my lipstick, fluffed my red hair, encouraged my long-lost smile, and stepped out of the cell. I shut the heavy, wood door with its larger-than-necessary steel handle and deadbolt.

I flew down the stairs easily, nearly airborne—my movements unencumbered, arms bare, legs shockingly free and enjoying the provocative breeze. My body had definition. I had definition. I was more than a blank slate for religious ideals to be written on now.

My parents were in the next room. They reassured the superior when she regretted my leaving and hoped it wasn't her fault. She didn't realize how ecstatic I was. Unexpectedly, she gave me a small box from the convent. I hugged my mom and dad, and then said goodbye—more to the convent than to the woman. That was the moment that ended my vows. I had fulfilled my commitments and could finally be released. The inmate was free.

Out in the car, I sorted through the box of items—a check for a hundred dollars from the parish priest, which I spent as fast as I could; a steel crucifix, which stayed in its box and got lost; my dowry, which my dad sent back; and a letter from a boy, which wasn't sealed. The convent had kept that letter for five whole years.

That boy was the Austrian exchange student from my senior year, who had partnered with me for May Day. As he predicted, he had entered a seminary in his country at the same time I entered the convent. In his letter, he wondered how I was getting along with my vocation. He signed it *Fr. Ulrich*. We'd called him Fred. I assume he's still in there. I still have the letter. He urged, "Do write." It was dated 1961. I knew I would never write to him because I didn't want to intrude or tell him I'd changed my mind.

Though my dad was quiet, the drive home was a whole lot better than the one five years prior. That trip had been completely silent. My senses were not silenced this time. This was the open highway, the *freeway*. We sped along the road like the wind and I drank in all the sights—the new fields of corn—three feet by the fourth of July—cows grazing, birds flying in the stunningly blue sky. The entire world seemed to celebrate my liberation. Had there been no sun in all that time? I'd never seen a brighter day. It was brilliant. It was all just brilliant.

My home had only been forty minutes away for all those years. I felt as though I'd been frozen in the Himalayas. I walked up our front steps exuberant but quiet. Freedom was massive. I wanted to do everything and nothing. I wanted to turn cartwheels, somersaults, and flips down the middle of the street. I wanted to jump up and down for joy. I wanted to call everyone from high school. I wanted to watch TV to fill in all the blanks, fall asleep sprawled on the sofa, sit on the front porch devouring good books, raid the refrigerator, and drive the car, all at once.

I put my feet under my mother's kitchen table. I was home.

My bedroom still had the matching purple rug, bedspread, and curtains. Purple! My bedroom was purple! I was delirious. I'd shed those robes, and my mother and I went shopping. I was the exact same size I used to be. My high school friends had become mothers with kids. I went to their parties and picnics and reveled in the fun. Still, conversation was pretty awkward. I had little to contribute. My friends had a stranger in their midst. It would take some generous patience. No one understood the colossal fracture between this world and the one I had been living in for the last five years. Not a single other person comprehended the intensity of my experience. I'd been in a cage, made to believe that my true self would cause the damnation of my soul. I'd been lost at sea for 1,825 days and it might have fused into a lifetime, had I not seen that movie. I'd been such a kind individual that the Church nearly bamboozled me forever. I'd held on for dear life with diminishing hope, squinting to see clearly as I searched for rescue, my head barely bobbing above water, kicking away sharks or delusions of them, wondering how I'd gotten myself into such a predicament and if I'd ever get out. I never wanted to be tricked that badly again.

I was so glad to see my mother. My father too. But in so many ways, my mother and I were never separated.

On my bed lay a box with all my letters. My mother had saved them.

"I don't really know why, honey," she said. "I thought maybe you'd come home someday."

My eyes felt wet, but nothing fell from them. I opened one to read, the words and practiced handwriting were all from a stranger. "I love God so much," I'd written unabashedly, the one passion I'd been allowed. Who had I become? Nobody. I wasn't anybody at all. I'd disappeared.

A boyfriend stole that box of letters from my house and left a piece of his art in their place. But he can have them. I never liked them. I never read them. And I'm glad they're gone because, except for the "Dear Mother" and "Love, Gretchen" parts, the rest were just lies trying to convince family I was happy.

My psychological state took longer to heal than my callused knees. I found it difficult to forgive myself for being so duped. I had recurring nightmares for over twenty years. In them, I'd always be locked in a room, banging with my fists on a door, pleading with nuns to let me out. I'd dissolve into sobs and collapse to the floor. Then, I'd awake in a sweat. My mind released pent-up emotions in my sleep, without needing my conscious help. I tried not to pay attention to them, to shake them off each time. But I noticed when those haunting remnants stopped, right after I paid a reunion visit to the Motherhouse twenty-five years later. I found that room, walked in, shut and locked that door, stood a minute, then opened the door, and walked out. For several years I had exhilarating dreams of flying—out in the darkness with the stars, high in the sky, just my body in a nightgown, horizontal in the night air, no metal plane. Just me. Soaring.

I'd made a five-year-long huge mistake that I could never undo. It separated me from my family and marked me forever different from my siblings. They couldn't comprehend the internal struggle I'd had, debunking the brainwashing. Elizabeth, who had taken my entry into the convent particularly hard, wrote to me years later: "I sure thought you wanted to be there. I didn't know you were so unhappy. You would always sit prim and proper when we visited and talk with proper diction. You were stiff, not relaxed and I thought it was because of your 'holiness' in being a nun. So the vibes were not good for me when I visited. I think I was upset because you changed. You were very stand-offish."

But it was so great to be out of there. I was nearly manic like a little kid—happy, carefree, in love with a great big world, but overwhelmed by it and immature.

In my first few months home, although each knew exactly where I'd been, amazingly five guys asked me out anyway. One re-enlisted in the armed services after a couple dates. Another got back on his motorcycle after a month, without ever attempting a kiss. One I was especially fond of died as a result of military service in the rainforest of Central America. A fourth returned to his university to finish his law degree. The fifth, Charlie, said, "I want to get you pregnant." I'd left the convent in June. That was August. He was definitely jumping the gun. He wasn't what you'd call a stand-up guy at that time of his life. On one date at a nice restaurant, he ordered some wine with whiskey chasers and cordials following dinner, and when we danced, I became dizzy. He laughed when I said I'd better sit down. Afterward, he drove down Main Street and pulled into a motel parking lot.

"What are we doing here?" I asked, barely able to enunciate.

"I got us a room," Charlie said.

"You're crazy. I'm not going in there."

"You mean to tell me that I spent all that money for dinner and drinks on you and this is the thanks I get?" said that nice young Catholic boy.

"Take me home." I was so accustomed to being treated poorly that I continued to date him and continued to fight him off. *I guess a bad date is better than no date.*

One night, he climbed the rose trellis up to my purple bedroom and wanted to climb in. "If my dad had a gun, he'd shoot you. Go away."

I attended summer session at the very same university I had initially enrolled in right after high school. Usually, my brother drove me back and forth between cities, sharing his stories of army life with me. But one particular weekend my sometimes-boyfriend Charlie drove me the forty-five minute return trip on a Sunday evening. A torrential downpour took us onto the shoulder of the two-lane road numerous times and other cars came within inches of sideswiping us. My life passed before my eyes for three hours and when he finally pulled into town, my dorm was locked and our only choice was to spend the night in a motel. I collapsed onto the bed, seconds from sleep, when he plunged at me and took what he wanted. Finally, I decided that no date was better than a horrible date.

I tortured myself over that highly personal theft and was frantic about pregnancy every minute of every day and every night for well over a month. It wasn't much of an awakening. There was nothing wonderful to celebrate. I hadn't freely given in. I just didn't know how to resist. I was accustomed to following orders in the Church military. I hadn't been given the behavioral tools other twenty-two year olds had acquired.

Like the active Catholic that I still was, I went to confession. "I had sexual intercourse," I told the priest.

"Are you sorry?"

"Yes."

"Then you must promise not to do it again without the benefit of marriage."

I didn't like his tone. *Yes, Father* was no longer welcome vocabulary, so I resisted. The words that came out startled me, "I'm not promising you anything."

"Without repentance, you won't receive my absolution."

"Okay," I said without attitude and I got up and left. I heard shuffling, so I decided he peeked around the curtain to see who the insolent female was.

Of all the ironies, I enrolled at the local Presbyterian university. Except in childhood, all of my interactions with people had been with Catholics. What would I say to a Protestant?

With credits in hand, I visited the admissions department. "We would be honored to have you as a student. You have a lot of theology credits on your transcript, would you be interested in teaching religion?" the counselor asked with a grin. I thought it was humorous too.

The university was going through Rush, as there were many Greek houses on campus. It was a week at the beginning of the term when new students were invited to join sororities or fraternities for social camaraderie and other exclusive collegiate support. I got asked to a sorority meet-and-greet. But when those cute girls referred to each other as *sisters*, stood, prayed, and sat down at a long table accommodating twenty, anxiety gripped my insides and I began scheming for a polite way out of there.

I lived at home, so meeting people on campus wasn't easy, because I was so reserved about my past. I shared my background with one co-ed, who then gave me a wide berth. That was my cue to tread carefully. What would I say to people after hello? Non-Catholics I eventually got to know never spoke of sins, as if they had *no idea* about them. Evident to me was the lack of women making even occasional attempts to imitate the Blessed Virgin. They were more like Eve, with her edge of fun and excitement. I had entered a different world. There was such a mixture of colorful personalities. I liked making an assortment of friends from different backgrounds. I let go of the idea that the world should convert to a single religion. Rather, we should co-exist, like a good stew where distinct vegetables and meat in the same pot of gravy complement one another, and not one ingredient is superior to the others.

I felt lucky attending Homecoming with a Jewish guy that I'd never seen prior to the moment he asked me.

"Hi, I'm Steven. Are you Gretchen?"

"Yes." I blinked, somewhat startled.

"Would you go to the Homecoming dance with me?"

"I don't know you, Steven. Why are you asking me to the dance?"

"I've seen you around campus. I'd like to get to know you better."

I had no good reason to turn him down. He was nice-looking, no visible signs of quirkiness. I was the one with a past. He picked me up at my front door and spoke all night about a certain fraternity keeping him on the fence about joining. He said it was because he was a Jew.

"Why would fraternities care about your religion?"

"Jews aren't usually accepted into traditional Greek houses. On larger campuses we have our own fraternities."

"You mean they'd discriminate against you?" I asked, not having a clue about anything.

"It might even be on the books. I can't be sure, but I'll know soon. I fit all the other criteria. When they see me here with you it should solidify my chances, so if they don't let me in, I'll know why."

"Oh I see," I said, but didn't. It was an odd sort of flattery. I was relieved to attract male attention but had no clue how to interact. He never asked me to dance that night. We just walked around. I eventually lost sight of him around campus and I assumed he had gotten tired of the isolation, like I once did, and left. I wondered why people held onto religious resentments for centuries.

Though social activities were an integral part of college, I didn't participate in anything. The panty raid I witnessed—coeds throwing panties out dorm windows to guys—was shocking and confusing to me, the little ex-nun. I didn't mean to be like that, judging everything that presented itself in my new surroundings. Students knew how to act, how to walk, what to say. This was their world and I was an interloper, thrusting myself into a place without the necessary savvy to do so. I bravely attempted conversations while waiting for classes to begin, with girls that looked amenable. Talking about my studies seemed the easiest way to get started. But most everyone had friends and didn't need a new one, especially one with reservations. I had to speed things up regardless, push myself forward, and risk making errors in judgment in order to have an actual life. I certainly would not run back to the convent, as had been a prediction.

I wanted to feel the freedom of my own devices after so many years devoted to doing what I was told. To me, having a few quarters jingle in my pocket was like carrying gold. The only thing I could think to do was buy two candy bars and a Coke every day. Self-indulgence was a novelty. Occasionally I'd go to the library where the quiet was familiar. But then, an adjunct professor sat down right next to me one day, when there were plenty of empty tables. Within minutes I felt his shoe tap mine. I moved mine away thinking he'd accidently slipped into my space. He did it again. I kept staring at my book but was no longer reading. Then again. What was this, high school? He nudged my foot deliberately and didn't pull back. I held my breath. My face flushed. His foot pressed mine even harder. I sat paralyzed. Both of us pretended to read. I didn't know how to handle it. I knew it was odd. I let it linger trying to figure out what to do next. Finally I glanced at him. He didn't look up. I slowly pulled my foot away, pushed back my chair, stood, picked up my books, and left the building. But that incident repeated itself two more times, him coming over, sitting down, and nudging my foot. I knew it was weird, but I didn't know what else he was capable of. I stayed away from the library for weeks. I saw him in the hallway once and watched him enter his classroom chatting with students. He was quite good looking, silver streaks running through his crop of good hair, his face well-defined with regular features. By exterior accounts, a favorable man. But what lurked beneath his surface? I wasn't sure what to expect from a man's intentions, but that business turned my stomach. I'd always tried to evade trouble. What helped me that day? I'm not sure. I'd chosen to escape the protection of the rose bush hedges, and now I'd stepped into a carnival of games. Which ride would I get on?

Chapter

16

I saw that professor nudge a couple of other girls' feet. Then he disappeared off campus. Two and a half years of college under my belt, and a number of easier friendships born out of an interdisciplinary class, I was in my final year of studies, no further along in dating, came home one afternoon, opened the front door, and heard a voice I didn't recognize. Dropping my books on the table, I saw a handsome man visiting with my dad in our sunroom.

"Coleman, I'd like you to meet our youngest daughter Gretchen," my father said. That tall fellow stood and both men focused their attention on me.

"My grandmother's name was Gretchen," he said, reaching out his hand.

"Really? That's amazing," I said, smiling broadly, touching his hand briefly.

"Yes, Grandmother Gretchen on my mother's side. I don't remember much about her, I was pretty small. She was a lovely woman and a violinist."

"What a wonderful coincidence," I said, probably blushing.

"It's a beautiful name," he said. "My name's unusual too, at least in the North. I have three last names, a Southern tradition. Coleman Taylor Mobley, the Third, but I don't use the third.

Northerners think it's too snooty, too many embellishments."

"Coleman is one of the good reporters from the newspaper," my dad said. "He's interviewing me for a story."

"Who is that guy?" I asked my mother in the kitchen.

"This is the first I've met him. Go give them more coffee, honey," she said with a smile and a twinkle, pushing the pot at me. Face flushed, eyes alert, I happily refilled their cups.

"What are you two talking about?" I asked, pouring.

"One of my jobs at the newspaper is to cover the city beat, so I'm here to fill in all sides of a story before putting something in print."

"Coleman is one of those rare newsmen," my dad said. "Most reporters wouldn't go to this much trouble. They just print what they think they heard."

"The newspaper has several cub reporters, most right out of journalism school," Coleman said. "Half the time they don't un-derstand what they're hearing in the meetings, just copy down the agenda, and throw in a few quotes to bulk it up. Whereas, I've seen the world and can put some experience into it." *Seen the world...*

"Coleman is the exceptional writer. It's good to know there are reporters with integrity."

A little while later, Coleman stood, thanked my mom for the coffee, my dad for his time and quotes, said it was nice meeting us and that he had enough material to finish his column. We three said it was nice meeting him, humorously sounding like a choral group due to too much enthusiasm on everybody's part.

"Come back anytime," my father said, sounding like he meant, *"Take my daughter."*

It's still vivid in my mind. The inflections in Coleman's voice are forever etched in memory. They linger as if they'd just happened minutes ago. The second he stood to greet me I felt a rush. His camel coat was on by the time I thought to check if he was wearing a ring. He had a notebook in one hand, left hand still in his pocket. I couldn't tell. Then, as if my curiosity had dragged it out, there it was. No ring! I imagined we'd see each other again.

A week later I thought I'd probably misread the situation, until the phone rang late one afternoon and he asked me out to dinner.

"He's a fine, Catholic young man," my dad said.

I think I latched onto Coleman because he was the exact opposite of my father. Both men were quite strong, quite intelligent, with convictions, but my father carried the weight of the whole world on his shoulders, whereas Coleman threw all caution to the wind. Some people gravitate to what's missing in their lives, while others stick to what they know. Coleman was the embodiment of the free spirit I now longed for.

Coleman's English-Irish personality was such fun, whereas I bore twenty-four years of structure. "My heart nearly stopped when I saw he wasn't married," I wrote in my diary, whose spine is completely broken now. It bulges with letters, cards, newspaper articles, assorted programs from plays we attended, and love notes. "Where have all the flowers gone? To my true love's cheeks!" Coleman wrote on little cards that he tucked in bouquets and signed, "To my darling Gretchen. With love, Coley."

Other entries read that we had dinner at The Red Baron, went ice-skating, and kissed on Valentine's Day. He sent flowers with a card, "Say you'll be my Valentine or I'll hound you till you do!"

He was thirty-two and I was twenty-four, two and a half years out of the convent. I met Coleman's friends and colleagues who said how happy he was now that he'd found me. We were only thirty-six days into the relationship when he brought up marriage. I didn't mind. I really liked him.

I told Coleman about my diary early on. "Keep writing things down," he said, not an unusual statement for a journalist. I wanted to treasure our story so I could look back over things in my old age and share them with offspring like my own parents had, keeping memories of past generations moving forward.

He valued his family's gentle Southern history and was especially fond of his mother. *A man who loves his mother will love his wife,* I read in a self-help book about how to win a good man.

"My mom's had it rough," Coleman said on our first date. "My father died and left her with three young sons. She remarried and had three daughters, my sisters, and then her second husband died. She's raised six kids by herself."

"That sounds so hard. How is she now? Where are you from? How long have you lived here?" I pelted him with questions that first evening.

"I was born in Birmingham, Alabama. Most family members are scattered now. My mother moved us north for a fresh start. I've lived here two years." He was so interesting to me. Southern stories sounded sensuous and soft.

He stopped for a sip of coffee, several spoonsful of cinnamon ice cream, and then picked it back up, "I taught at a small college and ran the debate team, but I didn't like the life of a professor. Being a journalist suits me better. Another reporter and I share the rent in an apartment close to the university."

"That's my university. I'm there every day. I'll graduate in a year, certified to teach in public school," I said.

"I attended Catholic school up to third grade, but was miserable, so my mother transferred me into public. My grades were never as good as they should have been."

"Why was that?" I asked, knowing mediocre grades reflected preoccupation with something.

"Most likely the loss of my father early in life caused my troubles. I didn't pal around with a group of guys during my adolescence. Tom was my best friend—you'll meet him. We played a lot of tennis. We made a pact to marry girls from good families someday. On Saturdays, I'd sneak off to the theatre alone, but never told my mom because she wouldn't have approved. I didn't get along very well with my stepfather, so for high school I attended the local seminary for Catholic boys run by Brothers of the Sacred Heart. The theme of that place was to envision spending a lifetime in the Church."

"I was miserable in a convent for five years. Nuns told me I lacked the courage to stay, but I knew I was braver in leaving. I can't believe I'm sitting in this restaurant having dinner with you right now."

"People reject the strict life the Church uses to sustain itself," he said, putting a spin on it.

"Did you like the seminary?" I switched the focus, as he stared at me like I'd just revealed something he preferred wasn't true. In my mind, a girl who became a nun carried more baggage in society than a guy who went off to the priesthood.

"It suited my needs at the time, but I had lots of fights."

"There were fights in a seminary? Over what?"

"A couple guys called me a sissy, so I beat them up to prove I wasn't."

"That's so mean—why would anyone call you a sissy?"

"I wouldn't join their football team. I preferred tennis."

"I don't think that makes you a sissy at all," I said, wondering if it did.

"I lasted three and a half years in there. Then one Sunday, my mother and oldest brother came for a visit. 'Are you happy here, Coley?' they asked and could see that I wasn't. 'Not particularly,' I said. 'Let's go then,' they both said. 'Get your stuff together and leave with us right now.' So I did, I left that very day. I was gone in an hour."

His escape sounded as easy as mine should have been. My brain whiplashed painful, debilitating memories and I felt weak that I hadn't been as clever and honest as he was. After that first dinner, we began a dating frenzy. Though we combined over eight years of monastic life, we never shared those awful stories. The convent had been a terrible nightmare. Coleman had a wealth of other experiences and I wanted to hear them all.

We drove to Chicago so I could meet his mother. Sarah had just turned sixty. Her Southern drawl carried a charming, gracious lilt. Coleman and his mother were great friends. Their conversation flowed easily over the next two days, addressing family, politics, book reviews, and everything fine arts related. We attended a ballet at the Auditorium Theatre, with seats in the highest balcony so the dancers appeared tiny, as if the stage were a music box.

"Oh, Coley, I wanted you to marry that pretty blonde you brought last time," Sarah said as we found our seats. Her rudeness stung bitterly, but I didn't speak up. I was still accustomed to masking my truth, so I laughed at her remark. Coleman quickly cleared his throat, pooh-poohed her comment, and redirected my attention to the playbill. Within a month, Sarah wrote, "How's our Gretchen? I think of her so often and feel like she'll be the ideal daughter-in-law." *What changed her mind?* Sarah tutored me in bidding hands of bridge, her daily indulgence born out of a Southern tradition where refined women played rounds of cards while Mammy minded the children. "You're so smart," she said. I wondered if she meant I was smart because I was dating her son, since I was not in the loop of most of their conversations.

I met his high school age sisters that weekend. I couldn't even keep pace with them, social skills terribly deficient. We stayed two nights—him on the sofa and me in a bedroom. I knew he'd sneak in for some snuggling and I waited for the creak of the door. Suddenly, it was morning and I was startled by the sunlight.

"Coleman, why didn't you come in my bedroom after everyone fell asleep?"

"My mother wouldn't have approved and don't forget my teenage sisters are here," he said, not sounding as regretful as I'd wanted.

Driving back home, our radio blared, "I will not seek, nor will I accept, the nomination for President of the United States..." We stopped along the highway for a bite to eat. Coleman opened the restaurant door and made a grand announcement.

"Ladies and gentlemen, the Vietnam War is over! Lyndon Johnson has just turned down the nomination on the radio! The war is over! The war is over!"

Well, it wasn't, but he was undaunted, his arms in the air, while the rest of the diners and I went mute. People turned and stared, then shrugged and turned back to their food and new conversation I am sure. We found a booth and ordered.

"What made you do that?" I asked from behind the menu.

"This is history in the making. These people are numb and apathetic," he said.

Feeling numb and apathetic, I didn't know what to think of his grandstanding. Perhaps my personality really was bland from his perspective. But how could it be anything else? I'd been nothing but a carbon copy nun. His behavior startled me. It wouldn't be the last time. What a combination we were. Shy me, outrageous Coleman. He told me years later that because I'd let him get by with that impulsive display, he knew our relationship would survive.

"I didn't let you get by with it. I did object."

"No, I mean that you didn't leave me."

At Easter, Coleman's mother and sisters came to our home for dinner. My whole family was there, so thirteen of us crowded around my mother's table. The conversation was awkward, arch-conservatives meeting heady liberals. My mother's food was delicious.

"It's a beautiful day, Gretchen, let's take a walk," Coleman said. Out the door and around the corner he took a ring from his pocket and slipped it on my finger.

"Gretchen, marry me." And he bent down with a kiss to my lips.

"Okay," I said, surprised at how easy a proposal was.

That diamond was huge—nearly two carats. Heavy and loose, it turned over on my finger, following gravity.

"It's a family heirloom," Coleman said as we finished our walk. "My Grandmother Gretchen had two diamond earrings. Each one has been remounted into rings. My mother put this one in safe keeping for me until I chose a wife. Neither of my two brothers showed an interest. The other diamond is on the East Coast on another family finger." Coleman called them The Mobley Diamonds.

"It's beautiful, Coleman." We exchanged another kiss. A peck, sweet and lovely.

"We'll take it in for sizing and cleaning and then get it insured tomorrow," my fiancé said.

"A bloody nice ring," said one of his friends.

"Absolutely smashing," said another.

"I'm flabbergasted," said a third. I was engaged to a journalist with a Master's Degree in Political Science from Georgetown University. He was a really nice guy, with a big personality, a fearless love of adventure, and a capacity for both profound and congenial conversation. Offspring would be assured security. In little over a month, I'd gone from lonely co-ed to desirable fiancé. I wanted to marry my Prince Charming. I knew he was the one for me. Everybody said so.

"You two are meant for each other," some said.

"The perfect couple," said others.

Cinderella found her Prince.

Chapter 17

Having lived for five years under a vow of poverty, my hands needed coaxing to feel comfortable wearing that big ring. I wanted my high school friends to show enthusiasm and warmth for my engagement, and they did, but that big sparkly diamond also caused eyes to widen and brows to lift, as if I was attempting to climb to higher ground than them. I learned to play a Bunko table game that encouraged gossip more than any skill. Others talked about married life, babies, and childbirth, while all I could contribute was a roll of the dice. My conversation was uncool and strange. I smiled a lot.

A single rose arrived every Saturday morning until the day of our wedding. "My Darling Gretchen," the attached cards read for one entire year. Coleman was a romantic.

I began student teaching, while he was a reporter on second shift. Sometimes I would meet him and his cronies at Ruby's Tavern after the news went to press. Stuffed into a couple of booths, they debated everything that came over the wires, succulent dialogue for my starving brain. They were restless from digesting eight hours of straight news—sweat on their brows, sleeves rolled up, ties loosened, eyes bleary from reading and writing, ordering rounds of beer and nuts and sandwiches. I got completely left out, but a rush of news and information was what I craved. In my ear Coleman said, "Don't worry about keeping up. We don't expect you to contribute. We eat the news day in and day out. We like having you here." I was in his world now. And he was taking such good care of me.

It was the late 60's, Vietnam was still snuffing out lives by the hundreds of thousands. Everyone was consumed with that war.

"Are you afraid of the draft?" I asked Coleman one day.

"No, I'm too old now. I've reported to my local recruitment office every year since I turned eighteen. I spent the wartime getting two degrees. I was classified 1-A," he told me, reaching into his wallet, showing me his draft card to prove it.

With wars and assassinations headlining the news, I thought about hatred and remembered how mine had been generated. Like me, Catholics love their religion. But what I once held closely to my heart, had turned to torture and made me flee from memories of pain mixed with delusion, blanketed with ardent affection, so that it became so laden with layer upon layer of complexity, love sat beside hate, those two emotions tightly intertwined as opposites with exceptional passion. Still, the world was changing and so was I. The musical, emotional, and poetic strength of Joni Mitchell, the writings of Germaine Greer and Betty Friedan, and the openness of *Ms. Magazine* editor, Gloria Steinem, convinced women to think for themselves. We were now encouraged to reach for higher education, stop competing with each other for male attention, and adopt the abbreviated *Ms.* to hide our marital status like men could. I absorbed what I heard into my evolving self-perception.

"Go to feminist meetings so you can catch up," Coleman said. "Those discussion groups are cutting-edge and enlightening."

Women crowded into each other's homes and talked about careers, vaginas, glass ceilings, dressing for success, changing laws, running for office, no longer being housewives, replacing 'man and wife' with 'husband and wife,' and getting out the message that absolute male dominance need no longer be the norm. Women weren't victims. One book, *The Flounder* by Gunter Grass, claimed the human race was once female-dominated. A remarkable idea for me. I'd just come out of a society where women were covered head to toe and men, the priests, ruled without restraint. All those new conversations dazzled my brain, but improved my self-worth.

Society wanted everybody married. If you weren't, there needed to be a reason, especially in a small city where people depended on each other for news. We were both part of the Catholic community. Coleman was very active in his parish. Someone said he was one of the city's most eligible bachelors. He was gregarious and treated life like an adventure. He fit easily into my family. We all wanted him around. He took me to the city of his youth to visit close family friends. We were invited to spend the night at one home. When his friends asked if we wanted one bedroom or two, I was disappointed with his answer.

"No, no, separate rooms. The Catholic Church, you know," he said, sprinkling his response with laughter.

He was seven years my senior, so I let him decide. I believed all Catholics probably followed Church rules regarding sex, though I suspected some winking was going on. I didn't mind too much that we weren't exploring. With Coleman, I felt more curiosity than craving. This new man, rich in experiences—this I-have-seen-the-world person—easily distracted me with his interminable appetites.

Coleman read poetry over the phone. His letters began, "My Darling," and, "Sweetheart." He said memorable things, "Love is forever you. The honeymoon goes on forever when you're size eight," which I was. I took that to mean that I was his definition of love. And as long as I looked attractive to him, we'd remain life-long partners.

"All your good parts are hidden," he said the one and only time I allowed him to see a picture of me in the habit.

One day, he threw me over his shoulders and carried me across the street when I said I didn't feel like walking anymore. He commissioned an artist friend to paint my portrait in oils. He spoiled me to pieces with his compliments and eagerness to please. Anyone could tell the man loved me. Anyone could see how fortunate he felt in finding me.

Coleman took me to visit his former seminary so I could meet some priest friends.

"I don't want to go in there. It looks like my convent." I reared back in the car seat and braced my arms for a second as I stared at that large, red brick complex. Surrounded by a gate and sprawling lawn, it was exactly like the building I narrowly escaped.

"Don't worry. We'll only stay half an hour," he said.

"You don't understand. I really don't want to go in there."

"I want you to meet my Provincial, Father Westfield."

"You go on your own."

"Let's just see if he's here. We'll say hello and then leave." He opened my car door and took my hand.

"I don't like this," I said, my voice raised a pitch.

"Gretchen, I want to introduce you. Do this for me. These are important people from my past."

The housekeeper whispered from behind the door, "Everyone's gone on summer retreat."

As we drove away, I took a deep breath and my heart slowed to a normal pace. Coleman and I had better things in common than traumatic religious experiences. Our love of music, extended families, creativity, and enthusiasm. I remembered a young man who'd been in the seminary, then left and objected to the war, going to prison for a year. "I met nicer people in prison than the seminary," he told me. I recognized the culture.

We went window-shopping downtown one evening.

"That's the exact pattern as my mother's," Coleman said when I pointed out my favorite silver. We both had Irish backgrounds, fair skin, and freckles. Occasionally, he sported a red beard, a perfect match to my hair.

"I rode all around Europe on my scooter three summers ago," Coleman said. He shared more of his personal history while the two of us packed activity into five days of every week. "As a single guy traveling alone, it was easy meeting people. I got invited to homes and ate around family tables. I spent the night with some of them and saved money that way. I learned to negotiate prices, got the right exchange rate at banks or train stations for any European currency, learned to haggle with merchants, and when I used their language I got even better deals. I lifted my scooter onto the Eurail when I needed to make better time. I plan to return every three to five years. I want to show you all those same places."

"I've never known anyone who's done that. I'd love to go to Europe."

Coleman was proficient in French, could manage in Italian, and spoke some halting German.

"Coleman, I didn't know you also spoke Italian," I said over dinner at the Italian Village in Chicago, when we drove north for a weekend.

"It's just Church Latin," he said with a shrug.

"But you ordered our food!"

"C'est la vi."

"And French too?"

"I speak well enough to have led bus tours in Montreal one summer." He was such a talker. His thoughts were restless and always looking for an audience. He was a genius at capturing center stage and his personality filled up a whole room. I'd never known another person to use language and presence so well.

"Coleman, stay for supper?" my mother frequently said, and he would. They shared Irish lighthearted natures and Coleman admired her home management skills and devotion to my dad. He and I sat at the piano and sorted through stacks of sheet music, finding hundreds of songs. As I played, he sang to me in his beautiful baritone voice. Beethoven's *Ich Liebe Dich (I Love You)*, a German melody, proved his love as his voice caressed those sweet tones and the lyrics awakened my heart.

"Gretchen, you need to see some foreign films," Coleman said. "They'll encourage your sensibilities because they're very avant-garde"—an intriguing new concept for me. In between my college classes and his job, we sought them out. Most jolted my middle-class grounding and I took on more radical ideas. Then we saw *Barbarella*. No longer a *Sound of Music* girl, I now craved a body as efficient as Jane Fonda's. Coleman seemed eager for me to see *The Fox*, a startling film about lesbians. It was quite intriguing, though nothing explicit happened, so I remained basically naive. I loved the idea of strong women and thought they were onto something. I committed a mortal sin by watching *Rosemary's Baby*, but never once considered leaving the theater, but I expected a lightning strike after that devil-baby was born. *The Graduate* poked fun at my values and liberalized my thinking about sex. Coleman took me to see *A Clockwork Orange*. Scenes of gang rape flooded the screen. I couldn't sink any lower into my seat. I pleaded to leave after five minutes.

"But this is a classic," he said.

"What difference does that make? I hate it."

I spent most of that unsettling film pressed against the back of my chair. I clutched the armrests, closed my eyes, and held my breath for as long as I could. My mind still reels with those decadent murder scenes whenever I hear the song, "Singing in the Rain."

We saw a sensuous film from Japan, *In the Realm of the Senses*—two crazed lovers in a lovely teahouse setting, made high ceremony of strangling one another with gorgeous silk scarves, in an effort to reach the highest orgasm. Music, scenery, and sensuality flooded the mood with intrigue until the male lover died in bliss. I had no idea why people wanted to do those things.

"You can do anything you want to my body. It's the words you use when you communicate with me that have to be carefully chosen," I heard a movie-goer tell his girlfriend as we exited the theater. That was certainly a provocative statement. I imagined what *anything done to my body* would be like—raw passion, everything touching. I no longer worried about impure thoughts. Visuals popped up one after another as I thought about how naked bodies might slither and slide, caress and fondle, rock and roll.

I couldn't figure out Coleman's motivation for taking me to *Theresa and Isabella*, a film about a couple of young French boarding school girls. The theater was dark and empty except for two other people.

"I don't want to see this," I said within minutes, as those two young girls began to explore. "Let's leave, please."

"Wait a minute, wait a minute," he said, slightly irritated. Then, in the next hushed, camera-peering, skirt-lifting, closing-in-on-some-virgin-flesh second, Coleman said, "Go!" We bolted from our seats and left the theater.

"The fresh air feels good," I said. "I'm glad we're out of there."

"I couldn't identify with Isabella," he said, chuckling.

Thinking back now, he had access to the reviews of every film in the world. I hadn't understood why we were always in those audiences, seeing those films. Each one invoked awkward questions: *What sort of people strangle one another during sex? How much farther do you think those French girls went? Why would perverted sex and murder make that film a classic?*

"Sex is complicated," he said. It was embarrassing that I had so much to learn. "According to people I talk with," Coleman said over coffee at a local diner, "it's ninety percent of the trouble in a bad marriage, but only ten percent of the trouble in a good one."

We didn't see any more blatantly sexy films after I suggested we see *Valley of the Dolls* with Patty Duke.

"I hear it's good," I said.

"No, the critics slammed it. It's all about the drug scene. I'm not wasting my money."

End of discussion. I didn't understand his resistance. It was such a popular film. I wouldn't learn about its subplot for decades. It was all about how illicit drugs ruined the lives of people who were desperate for the good life. One of the husbands hid his sexuality behind an unfair marriage. *A Man and a Woman,* a French film and the ultimate "date" movie, was sensuous and I waited to be kissed afterward, but Coleman never moved toward me. Both of us enjoyed *The Student Prince,* "a light opera where, in the most memorable scene," Coleman said, "handsome male university students in red jackets lift their beer steins and sing in harmony."

Honestly, I'd have spent a lifetime exploring music, literature, architecture, drama, and dance with him, which is exactly what he had in mind—partners for the arts.

"Gretchen," he said, "I have to live a creative life. Let's go to Europe for a second honeymoon next summer."

Just thinking about Europe made me delirious.

"A significant trip like that requires a journal," Coleman said.

I kept a diary throughout our engagement, our eventual Chicago honeymoon, and later, I kept another traveling all around Europe. Now, fifty years later, those writings reflect my sheltered life. Had I deliberately put my head in the sand? "My fiancé stood me up," my diary reminded me of the time I'd been left at our favorite coffee shop. "I waited on his front porch for an hour but he never showed up. I could swear we had a date." "We were supposed to meet at a deli but he never came." "You went to the wrong place," he said. Things like that gnawed at my common sense like a puppy on a bone.

"You mean you were waiting for me somewhere else? Where? I waited forty-five minutes. How long did you wait?"

"It doesn't matter," Coleman said. "We're both fine now."

We saw each other nearly every day, so when I wouldn't hear from him for a while and he'd call without explanation, I wondered why.

"Don't engaged couples keep closer ties?"

"You're too dependent on me."

"But couples talk about these things, they fill in the gaps. I'm not badgering you. I just want to know what you did today, that's all. Isn't that normal?"

Many times after class, I'd stop at his apartment and cozy up with him in bed. We'd strip to the waist. It was special when we curled up together, cuddled, embraced, and shared one or two kisses.

"This is like a married day," he said once.

When I contracted the flu, he came over and gave me a back rub and kissed away my tears. He cleaned his apartment if he knew I was coming over and cooked spaghetti. We sailed in summer and ice-skated in winter. We danced at a local dinner club. We made linoleum block art prints together on the kitchen table and learned to make pear jelly and chilled straw-berry soup. We won a trophy in a sports car rally. We rummaged for gold in a Colorado stream and dined in the elegance of the Stanley Hotel nestled in the mountains of Estes Park. We stayed in the French Quarter in New Orleans and heard music pour out of musicians' tender souls. He sang at weddings, while I sometimes played the organ. Often times he broke out in song in the kitchen, or the car, or just walking down the street. On the spur of the moment, he took someone's last sentence and put it to music. *I have lost my keys,* he'd sing. *We need something to eat. It's almost time to leave. The laundry's piling up,* would escape from his high spirits and we'd laugh out loud at his musical interludes. I never knew people who did that. Just broke into song at the drop of a hat over nothing at all. We listened to the music streaming out of the Metropolitan Opera of New York on the radio. He introduced me to Gilbert & Sulli-van from Martyn Green's *Treasury of Complete Librettos of Eleven Operettas* and we sang those songs together at the piano. "We Sail the Ocean Blue" was a favorite. He bragged about me to everyone, "Here's my beautiful Gretchen," "Meet my sweet fiancée." I felt like Cinderella.

Yet, some of Coleman's friendships were unsettling. There was an interesting man that Coleman was fond of whose wife repeatedly tried to share prayer leaflets with me.

"These booklets have helped my marriage," she said, "call on The Lord as things get difficult, and they will. Jesus will get you through the tough times," she said moving in too close, attempting to focus my attention as she quoted chapter and verse off the page. I barely knew that woman. She was very attractive, very nice, but she seemed unhappy.

"Did you tell her I'd been a nun?" I asked Coleman. It became irritating having to continuously turn down those prayer books and I avoided making eye contact, so she'd stop seeking me out. I never talked about Jesus in social situations. Jesus belonged in church, not at picnics, parties, or casual gatherings. I wasn't comfortable with evangelizing. I had my own way.

"She means well. Be nice to her. She nearly drives her husband crazy with her female excesses, but she's a good person." He shared that their bedroom was too frilly for her husband's tastes—ruffles, canopies, pastels, diaphanous fabrics, scented candles.

"What does diaphanous mean?"

"See-through," he said, looking at me like I didn't know anything.

Some other friends he spoke of I'd never meet. In a way, it seemed deliberate. There was a fireman who was his tennis partner, a local pastor who he admired, and another man who collected armor from The Middle Ages. Then, there was Thomas.

"Thomas is new in town and having trouble making lasting friendships," Coleman said when I asked why he was always showing up. We became a threesome, and it soon felt natural when he joined us. He was a nice guy. If he was lonely, that seemed reason enough to help him out.

There's a year's worth of diary entries with Thomas showing up unexpectedly: "Thomas joined us for lunch at The Village Inn..." "Thomas and Coleman came over for the birthday party..." "We went out to eat and Thomas was there. He joined us at our table..." "Thomas, Coleman, and I went to Chicago together..." "Made stir-fry chicken for Coleman and Thomas." "Missed Coleman today, Thomas said he was still sleeping..." "Coleman came over with Thomas and we watched a movie..." "Went to Mass with Thomas and Coleman..." "Coleman worked late, then he and Thomas went to an overnight party..."

"Grown men don't have slumber parties," I said.

"Don't be ridiculous. We watched movies and ate popcorn."

"But your apartments are two blocks apart. I never heard of guys doing that."

"You're overreacting," he said. My remarks were appropriate, but when he'd blow them off as nothing I sent them straight to the back of my mind, where they could annoy me in secret. Two days before our wedding, Thomas ended up in our wedding party at the last minute.

"I owe him a favor," Coleman said.

"What favor?"

"I just owe him a favor."

Three years into our marriage, Thomas moved three blocks from our home for a few months.

As our wedding date grew closer, I began to waver, but Coleman would rally with more diversions, very talented that way. We traveled east and south to meet more of his relatives. They were all very fond of him. He showed me a photograph of a lovely, white, Southern home with a broad front porch supported by pillars. In it were his mother, father, their three boys, and the owner of the home, Grandee—his great-grand-mum. Looking at the picture with three-year-old Coleman and his family further endeared him to me. Southern heritage appeared gracious.

As he told me about various family members, it sounded like a Who's-Who in old society: someone in his family had actually written a dictionary, an uncle had a byline on the front page of the *New York Times* for years, his mother belonged to The Daughters of the American Revolution, and his very accomplished Grandmother Gretchen had made her violin debut at Chicago's Orchestra Hall. That concert's program was framed on the wall with a photograph of her seated in a beautiful white gown, her violin on her lap. She was lovely. There were so many stories about growing up in the South, about his family's property having historic value.

"My relations were not substantially wealthy," Coleman said, "but we were treated as part of the upper classes because we were thought to be intellectuals and fit into high society for that reason."

Our first Christmas as a couple, two months prior to our wedding, he bought me a luscious mink boa. Lifting it out of the box, I thought my fiancé had some misunderstanding of my needs.

"A big diamond and now an expensive fur? You've known me long enough to realize I have no matching wardrobe," I said as gently as I could.

I realized I was headed into a life for which I had little background. He spent months of his hard-earned money to prove his love, so I celebrated his enthusiasm too. The next week, we went to an elegant boutique where he purchased two tweed suits for me that looked great with my hair, he said. He brought the boa along to make sure it could be worn with whatever we finally chose. He never wanted that fur left in its box.

"How can you afford such luxuries?" I asked softly.

"I want my wife to fit easily into society, you'll look wonderful." He liked that boa better than I ever did and showed me how to clip it onto the lapels of my tweed suits or twirl it in a circle as a hat or a muff. I still have that mink boa. Barely worn, it's in perfect condition.

"No need for special treatment," the furrier said. "Just lay it over a hanger in your closet with tissue paper lightly atop so it can breathe. It'll stay beautiful for a lifetime." So that's where it's been, in one closet after another just hanging. I wasn't one to toss blood onto someone's mink coat. I simply never wanted those animals slaughtered for my warmth. I was grateful my boa had no head, tail, or appendages.

Now, both sides of my family had some history too, but we were not heavily laden with degrees from prestigious universities, like Harvard, Yale, Stanford, and Georgetown. Though both my mother and father's sides had accumulated and lost fortunes, we carried our heritage in a different way. We also appreciated genealogy and good music. We read books and enjoyed art, but we were regular people. We kept grounded with our fishing trips. By comparison, members of his family, though nice, seemed a little elevated.

"I don't want you to be low class," he said.

"I don't for one minute think that I am. Is that how you feel about me?"

"No, no, no, but people should always seek to lift their experiences."

I was getting a different feeling about this fiancé of mine. Was I his Eliza Doolittle from *My Fair Lady*?

Two months before our wedding, I wrote in my diary, "I feel depressed. I have doubts about everything."

The next day, the entry read, "Over the phone I confessed my doubts and hesitations. I told Coleman how different he was from my family. How I feared marriage with him. He said he wanted to talk at supper. At the kitchen table I tried to explain my distress at entering a life that felt alien to mine. Everything about him was so showy and I wasn't that way."

"I don't think I can keep this up, Coleman. You're so different than me. I'm not used to fancy socializing. I don't know how to keep up conversation. I have nothing to add. I get flustered and people don't respond to me like they do to you."

"Don't worry. We'll do this together. I'll help you. We'll be fine. Everyone loves you. Just be yourself. We're lucky to have each other. They say opposites attract. We'll make good partners. We'll have a great marriage."

His words comforted me, so that when I shut my diary, I sealed my uncertainty in its pages. I liked the idea of a *partner*. I needed a good friend after feeling so solitary. He'd been warm toward me everywhere we went, pulling me close, including me in conversation, and encouraging me to go beyond my immediate experiences. Constantly at my side, he was tender and sweet, and loving the twosome that we'd become.

"Your father just returned from a visit with our family doctor," my mother said a week before the wedding. "The doctor wanted to talk to him about Coleman," she said.

"What about?"

"He hasn't said."

We both glanced at him sitting in his chair, his eyes buried in the newspaper. My mind raced for a moment, then I forced it elsewhere. "How can I help with supper?"

The wedding was tomorrow. Prior irritations that I had flung to the back of my brain decided to emerge and tease me again. I'd become so accustomed to my own conflicts: *What was or wasn't a sin? Was or wasn't there truly a spirit world? Did or didn't I have a true vocation?* One more complication hardly seemed remarkable. I remember wondering if Coleman could be *one of those people*. I had no clear thoughts, no specific anything. Only hints of unusualness, difference, nuance, that I'd had to piece together from nothing more than raised eyebrows or whispers. Just like the women the convent kept under watch for certain reasons, where eyebrows went up, faces exchanged unspoken messages, and eyes might roll upward, I'd been left to figure out things on my own and I wasn't sure what any of it meant. But I thought it involved sexual conduct so I decided to push my fiancé a little to settle some nerves, to see if I could pick up signals or something.

"Please, Coleman, let's do it, let's make love. Let's see what its like," I said the day before our wedding, hidden agenda well-learned. We were doing a final cleaning in our apartment when I pulled him down on me.

"No, we can't. It's a sin. I'm trying to do the right thing here," he said.

"How can it be a sin? We're getting married in the morning," I said, me looking at him, he looking away.

"Don't pressure me, Gretchen." He turned toward me.

"But how can you refuse? I just want to be close to you."

"Oh, alright," he said, unbuttoning.

I scrunched down to accommodate him, but in less than a minute he rose quickly, pulled himself together, and acted like the Monsignor would nail an edict on our door.

"I'm not doing this," he said.

I hardly got a look or felt much of anything. I'd have to wait until our wedding night.

"What right does the Church have intruding into our private life?" I said.

"Stop acting like a Jezebel and remember your religion."

"A Jezebel?"

"From the Bible. It means a loose woman."

Let's see, I'd been locked away in a convent for five years, gotten date-raped by a phony boyfriend, tried at long last to strip away the mystery of lovemaking on the night before my wedding, and my fiancé had just called me a Jezebel.

Chapter

18

On a sunny but chilly day in February, guests packed into St. Boniface Church. My mother had sent out two hundred and eighty-seven invitations.

"Coleman certainly knows a lot of people," she said.

"Mother, he's traveled all over the world and made friends for life. People are crazy about him. They love him."

We'd gotten gifts, letters, and telegrams from acquaintances in countries scattered around three continents and multiple ethnicities. Even the Pope would be mentioning us in his private prayers because Coleman's Provincial sent us a card "Via Roma: I thought you might like to have the Holy Father's blessing on this great day of your life." Nuns that I'd known in the convent sent beautiful wishes that caused me discomfort since I'd judged them so harshly. But right next to the mixing bowls, can openers, irons, blenders, and practical household items, were gorgeous china pieces and heaps of antique silver on display. Great Aunt Kate took one look at the elegance, turned toward me, eyes afire, slapped her chest and said, "Who do you think you are?"

"Did you tell her you're Mrs. Coleman Taylor Mobley, the Third?" Coleman said later.

"Your relatives sent so many expensive things," I said.

"All that glitters is not gold," Coleman said with his hint of insight and fun.

"What?"

"It's from Gilbert and Sullivan's operetta, *H.M.S. Pinafore,* remember?" Coleman sang the first line of the lyrics. "*Things are seldom what they seem; skim milk masquerades as cream?* It means truth isn't always obvious, life is full of delusions."

Church bells bonged in the tower and ushers escorted guests to their seats. My father in tuxedo, my mother in taupe, and Sarah enhanced her coordinated pinks with a silver fox luxuriously draped around her shoulders. In the choir loft, my college piano teacher sat at the organ, accompanying Coleman's sister on the violin. Waiting in the sanctuary were my brother, Coleman, his brothers, his best friend from high school who married a girl from a good family, and Thomas who needed a favor. The Monsignor—the one my parents knew from their youth, who likely engineered my convent entry, and later came to talk me out of leaving the convent—was about to officiate the wedding. A couple of extra priests and an additional Monsignor were there too—Church hierarchy to sanction our marriage.

Across the street in a schoolroom my mother fastened the last few buttons on my wedding dress, ten minutes before the ceremony. My sisters, my high school friend Lisa, and Coleman's sisters made last minute adjustments on dresses, accessories, makeup, and hair.

Coleman sent over a gift for me, a small antique silver jewelry box that once belonged to his grandmother Gretchen. The silver lid bore an engraving, *Darling Gretchen, From Coleman.* My heart melted as I touched the delicate pearl necklace inside, chosen just for me. Mother fastened it around my neck.

Someone knocked at the door. My sister hiked up her gown to answer, then came over to me and said a priest wanted to have a word. We were just minutes from walking down the aisle, but there stood one of Coleman's priest friends, guarding his eyes from the women in varying stages of undress.

I barely knew him. What did he want? All the details of the wedding had been taken care of. Monsignor gave his blessing after only one Pre-Cana session instead of the required three. Three precautionary announcements in the church bulletin had alerted parishioners to the upcoming exchange of vows. People rarely questioned the actions of priests back then, so I gathered up the folds of my gown and train and went to the door.

"You need to make a confession of your sins," he said.

"Pardon me, Father?" I asked, thinking it was some over-zealous, last-minute cleansing by the Church.

"Coleman just made a confession." I didn't want my mother to hear that. "A few minutes ago, he told me what you two did yesterday. You need to ask God's forgiveness or this wedding can't take place. The Church won't allow you to receive the Sacrament of Matrimony if you're not in the state of grace."

"He did what?" I wanted to slap that priest.

"While Coleman is free to marry, you are not. Without the Sacrament of Penance your marriage won't be valid. In fact, you're forbidden to marry."

"There are two hundred guests waiting in church for us right now. The wedding's about to begin."

"There may not be a wedding this morning."

"People can't be sent home." Every swear word I'd ever heard was making its way to my throat, but I thought about how it would look. In my dress. On my day. I needed bliss. Where was my bliss?

"Just make a confession and get this over with."

"No." I took a step toward him and he backed out of the doorway.

"Simply say you're sorry and I'll give you my blessing."

"I'm not sorry." My voice was much calmer than I expected.

I remembered every single time I'd disagreed with the Church but kept quiet. Every blemish on the Church's snowy white reputation. The Monsignor who threw a fit and kicked me off the organ bench. Every superior who punished me for failures. Both Mothers General who wouldn't let me leave. Every priest and nun who didn't teach me to think for myself. Every sanctimonious judgment. Every action said to be a sin. Every warning that hell was always lurking. Every shaking finger. Every penance I was forced to make. Every ritual that went against God-given morality. If anyone needed to confess, it was the Church, for attempting to darken my wedding day.

"I'll give you my blessing anyway." He spoke Latin words and made the sign of the cross, as I turned and walked away from him. I hoped he liked the back of my dress.

"What's going on, honey?" my mother asked.

"Nonsense," I said.

During the ceremony I fought off anger and doubt. One moment we were at the altar and the next my feet were prancing down the stairs and out the church door. Flower petals everywhere, my veil kept blowing across my face. People cheered and cameras flashed. Next thing I know, Coleman and I are driving toward our honeymoon.

"Did you like my wedding dress?" I asked.

"It was fine," he said, "but it needed a plunging neckline."

Coleman had planned an incredible four-day honeymoon in Chicago, a surprise for me. He wanted to keep us very busy and make it memorable. We jumped into bed at a hotel and he turned over.

"You're going to sleep?"

"I'm tired," he said.

"Aren't we going to make love?"

"Let's get a couple of hours sleep first. It's been a long day. I need rest. We'll do it later."

"I've never heard of this. We've waited so long."

"I'm exhausted. Don't be pushy. I need sleep. Good night, beautiful wife." He turned and planted a kiss on my cheek, then dove back undercover.

Darkness, shadows, and slivers of light from under the door and behind the drapes kept me company.

Late into the night, covers ruffled. A body crawled on top of me and was inside.

"Huh?"

Coleman held me, called out my name, and brushed my lips with his kiss.

"I love you. You're wonderful," he said, then crawled off and went back to sleep.

Same darkness, same shadows, same slivers of light from beneath the door and behind the drapes. I practically missed the whole thing.

The next morning, we had a light breakfast in the room.

"Things went too fast last night," I said. "And why did you send Father to demand a confession from me?"

"I cleared my own conscience, but I didn't send him over. He did that on his own. You know how priests are. They think they have to be in control." I knew that as fact since I witnessed parish priests enjoying multi-faceted lives, while nuns never went anywhere, constantly under restrictions set up by those same clerics, and all the way to Rome.

We drove to the heart of Chicago's Loop and stayed at the St. Clair Hotel. It was a few blocks from the lake. In our room stood an enormous vase with a magnificent arrangement of a dozen gorgeous, long-stemmed, deep-red roses and shiny tropical flowers with yellow fuzzy stamen jutting wildly in all directions. It was as tall as the mirror and nearly as wide as the dresser. "To my beautiful new wife," the card said.

The winds on the streets of Chicago blistered our faces. We spent the whole day on Michigan Avenue. Every detail drew us in. Antique silver and furniture called our names. Each glass display stole our glances and begged us to purchase.

"This is overwhelming," I said.

"Treat it like a museum and enjoy," said my new husband.

At dusk, we escaped to the top of the Holiday Inn for cocktails in the circular restaurant. It revolved. Our table was by the windows. Coleman ordered two martinis, which I'd seen before, but never tasted. The oily drink slid around in the stemware. We toasted and sipped. The taste was unusual for me. Coleman wanted me to be sophisticated so badly.

"I don't like it," I giggled, squinted, and puckered.

"Sip some more and you will."

We enjoyed Lake Michigan, then toasted as night lights took over the city. I measured up, looked well-bred, smiled easily, and supported his every conversational thread about our wedding, the guests, the gifts, and the lovely party my folks hosted in their home. He brought up his charming mother and all his siblings, who were so very pleased for their brother. At Jack Diamonds, we shared a romantic dinner. I felt glowy after more alcohol moved through my bloodstream.

That evening we attended the newly released *Romeo and Juliet* film by director Zeffirelli. Those two young pups on the screen were filled with passionate love. My husband and I were both sniffling and I knew he'd soon take me in his arms, hold me close, and we'd roll around in delight, together at last.

"Too exhausted," Coleman said.

When he was asleep, I crawled into the bathroom, shut the door, grabbed a white bath towel, bundled it tightly, and buried my head deeply into its center. I cried hard on that cold, clean floor with its little black and white squares of porcelain tiles, somewhat uneven with a couple of diagonal cracks. I hadn't sobbed like that since the day I entered kindergarten, the day I entered first grade, the day I entered the convent, and now, the day I entered marriage.

"Couldn't we please make love?" I asked the next morning.

"Gretchen, this is one of the world's greatest cities and I have a lot planned for us. We have the rest of our lives to make love."

I said I understood, but I had no idea how physically painful sexual disappointment could be.

The cultural whirlwind began anew. We got dressed, bundled up, and were the first ones on the Magnificent Mile. We went shopping at Saks Fifth Avenue. Coleman took me to their millinery department. He loved hats and had a collection of them for parties. He sat me down at a lovely little vanity with its big oval mirror, and then walked around, gathering choices.

"Put this on, Gretchen."

"We're not thinking of buying these?"

"Just try it on," he said, placing one after another on my head without my permission. The ladies in the department were charmed by his daring whimsy. I was wearing a fine, knitted, pale blue suit and the mirror showed a lovely reflection, so I sat tall and attempted elegance. More hats arrived. One was fedora-like, really chic, navy, soft-brushed with a curving brim all around. It dipped over one side of my face. I looked like I belonged in the world of high fashion. The small sewn-on tag read: *Made in Switzerland.*

"Coleman, look at the price tag."

"Don't worry about it."

"But I don't want these."

He brought over a huge mostly white sombrero. The clerk fixed it in place. It cast a shadow over half of my body. The diameter had to be a foot and a half. The finely soft straw brim swooped down, out, and up, with attached navy circles in parade around my head. My shoulders slumped under the haute couture. In the mirror I saw a face full of surprise. Coleman loved it. My head was the runway upon which the hat could promenade. It was all about the hats. Whatever was going through his head, I couldn't venture a guess. Its sewn-in tag read: *Made in Paris.* I spoke with him out of earshot of the clerk who, though flirty, charmed, and exuding accolades toward Coleman, treated me like a frog.

"What are you thinking, Coleman? I've told you I'm not like this. I don't want these hats. I have no place to wear them."

"You can't let yourself be held back because others have no imaginations. The people in church will love you for it. You'll look fantastic. You'll be a trendsetter. We'll take these," he told the clerk, and she disappeared to find their boxes as my husband pulled out his wallet. I sat and stared, at myself, around the room, through the big window, then down at the avenue beginning to fill with shoppers. *He's not listening to me.*

Two hats were mine—ours—and out onto the street we strolled. Our circular boxes bordered on the obnoxious, held by fancy decorative ropes, they bounced off our legs at every step. We looked Hollywood bound.

We walked in and out of shoppes, stared into display windows, then found Tiffany's. Linking arms, we strolled the circle of cabinets, taking in the refined sparkling jewels. The refined sparkling clerks spun their polished sales pitches. Then we exited, one of us pretending we were too good for the likes of Tiffany's.

Coleman whisked me into a high-end boutique. As soon as we walked through the double doors, a man, eager to see us, exuded a charmed, "Good morning!" He told us how divine we both were, and that he had fabulous things for us. My brand-new husband stepped right up to an armoire, lifted an enormous mink fur from its hanger and onto himself. It came within inches of the floor. All I could picture was hundreds of little furry caged animals waiting to be skinned and sewn together into that coat. He swirled and pranced in that luxurious fur.

"That coat is for a woman," I said.

"Men wear fur coats too," he said and the clerk absolutely agreed. With that encouragement, Coleman opened the doors and stepped outside to view himself from a pedestrian's perspective, which alarmed the clerks, who must have wondered if a theft was in progress. We watched through the large storefront window as he viewed his reflection. Before anyone followed, he was back in and removing the coat, with the help of the clerks, who stammered in disbelief at what had just happened. Then Coleman strode out of the store and I chased after him.

"You're not into the spirit of the adventure," Coleman said. I lightened up and giggled, remembering where I was. Certainly not behind a wall or in a habit. I was in beautiful Chicago and though we were freezing, it was a festival of delights.

Arm in arm we went to lunch at Kungsholm, a single-story ornamental building where Coleman promised a big surprise.

By now, another surprise was not what I had in mind. But he was so excited with all his plans that I opened my senses and took it all in.

Inside, we were escorted to a dining area that seemed like it might have been someone's living room once. Everyone there was well-dressed and all conversations were in hushed tones.

"Where are we and what's going on?" I asked.

"We're having a Scandinavian brunch and then you'll see," he said with a twinkle in his Irish eyes.

Truly, that elegance was right out of the movies. Ambiance and music filled the air. We sat on soft-cushioned pale yellow sofas that wrapped half way around us, oval tables spread with fine linen cloths snuggled us in. Low ceilings and graceful chandeliers tranquilized the mood as we dined on tasty cuisine and sipped champagne, then onto coffee with sweet desserts. But there was something else lingering. I asked again to be let me in on the secret.

"Just wait, you'll see soon enough."

A man in a tuxedo walked to the center of the room, stood perfectly still for a few seconds, lifted a circular gong held by a cord, and struck a clear musical tone with a tiny brass hammer. He made an announcement in a voice so utterly cultured I didn't understand him, but he must have said, "Right this way." Every one of those beautiful people rose from their tables, gathered their furs, and along with us, followed the gentleman through a hall and into a petite theatre for a cozy surprise. Our box seat was to the right of the stage. Music began, the curtains parted, and I noticed the wooden stage floor had metal grid patterns of grooves imbedded into it. I leaned to ask Coleman what's this and he opened the libretto and pointed to the title.

"*Hush*. Just watch."

The opera was *Kismet*, and after the overture the most adorable marionettes appeared, being worked from below. I heard chains and gears, and could see someone rolling around on a wheeled cart underneath as the marionettes sang and turned and gestured. I was truly charmed by this fanciful ensemble. Everyone applauded and whistled and bravoed enthusiastically after it finished. Coleman was pleased with himself and I understood why.

"Coleman, you're wonderful. You've planned such unusual things for us. I'm so lucky. We're so sophisticated."

We spent the afternoon in the galleries of the Chicago Art Institute. I was awestruck by paintings and sculptures that went beyond religion. Anything could find its way onto a canvas or sculpted into form. I learned the beauty of ordinary things—humble peasants, soup cans, piles of garbage, utensils and tools, intensities of light and shadows, lines and swirls, intriguing sounds, and clumps of curiosities. We ate in an exquisite dining room with floor-to-ceiling windows overlooking the city and graceful gardens. Chicago, now my favorite new place in the world, had found its home in my heart.

That evening, we drove to The Candlelight Theatre, where we ate dinner while watching Neil Simon's *Star-Spangled Girl*. Afterwards, musicians struck up the band and we danced and swirled on the sunken stage floor. Coleman was dashing. I looked the part of a happy new bride, a vast improvement over my first wedding.

Back at the hotel, we both crashed as soon as our heads hit the pillow. The next evening, after another full day of activity, we attended the musical *Hair*.

"How did you like the nude scene?" Coleman asked at intermission.

"What nude scene?"

"What nude scene! You missed the nude scene?"

"I fell asleep. I'm exhausted."

"You fell asleep! My wife fell asleep in the nude scene! How could you do that!" His face turned a pale shade of red and his eyes cut clear through me.

Crowded into the tiny hall, some people turned and stared at us. He lowered his voice, but continued his insult, some of it in French.

"Nobody falls asleep in the nude scene. Why did we even come here? This is absurd! You missed the whole thing then. How could you let that happen? Mon dieu!"

Had my husband just lost his mind? He'd never acted like that before. I was ashamed that I'd let him down. We went back in for the final act and I thought, *"I can arrange a nude scene if anyone's interested."*

Back home, Coleman fumed about my *faux pas*, as he called it. Every time he told people I'd fallen asleep during American theater's most dramatic scene to date, he became angry all over again. I did what I could to soften his disappointment by making great suppers and remaining enthused. That was the first time Coleman had turned on me. It left me straddling the margin between loving and appeasing my husband.

After the honeymoon, he kept his old schedule, working until midnight, crawling into bed long after I'd fallen asleep. I'd often heard that the excitement went out of a marriage over time, replaced by a deeper, calmer love. Were we going to skip the good part? Really though, we had no time for lovemaking. Our weekends were filled to capacity. There was some minor sexual activity, but any adventures there were less than I'd anticipated or longed for. Of all the things to remember, what has stuck in my mind was how quickly we got through it. Two minutes. I remember two minutes. One of us always fell fast asleep afterwards. The other tossed and turned.

"Wait a minute," I said each time. "It's over? What about me? There's got to be something in this for me. Can't we talk about this?"

"We have the rest of our lives to explore sex." He'd always say so sweetly.

I knew that was a true statement. But, in that sense, I wished the rest of our lives could get there faster. We had such fun otherwise. Coleman was an entertainer and I was thrilled to be part of his adventures. He turned ordinary things into drama simply by bringing along his personality.

But there was always an inevitable, burdensome side effect for me whenever we did fool around. I made an appointment to see my doctor to clear up infections. He insisted Coleman was to blame.

"You and your husband are incompatible."

Chapter

19

I dismissed the doctor's comments immediately. I had no clue what he was getting at. Incompatibility was an emerging term tagged onto some marriages. It simply meant there were problems that needed solving. It could suggest lack of communication, arguments, or control factors. Its definition was broad. Should I listen to someone born in Sicily, divorced, and living in mortal sin with a second wife? I tucked his criticism into the back of my brain where it could fester for a few more years. I packed for Europe.

Coleman was never at a loss for planning something new. While other couples saved money for mortgages, he purchased airline tickets and wrote advance letters to Europe. He wanted to, and eventually did interview the head of the Neo-Nazi party in Hanover, Germany, Adolf von Thadden—so he could write off part of our trip. While other couples set up households, had dinner parties, and used their new wedding gifts, I rewrapped ours for safekeeping and put them in storage. Couples looked forward to the day when they could start a family. We were barely having sex. Producing children wasn't a factor. *Strictly for procreation,* the Church's words prickled my brain.

"Look Gretchen! Our tickets! We fly to Chicago on May twenty-fourth and the next day we fly to New York. Six hours later, we'll land in Iceland!"

Oh! The thrill of it all... I needed to pinch myself every day. Could anyone's life have been dreamier? I never imagined my Cinderella story would actually come true. I was center stage in the middle of a fantasy, ready to fly through the sky to a beautiful land across an ocean.

In the tiny Iceland airport, we stretched our legs and walked around while our plane refueled. An hour later, the jet was in a slow roll down the runway when it suddenly cut its engines. Out the window we saw a young man running, holding something in the air.

"My camera!" Coleman said. He'd left it behind and whoever found it was running it out to the stewardess. That pilot stopped for my husband's camera!

Landing in Luxembourg, it appeared the entire country had come out to greet us. There had to be a hundred villagers.

"Why are so many people here?" I asked.

"It's a favorite pastime. They want tourists to feel welcome."

We were celebrities. I wanted to pose for paparazzi. I waved enthusiastically to everyone.

"You know what they say about people who wave to strangers, don't you?" he said.

"No."

"It means they don't know how to engage in close relationships, so they reach out to people from a safe distance."

"Oh. I thought I was just being friendly." I quit waving.

I knew I'd like Europe. My ancestors came from there, so people felt like distant relatives. But I had no way to communicate with them. Coleman spoke with anyone and everyone, so I began to feel left out. I was forever asking, "What did they say?" "What did you say?" Coleman spoke French from the minute we landed.

"When will I get to have a voice on this trip?" I asked.

"Each morning, we'll buy a bottle of wine, great bread, dried fruit, meat, and cheese. It's an excellent traveler's diet," he said and sent me shopping with no grasp of the language or knowledge of lire, deutschmarks, or francs. I came back with actual food and he said how proud I made him.

"We'll use our remaining money to pay for entry into museums. Save all ticket stubs. I'll take the photographs. You keep the journal. Write everything down. The places we visit. What things cost. People we meet. Do it at the end of each day. It's not hard," he said.

"But I'm not a writer, you're the writer. It's not like I'll be writing a book someday."

"You never know," he said. He stopped what he was doing, stared over at me, lifted his eyebrows, and nodded once with emphasis like he saw into our future. He knew things. The moment startled me. His poignant look spoke volumes. I didn't understand, but noted the nuance.

We were a young American couple driving around Europe in our own VW Bug, somewhat poor, but free-spirited. I thought I'd died and gone to Heaven.

"Ich bin aus Amerika," Coleman said to each startled German face that opened a door to us. We brought along our papers, and photographs, and specific addresses so we'd knock at appropriate homes. He explained that we wanted to trace my lineage. Receiving warm welcomes, we spread my family tree on kitchen tables. They pulled out their blue, hard-covered booklets, which showed their ancestry—stamped, sealed, and signed by A. Hitler. Finding a match of grandparents back several generations, they patted my cheeks, "Yah, Grossmann!" they said. We hugged and feasted on whatever foods they brought from their cup-

boards. And who stole the attention and won the hearts of my long-lost relatives? Even in a foreign language in a foreign land, Coleman was a connector. One benign couple, whose three sons were all lost in the war, gave me a treasured letter typewritten in German in 1905 from Mr. Nicholaus Grossmann. He was my father's grandfather. The letter heading read, *Grossmann's Fruit Orchard und Vineyard, Hotel and Wine Garden, East Clear Lake Avenue, Springfield, Illinois.* It promised a large inheritance upon his death. Sixty-four years later, this dear feeble couple was willing to place that letter, which had become infamous among relatives over there, into my hands.

"We're taking a cruise on the Rhine River," Coleman said, and we spent the next sunny day pointing out castles nestled high in the steep hills that rise from the valley. As we sipped our warm beer, I thought my husband was the most brilliant fellow on the planet to figure out how to live so richly on modest resources. There was no real depth of friendship, but I knew I loved this man and I thought he probably loved me too. One perfect night, we slept in a Bavarian pension, which was a rented room in a private home, $2.00 including a continental breakfast—very lovely quarters on our tight budget. It was at the foot of the castle Neuschwanstein, which we toured the next day. Castles, castles everywhere. I was Cinderella. And my husband struck a likeness to the prince in the movie.

In each town, we pored over the pages of our guidebooks, kept track of our money, and stayed on budget. Our expenses covered inns, food, gasoline, and tickets to the Louvre, *Aida, La Trivia,* Notre Dame, the Roman Forum, Venetian gondolas, *Hofbrauhaus,* the Leaning Tower, and the Vatican. We saw Charlemagne's throne, giant glockenspiels, hidden quaint villages, and what seemed like every museum and cathedral ever built and opera ever performed. In Venice my husband told me about an order of nuns who lived on one of the islands that had a repository of sacred remains, and whose job it was to rebury each one as they reduced in size. I imagined those lives with horrified wonder.

For three months, Coleman made history come alive. He knew which wars destroyed which cities and which political parties were currently grappling for power. He compared the stories of former Kaisers of Germany and kings and queens of England. He explained arranged marriages. He identified every statue in every plaza and museum. He spoke of alliances between countries and strung together important dates. He named cathedrals and famous streets and articulated about art and architecture. His knowledge was more extensive than I'd realized and he shared it generously. I couldn't wait until we got to Rome. I knew all the saints.

"Let's stay in bed and make love," I said one morning. "We don't always have to be the first ones on the street." But we always were. We never stayed under those covers, but rather rose early just like two monastics.

"We're in Europe. There's a new city to explore. The sun's up. Let's get the day started. We'll tour and then get back on the road to the next town," Coleman said ever so sweetly each time.

Don't get me wrong. I was enthralled with Europe's beauty, a spiritual high, a romantic and intellectual whirl. But I wanted to celebrate with a sensuous treat as well.

We spent twenty-four hours a day side-by-side. I opened the guidebook and scoured the pages in search of places to go and things to see, reading countless paragraphs aloud to keep our communication going. But I started to become demanding, rude, and argumentative. We kept a different gait. Everywhere we walked, Coleman raced on ahead.

"You walk too fast," I said. "Don't you want to walk with me? We've got all summer together and it's lonely back here." I saw how other couples interacted with public affection and I began to realize that we might never get there. In a very déjà vu moment reflecting back to the convent, my heart was beginning to close down again.

"A wife's place is ten paces behind her husband anyway. If you can't catch up, that's fine with me," he said.

Ten paces behind. Why did he push me toward those feminist meetings? Why shower me with wonderful things? *He's teasing.* Then one day I just stood still. He came back to find out what the problem was.

"What is it? What *is* it?" His hands were fixed on his waist, like a parent disapproving of a child's behavior.

We ran through the argument again. But nothing changed. We each got to say our bit and be done with it. I spent half that second honeymoon staring at my husband's rear-end striding ahead.

I stifled all sexual energy. Castles, ballets, rivers, lakes, gardens, plazas, fountains with water spraying out of nipples and penises, Roman walls and roads, antiquities, mountains—everything was bigger than our feelings. It drove my hurt deeper inside me and I got out my shovel and tried to bury it.

One day in Germany, Coleman went out for an excursion with friends and I went shopping. I found the most adorable brown leather skirt with matching vest. I paired it with a long-sleeved, starched white blouse and stylish brown-heeled shoes. I looked very clipped, very chic, and utterly German. *Wait until Coleman sees how sexy I am.*

"What were you thinking buying leather! No wife of mine is going to wear leather! You'll have to take it back. Or I will. It's ugly, you look awful."

"But I love it, Coleman. I look European."

"Our budget didn't take shopping into account."

"It wasn't that expensive. Besides, I helped earn money for this trip."

"You should have asked me. We need to have discussions about this kind of thing."

I didn't take it back. I wore it the next day. When we got to Bavaria, Coleman bought me a German dirndl.

A dirndl was one of those flowery costumes that women wore in the home and waitresses wore while serving steins of German beer.

My husband said, "You look like the perfect hausfrau." *House-wife?* I didn't care for that word. It implied staying in the house and being a submissive woman for life. I could have remained a nun, if that was my goal.

But I did like the dress. It had a charming, softening effect. He took my picture in a field of red poppies for posterity and it turned out to be his most cherished keepsake of our trip. I still preferred the classic look of that leather suit.

"You must, you *must* go to Berlin! No, no, no, you cannot come to Germany and not go into the Eastern Bloc!" some of Coleman's old friends said over breakfast.

We drove all afternoon and arrived near the border between East and West Germany. We ate our breads, cheese, and meat, drank our bottle of wine, and then felt ready for the border and Berlin.

"Notice those East German soldiers' uniforms are Russian," my husband said.

"Why is that?"

"Russia controls this border."

Cars were lined up bumper-to-bumper on a curvy, unpaved road and moving at the pace of a depressed snail. For several hours, we inched along, seeming not to get any closer to the checkpoint.

"I think we've made a mistake," I said. "Can we get out of here?"

"The road's not even wide enough to turn our Volkswagon around. We can do this, let's try to be patient."

People got out of their vehicles to stretch, leaning against cars drinking wine, and picnicking in the grass, during long pauses in the movement forward. Those around us spoke mostly German and French.

"You Americans are on the wrong road," the French couple ahead of us said during our long wait. "Tourist roads are very speedy. The delays on this road are notorious."

My usually carefree husband had now become agitated by our mistake. In two hours, we had only moved a few car lengths. By ten in the evening it had grown pitch black outside. Further up, we could see pale lighting in an open area, where cars were being searched.

"What have we gotten ourselves into?" I asked.

"We'll be alright. We're Americans."

"What are they looking for?"

"Modifications on cars."

"What do you mean modifications on cars? What if this car has been modified and we don't know it?"

"Not ordinary kinds of adjustments. They're looking for gas tanks that have been shortened to smuggle people in and out of the country in recessed car spaces."

"Maybe this one is like that. We can't be sure." I peered into the rearview mirror toward the back seat, as if alterations to the vehicle could be spotted like unwelcome passengers.

"Ours is normal. We can fill the gas tank up to full capacity."

"How would they know? Are they car experts?"

"They have a long pole for every make of European automobile. They ram it into the muffler to see if something's changed on the model. If they're suspicious, they'll tear the car apart. They can do whatever they want in an effort to find smuggled goods and people, but we have nothing to worry about." His attempts to reassure me sounded half-hearted.

"You knew about this?"

"Well, I had some inkling. People said to expect interrogations and the French tourists ahead just told me about long delays."

"What if we can't explain ourselves? Your German's not that good. I'm getting scared."

"These soldiers speak Russian, but stop worrying. We'll be fine."

"But we took the wrong road, we're supposed to be with the tourists, we're already under suspicion."

My own German father's words came barreling into my brain, as I remembered his final warning to me, "Whatever you do, don't cross into a communist country." Here I was, doing just that. World War II had ended over twenty years earlier, but the Berlin Wall was only eight years old. Things were tense around there.

A couple hours later, our car crept up to the stopping point, which was swarming with uniformed soldiers carrying poles and flashlights and shouting orders all over the place. A soldier rammed a long pole into the muffler. Coleman rolled down his window and handed over our passports. The soldier studied Coleman's photo under the glare of a flashlight, turned the flashlight on Coleman's face, closed the passport, and handed it back. Then he opened my passport, flashed my face, flashed my photo, flashed my face, flashed my photo, he hesitated, then he walked away.

"He took my passport!" I lunged toward the window.

"Just sit tight. We'll be fine," Coleman said pushing me back in the seat.

"Easy for you to say. Where did he go?"

Two soldiers came back to the window. Something wasn't right. They talked back and forth, held the flashlight on my face, peered through the window at me, squatted down to study my face one at a time and then both together. They opened our door and signaled for us to get out of the car.

"There's going to be trouble," I said.

"Shut up, Gretchen," my husband said, which made me worry even more. They took our keys and pulled our car off to the side to accommodate waiting vehicles behind us. Now we were devoid of my passport and our only set of keys. I envisioned myself sitting in a cell. *Wouldn't be the first time.* Memories of me in another desperate place flashed through my mind.

We followed a soldier into a cold, dank little concrete building, where several lines of other shivering and exhausted people were shuffling forward in stupefied lines toward a counter. One woman and several soldiers were our interrogators. We looked back outside as soldiers ran their flashlights through the front, back, and insides of our car, luggage strewn wherever. The vehicle behind ours had everything pulled out, including the back seat. My nerves shriveled in the frailty of my body.

"Be brave. Stop showing fear. Try to look sweet," Coleman said. *Sweet?*

An hour later, a soldier returned my passport and handed us our keys and a foreign license plate without comment. In the dead of night, we pulled our car farther away from the inspection lines and tried to change rusty plates in the dark with my tweezers. A British couple handed us their screwdriver and we finished the transfer.

"What in the world was that all about?" I asked.

"You didn't look like your photograph," Coleman said with a shrug.

"That's my studio portrait. I'm out here in the hinterland without my curling iron. Were they thinking I was a stowaway?"

"Yes, probably." He didn't seem too bothered by that. "It's an adventure."

We found a pension and slept late into the afternoon before heading for East Berlin.

"Check out the fencing," I said. "There's barbed wire on top of all three of those tall barriers around that massive clearing. This place is eerie. Does this happen when governments ban religions?"

"Those trees have been sheared to barren poles," Coleman pointed out. "Look into those towers as we pass and see if there are soldiers in them."

That two-lane road ran a flat, straight line from where we had been, to where we were going. The entire road was abandoned except for our car. We drove in the left lane because the right one was peppered with potholes and completely impassable.

"Where is everybody?"

"Most Easterners don't have automobiles."

"But we're out here all alone. There's not another human being in sight. Where are the houses? What are all those tall fences for? How come there are no crops in the fields?"

Absolutely out of nowhere, an official car pulled up behind and flagged us into the right lane. Another search?

"They're coming back for me, Coleman."

Shouting angry commands in Russian, swinging arms matching their belligerence, they got out of their car and came at us. I'd never seen my husband so amenable.

"They're forcing us to use the right lane." He said, sounding sheepish and defeated.

"How do you know?"

"Look at them. It's obvious."

"We can't drive over there."

"We'll have to," Coleman said, and he slowed to a bumpy crawl, while they followed behind us on the good pavement for a very long time. They eventually drove off.

"I'm going back over to the left. They've disappeared."

Driving in the opposite direction six days later, Coleman had deliberately put the license plates on upside-down just for the drama of it all. He was a teaser kind of journalist, the kind that wanted a story behind every exciting experience. I reminded myself to breathe.

"Let's go to Italy," he said.

In Florence, we slowly and separately circled Michelangelo's *David* for an hour. We pretended to hold up the Leaning Tower in Pisa, fed the pigeons in Venice, and flushed out artisans fashioning colorful glass figurines in tiny back street shops. We were haunted by Dante's mask, and tried to imagine how long it took to thread the intricate tapestries and piece together the vibrant mosaics. We saw a ballet, and then drove to Rome for

Aida in the Baths of Caracalla where actual elephants were brought on stage for a role in the opera. We competed to name the saints on canvases, triptychs, carved doors, mosaics, and statues. We visited Saint Peter's at the Vatican, standing alongside hundreds of Italian nuns waving white handkerchiefs and shouting, *"Papa! Papa!"* We were within fifty feet of the Holy Father, Pope Paul VI, then watched in disbelief as a lunatic lunged forward with a weapon among throngs of worshippers and got carried out overhead by Swiss guards—the exceptional protectors of the Vatican for five hundred years.

I finally met Coleman's Seminarian Provincial, Father Westfield, who took us to the very top of the Basilica and we stood next to Saint Peter's statue, staring down at the plaza. Father told us the Church would be smaller but stronger someday.

We took pictures for our scrapbooks and headed to Naples.

We were robbed in Naples. We hadn't heeded the warnings to be careful of widespread thefts on tourists. Our car got broken into and we lost airline tickets, luggage, passports, Coleman's political research papers on Neo-Nazis, and both my dirndl and leather outfits. I sat down on the curb among the twists and turns of cobbled brick roads, clotheslines strung with colorful laundry between apartments, buried my head in my hands and sobbed loud and uncontrollably. People crowded around. I was beyond repair. I had no friends, no language, and my husband's passion for me had run out.

"Gretchen, pull yourself together," Coleman said tenderly.

"I don't want to be in Europe anymore. I don't understand anybody and you only talk to strangers. Not to me. I want to go home." Déjà vu on the pleading to be set free and go home.

"We still have money. We still have our car. They didn't take our rolls of film. And we still have clothes on our backs. We'll go to Pompeii and tour the excavations, get our minds on something else. Later this afternoon I'll go to the American Embassy and make a formal report. The airlines will issue us new tickets and temporary passports. We'll be fine." I lost count of all the times he had spoken those three words. But he always found a solution.

Separately, we meandered through empty, ancient Pompeii. Vesuvius' massive destruction softened my personal misery. When he found me a couple hours later, he shot a few photographs.

"Smile," he said.

"I don't feel like smiling."

"But I'm taking pictures for future generations."

"You don't need me to smile at this very minute."

We headed north to France. At Fontainebleau, Coleman rushed ten paces ahead, upsetting me nearly to tears.

"You're an ass." I said. I'd never sworn at anybody in my life and that word flew out of my mouth unrestrained and like it was comfortable.

"Where did you learn such a fowl word, and how dare you refer to me! You're obviously low class and don't deserve of my companionship. You can do this tour alone."

I walked around that castle by myself. I didn't care about Napoleon or Marie Antoinette's head. I was so bewildered and bitter. Swearing wasn't allowed when I was growing up. Certainly not in the convent. I heard my grandpa say "damn" several times, but he was a farmer and had earned that right, Mother told us.

The Eiffel Tower brought us back to clearer heads and better manners. We strolled along the Champs Elysees our first evening in Paris. Coleman walked on ahead, looking at the sports cars in large windows, while I stared at fashionably dressed mannequins in others. A Frenchman approached me and began speaking, *"Je suis fou de toi. Quel est le cout?"*

"What? I don't understand what you're saying," I said.

More fancy phrases out of him. He wouldn't leave me alone so I answered him in measured English, "Sir, I cannot help you. I do not know what you want."

He seemed personable, trying to make some point with me, pressing me with his French. Suddenly, Coleman charged toward us, yelling at the man, who was nicely dressed and looked to be a gentleman, so I was alarmed at my unusually uncool husband.

Coleman waved his arms, dismissing the man, who hurried away, turning repeatedly to give a look back over his shoulder.

"What did he want? What was he saying? I couldn't understand him. He seemed to want me to help him."

"He was propositioning you." At first Coleman chuckled, but then his face registered chagrin.

"What's that mean?"

"He wanted you to exchange sex for money and was asking what you expected."

"Really?" I stared after that retreating Frenchman and felt strangely flattered, desirable, and rather relieved. Coleman put an arm around my shoulder for a moment.

I was thrilled that nice bereted stranger hadn't even hesitated to approach me. He'd been wonderfully insistent. My mind reveled in that scenario, fantasizing about a Parisian gentleman sneaking me away from my passionless husband to give me a night I could remember. It brought me secret pleasure. It bolstered my self-esteem. I should have been ashamed of myself.

"I'm interviewing for a job at the UPI (United Press International), translating French into English. We'd be able to remain in Paris for a year," Coleman said, days before we were to fly home.

"Only if I get to go home first. To get my bearings. Then I'll come back with you."

In Germany, we sold our VW back to the dealership, secured new airline tickets, and ignored the farewells of the good people of Luxembourg, and boarded our return flight to Iceland. We spent two days on that island due to a stewardess strike.

"Let's take the mail route rather than a typical tour bus. That way we'll see the true countryside, picking up Icelanders from farms and villages along the road," Coleman said and was right, as usual.

We stopped in tiny villages. Our bodies turned lobster pink in pools heated by natural springs. The bus drove on a ribbon of asphalt among deserted mountains and hills of black lava, along grassy fields with grazing sheep whose wool draped over them like waterfalls to the ground.

"Gretchen, let's make love on these beautiful hills alongside this cascade of water. It'll be something we can tell our friends. 'We made love at the top of the world!' we'll say." He wrapped his arms around me.

"What?" I pulled away. "There were ten-hundred places we could have made love on this trip and you want me to strip out here in the frigid open air and lay on the hard barren earth without a blanket or anything? I'm freezing. What's wrong with you? People are just over that hill and heading this way. I'd never do anything that crazy."

"It doesn't matter what people think." Coleman said. "What matters is that we have this great adventure awaiting us—mak-

ing love on Iceland's lush's volcanic ash in this primitive sanctuary. Nobody thinks of doing that. Can't you see its a-once-in-
a-lifetime opportunity? Don't be such a coward."

"No, no, no. I won't do it. *I won't!*" I yelled at him in rage and
disbelief. "I am not taking my clothes off out here! I am not
going naked in front of the whole world!" I stomped my foot
and waved my hands, settling them at last on my hips and
scowling at my husband. I planted both feet firmly on the tun-
dra, brisk winds carrying mist from the falls onto my face. The
panorama of amazing Iceland surrounded us and I was tainting
the quiet beauty with my objections. Coleman was disgusted
with me for being such a nutcase, ridiculing my sanctimony,
my childishness, my foolish fears, and my lack of imagination.
But by now, I knew he didn't really want to make love as much
as he wanted the spectacle. A group of tourists trotted over the
hill with cameras and wide-eyed wonder.

"See, Coleman? People."

"It would have been a memorable story for them too."

We hiked over to the bubbling geyser just as it exploded up
and out into the frigid open sky. Watching nature spew boiling
water, I felt I understood that isolated lonely island.

Chapter

20

After three months of European travel, I was excited to start our real marriage. As far as sex, I figured there must be something wrong with me, and that I'd lost a lot of ground in the convent.

I returned to teaching in public school and Coleman went back to the newspaper. We took dance lessons and learned to waltz, twirl, and dip. We performed in the local theater. Coleman won a starring role in Gilbert and Sullivan's *The Mikado* as Pish-Tush, a nobleman from the town of Titipu, Japan. I was in the chorus of schoolgirls and I stared jealously at Yum-Yum, the love interest of Nanki-Poo, who was doomed to die, but didn't. On Sundays, we went to church, where I wore my fancy hats and tweed suits with my mink boa. Coleman said I looked great. I couldn't pray.

"Incompatible," my doctor's diagnosis crept into my thoughts. With regards to sex, yes, I could see that now. A year of struggling had worn me out and I knew I'd never experience the passion lovemaking was rumored to ignite. Coleman and I attempted intimacy, but it felt counterfeit. I was sick of that whole thing, realizing nothing would ever change. Still, I wanted a family. I thought a baby would fix us. And though there was not a prouder father in the world when our baby boy arrived, Coleman was upset when I first announced the good news.

"I have the best news." I said from the kitchen while he was changing from him work clothes.

"What's going on?" At the time, my husband was one of a few finalists for a journalism fellowship in Washington, D.C. He had big ambitions and a baby wasn't in the plan.

"I'm late with my period."

"What! Aren't you taking the pill anymore?" Now we were face to face.

"I told you they were making me sick. I think I might be pregnant."

"We can't afford a baby. Listen, Gretchen, we haven't discussed this. You never consulted me."

"Aren't you happy? Don't you want us to have a family? People get married and then they have kids. It's what couples do."

"I wanted to get married, but I never anticipated kids. You had no right to stop taking the pill without my permission"

"Who gets permission? I don't get permission. Nobody gets permission."

"Well, I'm half of this marriage and I wasn't brought in on this plan. Having kids is a very serious proposition. You planned this behind my back." He began to pace.

"No I didn't."

"You stopped taking the pill without letting me know."

"Every day, I got sick in the mornings at school. I said right to your face that I needed to stop the pill. You don't remember because you don't listen." My shoulders held their position, broad and steadfast.

"You did not tell me and I resent this. I have plans for my life and it never included kids. They cost a fortune. This changes everything."

"I thought you'd be happy." I stared at him, daring more argument. Why should I feel repentant? I wanted kids. This marriage was lonely for me.

"Maybe it'll be a false alarm," he said. "But I refuse to be one of those people who gives his life over to just raising kids."

Then one miraculous day, "You have to nurse our baby and join LaLeche," Coleman said. The LaLeche League was founded in this country by women in the 50's. They wanted American mothers to experience breastfeeding.

The Lamaze natural childbirth classes were becoming all the rage, as well. Local hospitals were eager to introduce the novelty of the French method that helped a woman give birth without medications.

"It's cutting-edge and we'll be among the first in town to participate in something barely discussed in polite conversation. Fathers won't feel left out any more. Childbirth is now a family event," Coleman said. So we practiced the birthing exercises with other prospective parents.

A week before my delivery date, my mother came over to see me.

"Your doctor's incompetent," Coleman said, having just learned he wouldn't be allowed in the delivery room.

"He's a wonderful doctor, he's practically part of our family," my mother said.

"He won't be delivering our baby."

"See here," My mother said. "Who's having this baby?"

"I'm firing you." Coleman told my doctor. "We're hiring the Lamaze doctor." Then he convinced both physicians to agree they'd cooperate. My doctor thought Coleman was crazy and told him so, but the Lamaze doctor thought he was spot-on.

"I'll handcuff myself to your bed as they wheel you into the OR," he told me and then anyone else who'd listen.

Coleman forgot the handcuffs and slept through most of my labor and delivery. When he was awake, I swore every cuss word known to mankind and Coleman called me his wanton fishwife. Honestly, I don't know where those awful words came from.

Our baby was beautiful and Coleman named him David, in honor of Michelangelo.

"You named your baby after a statue?" my doctor said.

"No, we named our baby after a great work of art!" Coleman said, and wrote a charming tribute to our son in an editorial piece for the paper where he worked.

After delivery I had an outbreak of eczema all over my face. For the first time in my life, I made a choice not to attend Mass on Sunday. No elegant hat from Switzerland or Paris could hide that mess. The skin around my eyes, forehead, cheeks, neck, nose, and chin peeled, leaving puffy red blotches and ugly white flakes on every available skin cell. My baby didn't mind that I looked like a reptile, but polite society would surely talk. I looked hideous.

All that day, I breathed lightly and tiptoed around the apartment waiting for lightning to strike me dead. When it didn't, I stayed away from Mass the entire month, and later, forever. I went to see my doctor early in the outbreak. He asked me if I was happy in my marriage.

"Of course. I love my husband."

"Clearly something's making you sick. Eczema stems from nerves. I think that husband of yours is the cause. This isn't some little rash. Your face is in full display."

"How could a skin disorder on my face come from my husband?"

"Because you're convincing yourself to be happy in order to make the marriage work. I've known your family a long time. I delivered all you kids. This husband of yours doesn't fit in." I thought the doctor probably resented Coleman's prior insults.

"I think you should leave him," he said without flinching.

"I just got married."

Prescription in hand, I told Coleman the doctor said the eczema was his fault.

"That's ridiculous," he said.

I was unsure if anyone was to blame for my affliction. All I knew was that our marriage wasn't like my parents'. My husband was unusual and referred to himself as a creative thinker, a pseudo-intellectual. Sometimes, I just wanted us to be normal like everybody else.

Coleman insisted we purchase a piano and a sewing machine to enrich the household with what those two things could offer. "It's up to the woman to educate the children in a family," he said. We hosted formal dinner parties in our four-room apartment and Coleman taught me how to properly serve a multi-course dinner. We began in the front room with perfect conversation matching perfect pauses, while sampling the appetizers I'd slaved over. Then, we moved to the dining room—not a foot from where we began—and drank our first goblet of perfectly selected wine. I commenced a ritual of clearing smaller china, sterling, and crystal after each course, giving eventual maximum view to the elegant, subsequently larger dinner plate beneath. It accommodated an entrée that I brought from the kitchen upon a return trip. The pomp and circumstance continued all the way through to dessert and coffee, after which I blew out the candles—my hand cupping the flame from behind—so we could all retire to the front room where we'd started. The conversation wound down while we sipped our cordials and mixed a sprinkling of laughter with our evolving attitudes. I attempted to master the art of fine dining just like my new husband wanted me to. I realized my diamond fit the scene, but it felt heavier and heavier on my finger.

"Why couldn't I just put all the food on the table at once?" I asked my husband before guests arrived. "How should I know when people want the next course?"

"I'll give you a sign," he said, and he did, nodding his head and softly, secretly tapping my hand when he thought I should move on to the next prepared item—clear through to the toast at the end of the evening. By that time, I was a wreck.

"Whew! Coleman, I couldn't enjoy myself. I kept waiting for your signal, and serving dinner in increments was too much pressure. I was on the edge of my seat the entire time. I couldn't even enjoy the conversation."

"You did just fine. We got to show off all our beautiful things. You went to too much trouble with the food. You could have served hot dogs on our china. People care more about the ambiance than the food. And don't worry. I'll manage the conversation. It'll get easier in time, you'll see."

"You didn't like my chicken croquettes with capers and sauce? I worked all week on that recipe." I plopped down in a chair.

The only way to get along was to go along. I didn't keep my mouth shut, but I sure did try to please him. It seemed important for him that we impress.

While Coleman went to work in the daytime, I stayed home with our son and frequently got together with my mother and two sisters and their babies. I'd finally caught up to their lives and loved the visiting I'd missed for too many years.

Our family budget got tighter, so Coleman found a position with The Illinois Arts Council in Chicago as their public relations person. It meant more money and a big move, but wretched bickering began all over again. "We're both moving to Chicago. Both of us should pack, I said.

"Put it into a manageable timeframe," he said. Take your time and do a little bit each day."

"But I need your help."

"Packing is woman's work."

"That's not true. I can't do it all. I have a new baby to take care of."

"My work is outside the home. Yours is in the home."

"What about women's liberation?"

Arguments fell on deaf ears. I was becoming Coleman's workhorse. That's what marriage meant for me. I could have stayed in the convent. That bridegroom never helped me out either.

"You used to be so charming," I said. "Where's the writer of all those beautiful notes and letters? The boyfriend who sang me love songs? Where's the man who sent me a rose every Saturday morning for one whole year? Where did he go? Aren't I your sweetheart anymore? You used to put me first."

I did all the packing—the second time I'd boxed up our things—right down to the last paper clip at the bottom of the last drawer.

In Chicago, I was Coleman's wife and the mother of an adorable baby, yet not even that brought me the tenderness he exhibited prior to marriage. Being a wife looked so sweet before I actually became one, just like being a nun looked important when I was young. I took on everything that needed to be done, otherwise the institution, as he called our family structure, wouldn't flow. I knew the value of hard work. I organized and managed. Our baby's needs were taken care of first, our shelves were full, the house was clean and stylish, we had suitable clothing, food was on the table, and there was a rhythm to each day. Though the face in the mirror each morning didn't smile back, there was something that I liked about the new me—married, motherly, attempting to support my husband, and trying to look healthy and fit. I missed my family and my hometown, but the pulse of the city with its everyday beauty of amazing architecture and cozy neighborhoods energized me. Jogging was all the rage. I read a book called *Marathon Mom*, bought tennis shoes, and became a runner. *Getting in touch with your body*, was a new phrase. If looking fit would win me favors, and that book promised it would, then I wanted some of it. Physical fitness made me more noticeable. I met other moms with toddlers and swapped baby stories, though I couldn't participate in conversations about facials, manicures, pedicures, or lovemaking, since I knew nothing of them. I wasn't anyone's first choice for a casual get-together, but I made an effort to participate in group gatherings.

"Appearances are everything," Coleman said many times, which is why when I got a haircut to within two inches of my scalp, I thought he'd love it. I looked like Joan of Arc, who sported a boy's cut to become a soldier for the Lord. People said I looked chic. They said I was making a statement.

"How could you?" said my husband. "Have you taken leave of your senses? What have you done to yourself? What's happened to your hair? You no longer look like a wife. Why did you do this?" he went on and on.

I didn't think there was a specific way a wife was supposed to look, but for a mother with a baby, it was perfect. I kept it short for years. He had that same kind of reaction whenever I wore my jeans. In winter, I lived in them. He swore he'd send to Austria for five dirndls.

"You'll have a dirndl for every day of the week."

I watched the mail for a package from Europe, ready to intercept and return its contents. Nothing ever arrived.

Sarah, Coleman's mother, found us a place to live, a charming coach house attached to a mansion owned and renovated by the Dean of Art and Architecture at the university. The dean and his wife, both architects, taught me that preserving beautiful old buildings tied people profoundly to their own histories.

"We want to help restore the university's neighborhood," Leonard and Virginia Currie told the chancellor, who objected.

"You can't live in that run-down neighborhood. It's a slum, it'll be demolished within the decade, consumed by corporations," he said.

"We're both architects. We design and preserve buildings," the Curries said. "These homes are worth saving. The neighborhood should be returned to its original beauty. We'll purchase the mansion on the park and show you a revitalized human spirit." And the first renovation in that area got underway.

Little by little and one house at a time, people discovered the neighborhood and began to gut, strip, sandblast, silicone, paint, polish, and tuck-point old buildings. Several apartments went up in different pockets, mixing new with old. Architectural integrity and uniformity kept the neighborhood visually pleasant, but the Italians held it all together with their cultural passions.

Italians owned the hardware store, the barber shop, and the great restaurants where the sauces competed for raves, the pasta was always cooked to perfection, and the spumoni was creamier than anywhere in the world. Rather than say goodbye, Tony, who ran the fruit stand, told all the women, "Stay beautiful."

"Don't pay your bill today, we might not see you again," said Paul Chiarugi, as his wife Rose walked my toddler to the back of the store for a cookie.

"Take two or three," Rose insisted.

Italians owned the corner storefronts. They owned the best bakeries with stone ovens disassembled, brought over from Italy, and rebuilt. The bread was crusty on the outside, soft in the center, and unsurpassed. The two brothers, Luigi and Al Davino, baked until early morning, and could then be seen playing cards in the large storefront window, still in their long white aprons and covered head to foot in flour.

Italian grandmothers walked in their black stockings, black shoes, black dresses, and black headscarves to mourn their deceased husbands. I thought they looked like postulants. The women that did speak English would stop me as I pushed my stroller and ask, "Where is your family from?"

"The Midwest."

"No, what country?"

"I'm German and Irish." No one had ever put that question to be before. I liked it. It boosted my historical commentary— the bigger picture. I felt less lonely. Ancestral hovering was meaningful to me.

"That's alright then, that's good," they said.

I hadn't realized there'd be that scrutiny, but Italians had lost much of their ethnic neighborhood to urban renewal, the construction of a university, and every expressway encircled it.

Some Italians still owned entire apartment buildings where extended families raised one another's children with plenty of it-takes-a-village attitude. Young Italian boys played rock-paper-scissors for hours on the street corner and drove everybody nuts, but it was part of the rhythm of every night.

Even though people were friendly, they weren't my family. I wanted to put my feet under my mother's kitchen table. I felt like I'd lost too much time in the convent that I could have spent with my loved ones and now I lived two hundred miles away. I wanted my relatives to uproot and move north.

In our new neighborhood, like-minded people found each other. Coleman was a magnet for a crowd. People were in and out of our coach house daily.

"It's the neighborhood's Golden Age," he said. "It'll eventually grow bigger. What we know as cozy will one day be another great Chicago neighborhood. We need to take advantage of that."

Every summer evening, men beat exotic African rhythms, families and friends picnicked, and groups of students played touch football. Multiple races of people poured into our park like a little United Nations.

"Let's ride our bikes over to Taylor Street for Italian ice, or Chicago hot dogs, or fresh donuts, or Italian beef sandwiches," Coleman said all of the time.

What we weren't doing was attending church. We two former monastics avoided formal prayer altogether. Previous obsessions with religion vaporized. Barely twenty-five dollars to spare from every paycheck, having been on the inside of all things church-related, we weren't of a mind to tithe to the Church by denying ourselves our own pressing needs.

Occasionally, we'd have Sunday roast at Sarah's house and Coleman was able to visit with his siblings. Ivy League educated, incredible bridge-playing skills, musicians, scientists, and boasting verbal acuity, I was astonished at the quick wit and humor interlaced with such heady stuff. I'd been a sub-missive Catholic, whereas they were more prone to question authority. I tried to engage in the conversations.

"The food's delicious," I said.

Everyone paused, agreed, and then the high intellectual pursuit of their exchange began anew. They raised my level of awareness that our planet was headed for trouble, so they ac-tively participated in early conservation efforts. I learned that Presidents Nixon and Carter—from opposing political par-ties—each enacted laws that had we enforced them, our polar bears might still have a playground, I've since reasoned.

Whereas we stayed in constant contact with Coleman's fam-ily, it was a struggle to reunite with my own. Though Coleman liked them personally, he thought they'd hold him back from his need for a creative life. That's what he said.

"I had to get Gretchen away from family," he told friends when we moved up north.

"Don't you mean *you* needed to get away from family?" they said.

It was a lonely existence, once again. The weight of it all didn't come from a long robe this time, but from a longing for companionship. I loved the city, but I wanted to explore it with Coleman by my side.

"No one's responsible for another's happiness. Go meet peo-ple," he pushed when I told him I spent too much time without him. "This is Chicago. It's a very big city. There's more to do here than one can pack into a lifetime."

"But Coleman, you're supposed to be my best friend," I said. "You hardly spend any time with me." He loved people. He en-gaged them. I was still hesitant. I held my distance. He could make immediate confidantes out of strangers, and savor long and true relationships with people over many years. Just like in the convent, my experiences of friendship barely grew beyond the superficial.

Instead of getting more of my husband, I got increasingly less. He started a neighborhood newspaper, *The West Side Story*. He went around to businesses and construction sites with a notebook and camera, gathering articles of interest, covering the politics of the neighborhood, and getting businesses to buy ads and people to contribute features. It was the year of the Democratic Convention. Hippies were still having some influence in music and politics, the Chicago Seven trial had just ended, and conspiracy theorists had made names for themselves.

Coleman began his paper around the same time I delivered our second baby. *If having one baby helped me feel married, two would be even better.* Truly, I can't remember any romps in our bed, but there must have been at least one more.

He failed to visit me in the hospital for several days after our second boy was born. I was there for over a week because I had the Rh negative factor, which caused complications for our baby.

"I had to name our baby by myself, Coleman, the nurses were mad at me for the delay, so I finally told them to write down Thomas, after your best friend."

I'd seen Coleman lose his cool several times, but that time his hands flew up in the air and he began pacing the hospital floor.

"You can't name him Thomas!" he said as I lay in the hospital bed, and his hands went to his head as he circled the room. "No, no, no! You can't name him Thomas!" he said, and I stared at him from my hospital bed as his hands grasped his head and he paced all the more.

"But I love that name. I've always loved that name. You weren't here to help me! What's wrong with you? It's a beautiful name. Why don't you like it?"

"You can't name him Thomas! You can't!"

Something wasn't right. My husband didn't overreact to that degree without cause. I could have backed down as soon as he objected. I wasn't that invested in the name. But I think I was subconsciously goading on him so I could get the full flavor of his objections imprinted onto my brain. He was coming unglued. I felt so sorry for him, but it made me mad. He didn't even know we had a sick baby. We argued for an hour until we finally agreed on a new name. The decorative birth certificate with little footprints and a shiny gold seal and ribbon, had a big cross-out on the name line with a new one written above it. Our second son was finally named Gregory. "Gregory the Great," we'd both finally said—an early Catholic Pope, who designed the modern-day calendar for the Christian world, and was credited with the Gregorian chant, beautiful music for our beautiful baby.

That temper tantrum wore us both out. Despite his dramatic moments, Coleman was intelligent, well-read, and at ease in any setting. I still felt uncomfortable in my own skin, a very unfortunate hindrance that I had no clue how to remove. When he applied negative characteristics to me—too sensitive, too serious, overreacting, narrow-minded—I took them to heart.

Three years into our marriage, I was the busy mother of two little boys. Coleman wanted my continued support of his newspaper. I watched my two-year-old, held my nursing baby in one arm, and pressed type and straightened margins with my free hand.

"Coleman shouldn't expect you to help with the newspaper,

and it's not good for the coach house to have a professional business in it. We renovated it as an apartment, not for a commercial enterprise," our landlady, Virginia Currie, told me. "Your husband's a good guy and a smart man, everybody loves him, his paper is exactly what's needed in the community, but he's expecting you to carry too big a load."

After the paper was printed and stacks of them brought into our living room for distribution, our two-year-old walked alongside me, pulling his little red wagon loaded high, while I carried the baby on my back. I thought about how my father carted coal for his home as a little kid, only we weren't in such dire straits. We delivered papers house-by-house, up and down sidewalks for two days, while Coleman and his young crew took piles into apartments and stores.

"My paper makes a valuable contribution to the neighborhood, serves the people, and helps unify the community's expanding dreams. I need your help getting it out. The boys will learn some lifetime skills," he said.

"But David's only two and Greg's a baby."

I don't remember a rebuttal, but he always had one. Nothing I said ever mattered.

"Our apartment is totally consumed by your hobby."

"This isn't a hobby. It's a serious newspaper. I need you onboard. I can't afford to rent space, but as the paper makes money, I'll find a new place."

"But you don't charge anybody for it," I said. "How would it make money?"

"The advertisers pay for it now. More businesses will join, you'll see."

"It takes up half our apartment."

"Only for two weeks out of the month."

"Not everybody likes your paper," I said one especially mean day.

"It doesn't matter what people say about the paper, or me, as long as we're being talked about," was his journalistic bend.

I'd never heard anything remotely like that before. I thought being talked about was something people tried to avoid.

He worked hard pulling articles together, accumulating readers, and taking it to press. His personality won over advertisers who'd been in business for decades and didn't need space in any paper to keep customers. Coleman convinced them otherwise. Anyone could contribute news relevant to themselves or their businesses, clubs, schools, and churches.

"I want to be an important person in the community, and you'll be important too, Gretchen."

"Can't I just be a wife and mom?" I thought those were the most important jobs. To him, they were just titles.

I didn't think I could take much more. Coleman escorted me to local stores where wives helped their husbands. He asked those women to talk sense into me about the benefits of mom and pop businesses. Not a single one of them would.

The neighborhood boasted a frenetic pace. As soon as a new couple or new business moved in, the paper made an announcement. For two years, the paper continued to take over our living room until it all went to the press, when I could make a home again.

"A wife supports her husband," he said when I objected.

He shared cups of coffee in the homes of neighborhood women, who otherwise were supposed to be my friends, but given that he got to know them better—a personable fellow of wide interests, strong opinions, and a need for audiences beyond our front door—he became their confidante. He sat at their kitchen tables and heard their stories, saw their kids, shared his personality with them. He lavished all his charm on other people.

"You're always gone," I said. "The boys need their father around more."

"I enjoy visiting with people. Part of getting to know my customers is in sitting down with them and talking. Marriages become boring. I need broader interactions. Try being more like the other women in the neighborhood. They decorate their homes unconventionally. They entertain guests. They can speak on any subject. They are more involved with the neighborhood and activities." I knew these women, and what he said was true, but their husbands were not like mine either.

"Coleman is very intelligent and a good person. He needs to find creative outlets. I enjoy talking with him over coffee," women told me.

I resented his tête-à-têtes on so many levels. I had no special relationship with my husband whatsoever, but it seemed everyone else did. When our next-door neighbor confided in Coleman that she had miscarried, he gave her the longest, most tender hug, right there in broad daylight on the sidewalk. That was something I had never ever gotten from him. It was a wonderful sympathetic embrace. I stood there, watching them and thinking how very well taken care of she must feel. I looked quizzically at the back of my husband as his arms encircled her. They held one another, talking closely for what seemed an eternity, both knowing, but neither one caring in the least that I was behind them. Waiting. If it were a painting the artist wouldn't have bothered to include me on the canvas. She was a nice enough person. She walked her two little white schnauzers

three times a day in the park, dressed in brilliant, colorful kaf-
tans and turbans covering her long hair. Another sophisticated
female like others he admired. I understood her pain over a
miscarriage. Still, Coleman's behavior hurt me. And I didn't
understand it. I didn't know why I had to feel like the intruder.

"Why do you show women in the neighborhood your comforting side and you show me your criticism? Don't you love me
anymore?" I asked.

"Gretchen, I do love you. You're the one I married," he said,
and then went into the house as if the matter were settled. I
followed him in and got supper ready.

Chapter
21

I was only slightly comforted by his words. I knew every day couldn't be a fairytale. And how could I complain? I was forever grateful not to be in a habit. Two communities of nuns lived close by to remind me where I'd been. One group rented an apartment around the corner and wore jeans, while the other group were Italian nuns, barely spoke English, still wore heavy robes, and lived directly across the street behind the walls of the Church, rectory, and convent compound.

"Can you believe that nun asked me where the Eisenhower Expressway was?" Coleman said one day, and my mind snapped back to the most dreadful time of my life. Realizing that the nun could have been me, I was healed on the spot, resolving never to grumble again. At least I was out of there. At least I was free.

Coleman worked the late shift at his regular job and I stayed home alone five nights a week. When he said my pregnancy weight didn't bother him, it didn't ring true. He spent his time with the attractive women in the neighborhood. I continued my daily jogging so I'd feel better about myself attempting to draw his attention away from them.

I devoured the *Future Shock*, which I agreed with, but got so upset I threw that book across the room. The reality of that prediction scared me, as I recognized myself being overwhelmed by the acceleration of social change which I couldn't assimilate.

Living in an Italian neighborhood, *The Godfather* became the latest affection among readers so I picked it up. Same thing. I heaved it across the room unfinished. I wondered how much violence might be happening in my own backyard. I read every issue of *Newsweek* and *Time* magazines after putting the boys to bed, trying to absorb it to make myself smarter, and more desirable. In the *Chicago Tribune*, I favored the political column, the arts and book review sections, and the gossip and society pages. I wanted to lure my husband back with my own renaissance. I read about countries, their leaders, and things going on in our capital. Coleman wouldn't talk with me about any of it, distracted by other things. What did I have to do to be worthy of his love? Again, I was invisible, but still fighting for love and affection. I was learning new things, but what difference did it make? I'd be sound asleep by the time Coleman crawled into bed after work each night.

In the morning, I got up with my boys. Seeing their faces lit up my whole life. Pajamas off, fresh clothes on, they would head right to the kitchen for a breakfast: a small glass of orange juice, oatmeal or cream of wheat, milk, toast. They had good appetites. The cereal went on the floor, on the head, but some in the mouth. Spills never upset me. *Don't cry over spilt milk.*

Our little mother-son conversations were so precious to me. I hung on their every word. They filled the gaping hole in my heart where companionship and acceptance should dwell. I was finally a part of something special. No one accepted me more than my kids did. They were my best friends.

By nine each morning, they were ready for the outdoors. Whether rain or shine, cold or hot, we went outside twice a day to the little playground around the block. I didn't care if it took five minutes to get there or fifteen. Their center of gravity was close to the ground, so they noticed things I would've passed up. If they wanted to follow an ant along its destination, stomp on the dry autumn leaves to hear the crunchy sound, or grab a gnarly stick as a friend, it was all good. I waited and watched and talked with them, saying names of things, and opening up vocabulary. We all three stuck our noses in the purple and blue petals of the climbing four-o'clocks along the fence in late afternoon. Sometimes, they pushed the stroller, other times they rode. When they got to the Big Wheel stage, they raced down the block, careening into the playground, barely on one wheel. They headed straight for the swings. I would be hard pressed to say whether climbing up the slide or sliding down was their favorite part, but those steps were well worn down and shiny from their shoes by the time a contractor tore our playground apart and put up another apartment building.

My boys always got filthy. I was proud of their freedom to do that. There were teeter-totters, a merry-go-round, and two jungle gyms. They made the rounds. It was our time together and my favorite memories were born from them. I birthed those little boys out of my own body. Such a creation.

Somewhere around ten in the morning, Coleman got up and was out the door in short order. But on lucky days, he stayed in his pajamas and got down on the floor where he and the boys built things with blocks. He'd lift one, then the other high over his head or atop his shoulders. He took them to parades and baseball games. He began a collection of little wooden trains and set up tracks, turns, and bridges to run them on. Then, every little boy had to have Legos and Hot Wheels. They glued model airplanes together for flying in the park. There wasn't a more active family.

Coleman bought the first pop-up books and read with them in his lap. He took our sons camping. We all went fishing. He played water and sand games with them on Lake Michigan's beaches and took boat rides. He dressed up like an Indian chief at Thanksgiving and then Santa on Christmas.

Even though his father died when he was young and he never connected with his stepfather, Coleman instinctively knew how to love his kids. He wanted them to drink all the milk they needed and eat fresh fruits and vegetables. Besides the usual ones, they devoured bowls of artichoke hearts, cauliflower, broccoli, and Brussels sprouts.

On the few days when the paper wasn't consuming us, we bicycled to the lakefront, boys on the backs. Concerts were free. Museums were free. The parks were free. The views were free. Gas was cheap for a couple more years.

"Let's go see the sky show at the Planetarium. Then we'll head over to the Aquarium and watch the frogman feed tropical fish," Coleman said on Monday.

"Let's take a trip to the Arboretum," he said on Friday and we'd get on the highway and head west.

"Let's take the train downtown to Marshall Field's for ice cream," he said on Saturday.

"The Conservatory is free today," he said on Sunday, so we meandered along tiny rock pathways brimming with holiday flowers and cozy bridges, which arched over ponds of goldfish and splashy water. We relished those family expeditions.

Coleman frequently got complimentary tickets to a fine arts series. We heard and saw and tasted and smelled and touched symphonies, operas, cuisine, aromas, and textures. A bazaar for the senses. I was addicted to the Watergate Trials—*What did you know and when did you know it?* The question introduced by Senator Howard Baker which became the country's obsession. I became a news' junkie, sometimes forgetting that our marriage was empty without intimacy on any level. It was exactly like that vow of chastity and the solitude of the convent. My husband's coldness toward me had an unexpected consequence.

I had an affair. I didn't mean to and it still shocks me that I did. I hadn't awakened one morning and said, "I think I'll take a lover." The thought never entered my brain. I didn't even know what an affair was.

Our neighbor, Giovanni, and his friend showed up at our door late one evening after the boys were asleep. They were admiring the leaded glass in our foyer. I peeked around the corner to check who belonged to the voices spilling into our coach house. They were only a few feet from where I was reading and they were too loud for as late as it was. I recognized both men and opened the front door.

"Joe, meet the best-looking woman in the neighborhood," one said to the other.

"Me?" That was reassuring. When I wasn't in jeans, I wore skimpy shorts—my minimalist period, once I got past that gothic fiasco. But all that jogging had given my body definition and I was proud to show it off. I never wanted to hear anyone state that I'd been a former nun.

The two men had studied the window treatment carefully. It was of intricate design and widely admired. I chatted with them for a few minutes—very friendly. In an attempt to imitate other city women I'd met with enviable social personalities, I became enthusiastic, and stole their focus from the decorative glass. Both were good-looking Italians with wavy black hair, penetrating eyes, and their full-bodied luster of olive skin.

"Let me take Joe home and I'll come back," Giovanni said.

I wondered why he'd do that. But people were in and out of each other's houses all the time in that closely knit neighborhood. Still, it was very late. I knew him like I knew anybody around there, not very well. Coleman was due home in less than an hour and then we could all visit. I checked the mirror. I noticed how my cheeks flushed in excitement. In ten minutes, there was a knock on my door and I welcomed Giovanni into our coach house.

"This is nice," he said looking around. "Where's your husband?"

"He's at work. He'll be home in an hour."

He grabbed me, pulled me against his body, and planted a kiss fully on my lips, holding me up, as I would have surely buckled. That's all it took to push me over the edge. Without permission, my arms wrapped around him and my body clung like a dry sponge sitting on the beach, finally being swept away by the long-awaited tide. *Oh my God. I'll have to divorce my husband.*

Giovanni scooted me backward onto the sofa. My political magazines still sprawled open on the floor were now kicked aside and giving birth to a new preoccupation. He tugged at my clothes and I lay there practically naked with him on top of me, all boy and girl parts easily finding their natural pleasures.

"You're beautiful," he said.

While we made love, I was scared out of my wits, yet unable and not willing to push him away. He left quickly afterward and I shut the door behind him, leaning back against it. I breathed heavily, hesitant to even move from the spot. Then, it hit me.

Oh my God, I'd lost my mind! I was frantic with fear. I repeatedly checked on the boys, paced throughout the rooms, checked them again, wrung my hands, tried to calm myself, and looked at the clock, Coleman would be home in a few minutes. What had I done? What in the world had I done? The phone rang.

"Are you alright?"

"Yes," I said, sounding calmer than I should have.

"I just wanted to make sure you were okay."

"How'd you get this number?"

"You're in the phone book."

"Oh, right."

"Will you be okay?"

"I'm fine, don't worry about it."

"I didn't mean to do that to you."

"I'm okay. Really."

"Will you tell your husband?"

"Oh, no! I'll never tell anybody!" I sucked in my breath as if the secret was attached to it.

"If you need to talk, you can call me."

"Okay, but I have to go."

"You sure you're okay?"

I paused. "I can't believe I let that happen."

"You're probably starved for affection." I deflected that sudden pang of truth and snapped back to real-time.

"I have to hang up right this minute."

"You won't tell your husband?"

"No."

I'd completely lost my senses, all of them jumbled in a bewildered maze. In ten short minutes, I'd gone from saint to sinner. I suppose not attending church hadn't brought me any closer to God, but I'd been to Europe, where those Catholics were very casual about attendance. In this country, my soul was now destined for hell. My former elevated status for eternity, even my mansion and jewel-studded crown, liquefied the very moment I gave in to his kiss. On the spot, I was sorry and deranged, but how could something that filled my hollow desire, be so wrong? I paced like a complete lunatic desperate to escape an asylum.

When Coleman came home, I lay in bed stiff as a board, but fear had changed places with anger. I had the audacity to be furious with my husband. How could he abandon me to a cold marriage where I starved for tenderness and passion? He was supposed to be my lover. I was thirty-one years old, married five years, the mother of two little kids, and I didn't know the slightest thing about sex. Why was life's greatest joy denied to me? I stared out into the darkness of our bedroom, searching for explanation. My poor head was wild, seeking peace, finding insanity. My little boys had a bad mother. My throat swallowed hard, my eyes burned and brimmed with tears. *Jezebel.*

Sleep brought relief, morning brought reality. With my boys safely in the care of a babysitter, I visited Giovanni at his place now and then. How could I give up such a luscious experience? He was unmarried, so I didn't have that complication. A new word defined my state—satiated. It was like eating a plateful of the finest dessert. Yet holding onto a huge secret was no way to live. When I wasn't deliriously happy, it just ate me up inside.

From the depths of my soul, I was overjoyed to have someone touch me. I wasn't a pariah after all. I was lovable. It nourished me and I responded in kind, becoming especially sweet to my husband, no longer arguing, but going along, and a better mom than before. I'd completely disconnected from the person I thought I was—sin-free, straight-laced, machine-like—to having a natural feeling of spirituality—calm, easygoing, grounded at long last. I became my best self. Home at last as I reconnected to the little girl and brought her forward into womanhood.

After two years, the affair was over. It hadn't become a heart-felt relationship, more or less a hasty one, but the power of touch was enormously healing.

Coleman announced his newest passion one morning, "I've discovered an entire block of beautiful one-hundred-year-old mansions just north of the expressway, twenty-five of them, practically untouched, only in need of basic renovation. An elderly couple wants to sell for $25,000. It's a steal. Their mansion has three stories with fireplaces in every room, a beautifully carved, open and winding walnut staircase with an ornate newel post, and a huge kitchen with built-in cabinets. Everything's original. It has twelve-foot tin ceilings and walls in the foyer, hardwood floors with different intricate wood-inlay patterns in every room. It belonged to a grand family once. I have to take you there. We can't turn this opportunity down." He sounded more enthused than I'd heard him in a long time.

"But it's out of the neighborhood. What else is over there?"

"Right now the block is surrounded by union halls. It's not a real neighborhood, but the inner city is in its renaissance. We need to get in on the ground floor, buy while the prices are deflated. It'll be worth millions someday." Buying a house was more realistic than purchasing gasoline, which had doubled in price overnight.

"Do families live over there?"

"Everything is rental property, mansions carved up as apartments, but once a landlord sees money can be made, he'll be happy to dump the responsibility of upkeep."

"It sounds very risky."

"Have some imagination," he said so many times, "it could secure our future. At least go with me tomorrow and look at it."

"What are the schools like?"

"The boys are only two and four. There's plenty of time to worry about schools."

"I'm checking on schools before buying a home. I'm a teacher. I need to have my kids in good schools."

Other couples saw those beautiful mansions and formed an alliance. The city manager told our small group his office would abandon its demolition plans if we secured mortgages. Spurred on by unbridled energy, blind to all reason, before year's end, ten families purchased houses on that block and formed a historic preservation group. We moved into our mansion. It was three stories, in the middle of the block, with five beautiful fireplaces. It sported a winding staircase, three skylights, but only one tiny bathroom, and we could see our dining room through its rotting floorboards. The structure was solid, no woodwork ripped out, but softwood floors splintered tender flesh, so our boys wore coveralls to protect their knees. All day, I pulled splinters from tiny fingers and hands.

The kitchen was out of commission so I blew a lot of fuses until I learned to prepare meals using the stove in the kitchen, an electric skillet in the dining room, a crock-pot in the second parlor, and a hot plate in the front parlor.

Traipsing in and out of one another's mansions, neighbors shared stories, food, labor, dreams, and became fast friends, trying not to spoil things with too much obsession. Rehabbing was awful work and strained marriages. It was hard to run a home while living in a demolition zone. Each household shared food and wine around backyard fires, relieving tension and sore muscles. We borrowed tools, talents, and advice. Renovators scrounged the famous flea market on Maxwell Street early Sunday mornings, looking for heavy decorative doors and knobs, iron fencing and gates, banisters, leaded-glass windows and doors, fireplace facades, tin ceilings, woodworking, and whatever could be bought or bartered to restore our early-century beauties. I couldn't believe how much my life had changed.

"I quit my job," Coleman said one day. He left the Arts Council and returned to the world of news at The Associated Press. Our lives readjusted to his new job, our new home, and new people. But trouble lay ahead.

I finally made a friend in this neighborhood. Karen lived across the street from us on that historic block. Credentialed as a psychologist, she had unique insights and actually valued my thoughts.

"I'm starting a women's group, come join us," she said with a genuine smile.

I was a little on edge about joining a group of all women, but I needed help in understanding my complicated marriage. I'd been out of the convent eight years. Adjustment was taking forever.

"The other women are from Hyde Park with connections to the university," she added. They were so much more verbal than I was. Without much to offer, but nothing to lose, I'd try to fit in.

It took several weeks before I felt comfortable enough and then spoke about my marriage for the first time. "My husband and I have only made love a handful of times in seven years." They stared at me. "He thinks I should wear dresses every day and complains about my jeans. He hates my short haircut, says I look like a boy. He wants me to imitate his mother—coordinate hat, gloves, shoes, and purses, read what she reads, play

Bridge with her skills, match her wit and conversation, give cozy parties and exude her charm. I'm not charming. I don't understand charm. My husband is charming. He's very disappointed with me. Though he insists I can't do anything right, he wants me to do everything—help make costumes for his theatre group, partner with him on his newspaper, all while taking care of the mansion and kids." I paused. They stared at me without blinking.

"He wants me to be smarter," I said. "In our typewriter, I found a draft he'd written to my parents saying I swore at him, which I have done. In it, he claimed to be a good husband going to work every day, not smoking or drinking, and coming home every night. He wrote that I wasn't living up to my own mother's standards. He mailed the letter. And he's right. I'm not a good person anymore. I've had an affair."

I'd heard about their marriages for several weeks. I thought I was simply participating in the group. Though I didn't like the way my marriage worked, it's all I had, so I shared it. I waited for responses from the group, immediately wishing I could take it all back and run away.

"That's no marriage," one of them said.

Previous chatter subsided. Our children were in and out of laps, playing with toys, drinking milk or juice from bottles or cups, while the mothers adopted a new mood. Instead of insisting that my husband was gifted and talented—they didn't know him—they spoke calmly about how problematic my life was. Rather than criticism, everyone spoke words of kindness toward me. *It sounds like your husband owns you; everything revolves around his needs; you're lacking a partnership; his demands are damaging you.* That's when I understood the true meaning of the group's theme: to hear one another out, give respect for feelings, and offer feedback. I felt shaky, tears welled up, and I got up to gather things and my kids.

"Come back next week." *This is how women should treat each other*, I thought, reminiscing about my isolation and ridicule in the convent. *Why is this different?*

I knew I was an example of why women's groups were sprouting up. But my issues were not based on men and women jostling for understanding and equality. My issues had to do with *abuse* they said. Really? These women were barely acquaintances. Each one bright, each one well-educated. Their opinions stunned me. How far from their sense of right and wrong I stood.

"We'll reference your story as a marriage in crisis," Karen said the following week. She knew both my husband and me, so her statement was impartial.

I'd never spoken poorly about my husband because I assumed I'd look bad. Coleman won the favor of most everyone, but those women were suggesting insights into my marriage that I never dared to bring up. And no one condemned me over the affair.

I knew what Coleman expected from me couldn't be altered no matter the amount of arguing. Even though the Women's Movement was alive, and well into its second decade, he increased his criticisms toward me, and I'd become disgruntled and moody.

"Your family only talks about babies and dogs," he said, "while mine talks about ideas."

"First of all, we think babies and dogs are excellent subjects. And second, you never listened when they scrutinized the best deals in town, good investments, insurance policies, and helping one another with projects." Apparently, we all bored him.

My mind played havoc with my heart as I struggled to figure out who I was supposed to be. But as long as my children were happy and healthy, I could easily cook and clean for my husband. He did whatever he wanted and I worked with it. I was going through the motions every day, but I was not much more than a eunuch. I was my truest self only with my sons. With everyone else, my social evolution—arrested at seventeen—was still awkward.

"You can only be diminished if you allow it," a group member said and I learned something brand new.

I'd brought things on myself. My own devices, not my father, had landed me in the convent. My response to indoctrination and strictness had turned my personality toward approval-seeking behaviors that I had chosen for myself. The longer I'd wallowed in powerless circumstances and allowed disrespect, the more familiar it became. I was a victim of my own impulses. My approval-seeking had run its course. With newfound knowledge and courage, I had to change.

"Look, you marry who you sleep with, right?" Karen said, sending my mind in search of evidence. *That's how it's done?* The sheer novelty of that option threw my psyche into chaos, and then, lightning-bolt awareness. Clarity demanded I admit I'd been left out of a whole lot of what it meant to be grown—a full human being. I was among adults but not much more than a child. No wonder I'd made no strong connections. The force of a fraudulent way of life had dwarfed my growth. *"Your adjustment will be hard,"* Mother General had said.

Women's dialogue continued as background noise, while her statement sought common ground with my experience. Was the very thing that the Church chastised, actually the correct starting point for marriage? One of those women in the group was

Catholic and she hadn't waited. The others belonged to religions that didn't intrude. Theirs wasn't a sin. They carried no guilt. There was no Church peering into their bedrooms, shaking its finger, demanding penitence and control.

Tensions mounted between Coleman and me with my accumulating insight. "I can't take care of the boys, the household, and the renovation. I have to at least stop helping with the newspaper," I said.

"Fine, we'll see how you feel when the final headline reads 'Newspaper Folds as Wife Abandons Support.'"

"Print whatever you want," I said.

Renovating a mansion proved monumental. Neighbors offered to refurbish our wood floors. The day they were coming over Coleman and I had another round of arguing.

"I didn't give permission for people to come into my house."

"And you didn't ask me if the Joffrey Ballet could party here either. We can't live like this—it's too dirty. We need some relief. The boys get hurt every day."

"You're doing this to embarrass me."

"No, I'm not. Neighbors saw that we needed help and I jumped at the chance."

"You had no right to go behind my back like this and I won't allow it. You'll have to call it off." He began his pacing and hand-waving routine.

"But these are our friends. They'll be here in an hour. This is my house too!" Holding a handful of silverware, I lashed out with a large serving spoon, impulsively smacking Coleman directly below his kneecap—the exact place where a doctor would test knee jerk reflex. Only not just his leg, but his entire body sprang from the chair, pushed me down, silverware scattered on the floor, he hit me over the head with a handful of it, kicked at my head, at my back, and my legs.

"How dare you indiscriminately hit me!" he yelled.

How pathetic. The Cinderella girl crumpled in a fetal position and the charming prince towered overhead—the cultured, double-honeymooned couple, turned combatants. I wasn't hurt. Nothing was bruised. My ego hadn't even suffered. I wasn't exactly sure what had just occurred. The incident caused me to remember the beating I took as a child, but I was an adult now and not defenseless. After a minute, Coleman went upstairs, got ready for work, and then left. I got up and went after my boys who were playing with the neighbor's children. I fixed their supper. People arrived after a while and together we treated the floors. Several hours and sore muscles later, we drove to Billy Goat's Tavern for a midnight hamburger and Coke beneath the city.

I don't remember how Coleman and I slept that night, probably like always—two bodies sharing furniture, space in between. By morning, we could walk around without kicking up dust or taking on splinters. My marriage was in shambles, but those floors were gorgeous.

Chapter 22

It was horrible coming to blows like that. Everyone who knew us would have been shocked and appalled at our match-made-in-heaven. Our families, friends, and Church hierarchy, would have been scandalized. But it wasn't strictly my carelessness that caused this friction. We both harbored secrets. The two most significant men in my life had each raised a hand to me and I was the common denominator. I didn't know what that meant.

That same week, our little family sat down for supper. Coleman noticed that everything was on the table except the napkins.

"There are no napkins on this table!" he boomed.

My suppers were delectable and the flavors, aromas, and textures of the food would have satisfied anyone. Yet he focused on napkins.

"Where are the napkins? That's what's wrong with this marriage. My wife doesn't know how to serve her family properly." His voice escalated in volume, sounding like he was about to explode.

"I forgot them." I said coolly.

He started naming women in the neighborhood, saying he was sure they'd never neglect their families like that. They were fit mothers and wives and would have everything essential for a proper supper.

"My mother never forgot napkins. Your mother never forgot napkins."

So, I got up for the napkins. Once I sat back down, I served food onto the boys' plates and Coleman put out his.

"I am the lord and master, this is my castle, serve me!" he said as his fist hit the table.

"Coleman, you can serve yourself."

With that, he slammed his plate down on my hand, still holding the serving spoon, breaking it in several large pieces. He picked up one large pointed wedge, pushed back his chair, raised it over his head, and came after me. I bolted from the table, then turned to see him gaining on me like a mad man, weapon high overhead. At the door, he kicked me down the eight back-porch steps and I landed hard on the concrete below. I could hear my boys crying. He shouted that his mother would be coming over to take my place and that I was no longer allowed in the house, I was out of the family. He'd take the boys to Mexico. I scooped myself off of the ground, bounded back up the steps, opened the door, and stepped back in. My husband had lost his mind. The boys needed protecting. With obvious and intentional humility, I returned to the table.

"I love you, Daddy. I love you, Daddy," both boys said in a rush. I remained calm and told them that it was okay, the fight was over. I felt I needed to put those words in the air for everybody.

We quietly finished supper while I planned an escape.

"You know, the boys probably need a break about now. I could take them outside for some fresh air. Why not give me the car keys and I'll drive them over to the playground for some playtime?" I said, and he agreed.

We walked out of the house, acting like nothing had just happened. I chatted calmly with our sons, saying we'd have a nice time at the park, not to worry, their dad was being scary, but nothing else bad would happen. Once outside, I knew we were safe. I drove to my friend Marie's house, a single parent with two small children. They joined us at the playground, and as our kids played, I explained what happened. She was Coleman's friend before she was mine, and listened with perspective while I unloaded. With two violent episodes, I had to run my thoughts past an unbiased judge.

"I want to take the boys and go stay with my parents," I said.

"I completely agree, that doesn't sound like Coleman at all. You two need to separate for a while. You're both under too much pressure with that albatross of a mansion around your necks."

"What's an albatross?" I asked.

"Gretchen, come on."

Without extra clothing, but some money in my purse, I drove the boys for the next several hours to my parents' home, getting lost along the way. We arrived late at night. I was so worried they'd be upset, but when my father opened the door and saw us standing there, I said, "I've left Coleman."

"Good," he said, a response I hadn't expected.

In a few days, Coleman called. "I'm afraid of you and I hate our marriage," I said. "My parents think I should leave you and move back here for good."

"Come back. We'll get into counseling at the medical center. I'll arrange an appointment, just please come back."

I couldn't live with my parents. I'd become more independent minded than I realized. Coleman sounded rational and clear-headed. Counseling made sense. A trained therapist might be able to keep the marriage from disintegrating. By week's end, we returned to Chicago and we started therapy, physical abuse replaced by tension.

"You know, there's more of the same treatment if you continue to argue with me," he said matter-of-factly a couple times.

"We both chose to get physical. Couples have arguments, but they don't start swinging," I vehemently, sure-footedly spoke my truth.

"You provoked that behavior."

"We're both responsible for our own actions."

"I am not, and never have been, an abusive person. It was completely your fault," he said.

"You could have walked out of the house," I said.

I kept a low profile and continued to run the household. I still wouldn't put food on his plate. I remembered stories about my great-grandmother's marriage and used her strength as my example. Since I couldn't be sure Coleman and I wouldn't kill each other, somebody had to make a change. Four people were hurting badly—a mom, a dad, and two little kids. It was heartbreaking, but I grew confident that I could not remain in the marriage. After seven years of both of our best efforts, it wasn't going to succeed, and it shouldn't have.

I could rationalize the initial abuse, since I was the one who struck first, but that second attack was without justification. Without realizing the full scope of why we'd become enemies, we kept the appointments at the medical center.

"Gretchen is disrespecting our marriage by not putting napkins on the table," Coleman said. The counselor glanced at me for meaning and I glanced at her for the same. She handed us papers, escorted us to separate rooms where we checked off our spouse's faults from a long list. After three sessions, she gave us her assessment.

"I rarely say this to couples, but it's my opinion that you two shouldn't be married. Too many things are wrong here." We sat quietly and waited for more. "Gretchen, out of one hundred choices, you checked off twelve items that need improvement. Coleman, you checked off all one hundred."

My jaw dropped and my head whipped to face Coleman. His expression was unwavering. For all of those years, I had done nothing right? As much as I'd tried to fit in with his social circles, as much as I'd multi-tasked to keep up with his demands, it hadn't been enough? My skin went cold and my heartbeat echoed at the thought that I would never be worthy of his approval. I knew then that my situation lacked the same psychological security the convent lacked.

"Really? Nothing?"

"I don't feel you two will be able to continue the marriage without serious help. Gretchen, if Coleman truly believes you are solely to blame, then it's up to you. Coleman, did you mean to check off every item?"

"Absolutely. My wife isn't measuring up to the very standards set by her mother. She's welcome to stay in the marriage, but there have to be a lot of changes," he said like he owned me.

"If you want, I'll work with you, Gretchen. Are you willing to do that for him? Can you change in order to save the marriage?"

"I don't want to save the marriage. I have no idea how or what to do differently."

"Do you mean that, you don't want to stay in the marriage?" she asked, making sure.

"I don't want to be married to Coleman anymore." The words hung like leaded drapery around the small room.

"Coleman, you heard your wife, she no longer wants to be married to you. What's your response?"

"Well, I don't think she means it. No one in her family has ever divorced."

"My great-grandmother did," I said without hesitation.

"I'll continue to work with you, Gretchen. You want to be sure you're making the right decision, although I fully agree with you. The marriage is a failure."

"You should agree to the therapy," Coleman said as we walked over the expressway together, "my insurance will cover a percentage."

"Why just me? You think I'm the only one with a problem?"

He didn't answer.

I went to one follow-up session by myself. The counselor had me sit on the floor. She pulled over a chair and climbed on top. Standing high overhead and peering down at me she asked a single question: "How does this resemble your marriage?" I made an appointment with a lawyer.

All our arguing stopped after that. Coleman was like me in that he sometimes said things he didn't really mean. He was right. He wasn't naturally abusive, but then neither was I. Though we both lost control of ourselves, marriage to one another had negatively and dramatically changed us and the build-up was explosive. Why would a former nun strike her husband or turn to another man? Why would a former seminarian choose to ignore and abuse his wife? Neither of us was imitating things from our backgrounds. In seeking refuge in this marriage, we had both become severed from the good people we thought we were.

There was so much we were missing. The lack of sexual passion was the elephant in the room. I saw married couples hold one another and share intimate conversations. I listened to romantic music without personal experience. I couldn't remain forever removed from those sentiments and wondered how he could.

One Saturday morning, after the turbulence had ended, Coleman's mother Sarah walked into our house, carrying a book that she directed toward me without comment. In eight years of knowing my husband, his mother had been the primary woman in his life. He'd surely divulged our tensions to her. The three of us stood together awkwardly just outside the front parlor. She and I had never exchanged books or even recommended an author to one another. I stared at the cover with 'marriage' in its title.

"Is that for me?"

She still had a charm about her, her words delivered as one educated and refined, with a level of fun as backup. With a bit of nervous laughter, she casually said something about it being a book we ought to have in our home. I wanted her to know that I wasn't interested so my hands didn't reach for it. She held it out for a couple seconds longer, all of us staring at it. Coleman finally set it on the coffee table. I forget the rest of the visit only that, once I served coffee, I hid out in the kitchen with our sons until she left.

A week passed. After putting the boys down for a nap one afternoon, curiosity bubbled to the surface. The book looked interesting. Since Coleman hadn't picked it up, apparently it *was* intended for me. *Portrait of a Marriage* was the title, by Nigel Nicolson. It was a substantial book. On the cover was a man and woman's photograph. Vita Sackville-West was the lady. Her appearance looked luxurious, probably from the British upper classes of the early 1900s. She was a very dear friend of Virginia Woolf—perhaps her lover, the narrative said. He was Harold Nicolson, a Parliamentarian. The first part of the book kept my attention. The story unfolded slowly, steeped in descriptions of elitist traditions. I couldn't relate, but I kept reading. *Why me? Why this book?* I turned more pages, reluctance and worry slowed the reading. More than half a century stretched between that couple and me. Not until I finished the book had I settled the plot. Those two married people were respectful of each other, had a long-standing marriage of high-social influence, and, though fond, were never in love. The strong bond between them had to do with tradition, history, continuity, appearances, and wealth, things bigger than their own insignificant yearnings or self-determination. Without confirmed evidence, I found out Vita Sackville-West was probably a lesbian, and Harold Nicolson very likely gay. A relative wrote the book. Theirs was a marriage of convenience. Is that what we had? Was my mother-in-law's message that those two people made it work, why couldn't we? My insides were reeling, my head refused to acknowledge the obvious. I dropped the book on the coffee table.

Sarah had probably known for a very long time that her son was gay.

Chapter

23

I wasn't ready for that book. Denial is a phenomenon designed to protect a psyche from overexposure. Here's how my mind buried the obvious: *Isn't that an interesting book about excessively wealthy people? Privilege changes everything in a marriage. That husband and wife led totally separate lives. I imagine there are many eccentric people in England just like them. There's nothing in the book that resembles any part of my life. I wonder if my mother-in-law believes, like her son, that I needed to think more like a high-class person now that I lived in a mansion. She wouldn't be so forward as to hand me a book suggesting I recognize my husband or myself in its pages.*

And then I filed the book's fundamental theme deep in my subconscious and indulged my schedule. I was an active person. I helped strip woodwork, joined a group that started a preschool, and taught in it part-time, keeping very busy. I cooked, cleaned, and laundered. I mothered my boys. That book hardly crossed my mind. I left it on the table for my husband to read, but he never did. Other books of interest—famous artists' paintings and sculptures, Chicago history and architecture— lay on our coffee table next to the fireplace for conversation or perusal. That new book inhabited only a small space. I dusted it and put a vase of fresh flowers next to it. It was just fine with me that it sat there. I wasn't one bit worried about it. It had nothing at all to do with me. I wished the face on the cover would stop staring at me.

"You're both such nice people, it's a shame," Sandy, one of the six redheads on the block, said, once word spread about our impending divorce. "Neither of you gossip, you welcome people into your home, you have two young sons. It's sad." I wondered if people who didn't gossip were the ones getting talked about. I was no different than the next person with regards to rumors. I wanted in on things too.

"In my country, if a marriage is in trouble, both families plead to the couple: 'How can we help? You need money? We'll get you money. You need a house? We'll get you a house. You need a lover? We'll find you lovers. Just don't break up the family,'" said an insistent woman, whose son was enrolled in the preschool. That made perfect sense to me, but truthfully, I wanted out of the marriage and my family members would be the last people to try and stop me.

"Your wife can't commit to anything," another neighbor told Coleman right in my very own kitchen. "She left the convent, now she wants to leave you."

After a neighborhood meeting one evening, Howard, a member of the renovation group approached me. "Wait, I'll walk you home." We got outside and straight away, he asked me about my affair. I hadn't realized anyone knew.

"It's over now," I said.

"You two should get married."

"I don't want to be married to anybody else. I made Giovanni tell me he had no intentions of marriage, so that I wouldn't delude myself."

"You need a strong husband. It would be difficult for a single woman to raise two kids in this city. A new marriage would be terrific. He'd make a great husband," he said plainly.

"I won't even consider it. Besides, right now, I have a husband."

"Coleman is a latent homosexual," he said.

"Oh, he is not. What are you talking about?" I didn't look at Howard, thinking he would see the color drain from my cheeks.

"He's a latent homosexual."

"I don't even know what 'latent' means," I said. *Interesting, the word I chose to question.*

"Latent means something lays submerged in the psyche. In Coleman's case, it means that he doesn't act on his homosexual tendencies, he allows them to remain dormant."

I stopped dead in my tracks. If that man was going to tell me something in confidence, I needed to understand its meaning in measured, declarative sentences. I couldn't believe he was willing to go there.

"What are you talking about?"

"A latent homosexual is a man who, by his nature, is drawn to the same sex, but deliberately denies himself that lifestyle because he wants to live by society's rules." Howard continued, but I wasn't emotionally able to handle the truth. Rather, I noted that it was a nice summer evening, warm but not hot. Occasional cars drove toward the Loop, fifteen blocks east. It had grown dark, wisps of clouds hid the stars, but the moon was watching. Tree branches created shadows. Crickets were in full symphony. My boys were right upstairs, not fifty feet away, with Mark, an architecture student, who helped with renovation and taught them to play chess. Wasn't I fortunate to have bright kids?

I drifted back to the conversation. "I know where my husband is every night of the week," I said. How could Howard

realize something significant about my husband that I was un-
aware of?

"I didn't say he acted out his homosexuality. I said it's latent.
He may never act on it, may not even admit it to himself."

There was a statement I could understand—*he may not even
admit it to himself.* No one understood self-deception better
than I did. I could deliver a dissertation on that subject. I felt
an instant rush of compassion for my husband, brilliant at
self delusion, both of us geniuses.

"Has your husband asked you to stay in the marriage? Because if my wife said she was leaving me, I'd get down on my
knees and beg her not to go. I may not be the perfect husband,
but I love my wife. I'd figure out what she wanted and do whatever it took to make her happy. Has Coleman done that? Has
he begged you to stay?"

"No, he wrote me a list of demands and said if I were a better
wife, the marriage wouldn't be in trouble."

"Well then, I don't think there's any love there. You're practically out the door and he's piling it on. That kind of marriage
would be personal suicide. Coleman's a good man. He's just not
a good husband."

Homosexuality was emerging into conversation in the 70s, but
just barely. Psychiatrists no longer considered it a mental illness, California would legalize it in about four years, and parades, marches, and sit-ins were making the news. There had
been multiple signs that I'd ignored. Maybe I colluded with
Coleman, both of us eager to wed. I knew my husband had
unusual traits, which were so different from other men's, but
that's what made him special. That's what I loved about him.
What I didn't love, I tucked away. I had priorities—get mar-

ried, have children, fix later. Of course Coleman was a good man. He had far too many friends and family who loved him dearly, not to mention his own two sons. I tried to hurry my social development, jumping into marriage to keep up with siblings and peers. Ex-nun status was rank. No one was allowed single status without heavy social scrutiny. In a society with strict norms, marriage would assign us roles to play. I was good at playing a part. Coleman and I were perfect for each other at the time. I wondered who else suspected this crazy hidden stuff about my husband.

"I don't believe you," a girlfriend said when I told her about the abuse.

I knew then to be quiet and not circulate condemnation about a person so many people were fond of. Rather than turn to friends for support, I'd have to depend on myself. Thankfully, I had the wealth of my friend Marie's experience, who proved motherhood could be managed incredibly well, even in divorce. But I was so mad that dysfunction and incompatibility defined my marriage.

People didn't even know me that well. I'd been in their homes, and they'd been in mine. We shared food at picnics and worked together on projects. Now, I believed everyone knew about Coleman's sexual tendencies and probably my affair. They could look at things from an outside perspective. Sure, every household had its difficulties, but they had basic commonalities. We were an anomaly. I took books off the shelves written by the anthropologist, Margaret Mead, wanting to know if she'd found situations like this in the primitive cultures that she studied. While I read interesting things about men and women of small island villages, I couldn't find anything about a gay man's place.

Part of me thought my husband had played a trick on me. I'd been his front—plucked like a chicken from a coop. It hadn't mattered who the rooster chose to marry, any good hen would do. The other part of me knew Coleman hadn't realized his own nature, or had to relegate it into a file labeled *not-to-be-opened-ever*, so his basic motivation wasn't deception. I was more upset at being society's fool than Coleman's. Why hadn't people alerted me before I got married? I began to recognize our situation for what it was. There was no way to fix what we had. We were expected to live a lie. I knew the effects of that. Could I become invisible again to save the marriage, to keep our family intact?

I thought about the engagement period when I'd waited for more closeness. He'd written endearing notes and letters, sent roses, sat at the piano with me and sang beautiful love songs. I accepted those tokens as true, and they were on some level, but I also wondered why we rarely held each other and always stayed on the surface of conversation. It was probably the age difference, his wide range of experiences compared with my own. I allowed him the lead.

It's no wonder that the doctor from my youth tried to alert me to our incompatibility. Nearly thirty years later, I learned that other members of the medical community knew my husband was gay. Janice, a friend of mine, worked in the hospital as a scrubber in the OR at the time Coleman had surgery on a broken arm from an ice-skating accident.

"The patient lying on the table is a homosexual," the surgeon said to his staff once the anesthetic took effect. That was three months before I'd met Coleman. Some people were part of the gossip train, but I was more like my mother in that I listened, but never carried. I should have become savvier.

"The surgeon knew? You knew? Why didn't you call me?"

"How can one person know what is in the heart and mind of another?" Janice said. "People marry for a lot of reasons. It wasn't my place to interfere with that." Her explanation was honest. I wouldn't have shared something like that either. I hadn't realized that people got married for all kinds of reasons.

My mind plowed through buried irritants searching for the truth. All previous doubts that challenged my good sense came crashing in at once. I thought back to my wedding ceremony and all the guests. They all must have known. They must have assumed people could change, that gay people could alter their very essence. Where I came from, such a complication of nature wasn't even whispered about. Not to me. Everything was suspect, though sometimes, I applied meaning where none existed. Men that Coleman mentioned but never introduced during our engagement popped into my head—faceless individuals, just names. One day, I was washing dishes and then suddenly, my fingers stirred the suds meaninglessly as I remembered Thomas and all the time he and Coleman spent together. Some men always have that suspicious male companion, even when there's a wife. Another time, I shopped for groceries and recalled that we traveled far out of our way in Europe to Oberammergau, to buy a pipe for a particular man I hardly knew. What about the religious man who showed up at our coach house and was barely civil to me, but had known Coleman for years? My grocery cart parked and I stared at apples and oranges, seeing neither, while my head put pieces together every which way.

Days later, the boys pushed off the edge of the pool and Coleman's words echoed in the splash: *we have the rest of our lives to explore sex.* When? When would that time have ever come around? What about his rejection of my need for warmth, overreaction to our baby's name, my short hair, jeans, leather, the dirndl? Light bulbs popped, one, two, three, and then dozens—a stream of past visuals, people, places, conversations paraded through my mind like a line-up of culprits. I saw myself in the middle of Wrigley Field and the entire stadium was flooded in the giant glare of alleged truth, with me centerfield, tiny, diminished, and stunned. My mind froze, trying to halt the barrage I had to remind myself to breathe. So very hurt. So very deceived. I pictured the young girl I once was and felt such compassion for her. I was tricked into being the Bride of Christ and foolish enough to think being a real bride would be better. Such a silly girl to believe in a fairytale.

I kept the appointment with a lawyer. I had to operate out of knowledge, not as a victim.

"Illinois passed no-fault divorce," the lawyer said. "If your husband doesn't treat you right, you can dissolve the marriage. Describe it."

"One of us is the king of the castle. Sometimes, that same one is the lord and master. One calls the other a drone. There's been a constant demand to obey and another demand to make love. Honestly, we're not good at either. One of us is low-class and highly deficient when compared with peers. One of us works really hard and never gets noticed, while the other is consumed with self-image. One partner is boring, while the other is talented, exuberant, and scintillating. Both of us support equality of the sexes, but neither of us practices it. We both try to control the other. Neither is responsible for the other's happiness. One of us had an affair. There's been some abuse from both ends." I laid it out like a crime report.

"I'll draw up the papers," he said.

A boatload of testimony pressed me to realize my husband was not what I'd thought, but I needed to hear it directly from him. I couldn't go there just because my mother-in-law gave me a book to read or my neighbor exposed some alleged secret.

Arguments continued. "Gretchen's a blank slate waiting to be written on," he had told Mary Ann, my high school friend.

"You said I was a blank slate?" so afraid that I was, afraid I'd completely flunked life.

"Well, you'll have to admit you were behind in major developments."

"I'd been in a convent for five years," I threw my arms out just like he did when he was outraged. "You held that against me and used that to your advantage. I admit I didn't know as much about the world as you, but a blank slate? You assumed I couldn't think for myself? Was that your motivation to marry me? You thought I wouldn't know any better? I had no idea you thought so little of me."

"I'm worried about our marriage," I told Coleman the day after Howard spoke with me.

"Don't worry. Just remember your marriage vows to submit and obey," Coleman said.

"I never said obey. I said love, honor, and cherish. I would never have said obey."

"Well, that was a mistake. A wife should obey her husband," he said.

"Name one other woman you know that obeys. Neither your

mother nor your sisters obey. Who are you? I don't even recognize you anymore."

"You're the one who's changed."

Blank slate never accurately defined me. I always had my own mind. My character flaw was in not speaking up. I found my voice in the convent and amplified it in the marriage.

"Yes, I have changed and in a good way. You, on the other hand, pretend to be liberal-minded, yet behind closed doors, you treat me horribly."

And then he said something that I rejected, because it wasn't the whole truth. My heart pounded, but I let it brush past. It might have been why I stayed out of touch with reality on many levels—my impulsive nature, my over-the-top efforts to pretend happiness, the counting, immaturity, the nail biting, the anxiety—trying to repel old psychological wounds, but I couldn't be sure.

"You're rebelling against your father after all these years. Just be a good wife. Be like your mother."

I took off his family heirloom ring and put it in his hand. Thoughts of her gentleness brought tears to my eyes.

"I am like my mother. I was a good wife. You just refused to see it. Now, it's too late."

"Oh, I see." He pocketed the diamond. "Well, this is really something."

That diamond had not been chosen for me. I was a person of simpler tastes, it wasn't in me to flaunt. So much of our marriage had become an attempt to impress. Coleman had tried to write his expectations on my "blank slate" like a set of rules I was all too familiar with. The Church had tried to rewire my brain too. It almost worked then, but it couldn't be pulled off a second time. My goal now was to be authentic. Only one of us was disappointed with that effort. Since I had no emotional attachment to that diamond, I knew I'd be tempted to cash in its value, so I returned it to its rightful owner. It was never mine.

As the law decreed, divorce wasn't anybody's fault. Giving back the ring and then having Coleman served with papers were two assertive acts begging for strong reaction.

"You are nothing without me. You would never have had these great experiences by yourself. I broadened your mind and showed you an exciting life. I took you from a suffocating environment and brought you to live in a world-class city. I took you to Europe. Your life was boring and it will be boring again."

He was right about some of it. I'd never have had those adventures on my own. He was the master of creative living and I was his dreamy-eyed companion.

I turned to the law for help. I turned to the women's group for guidance. I got some therapy, I haunted bookstores, and I explored the spiritual high of a good diet and exercise to at least help my body feel healthy. I relied on the expertise of our marriage counselor to finalize my decision to leave.

Chapter
24

"**M**eet me in the coffee shop on the first floor before we go upstairs for the divorce proceedings," Coleman said. "A coffee, two sugars, cream, and a glazed donut," he told our waiter.

"Ma'am?"

"Black coffee," something I used to have in the convent—a drink just as plain and bitter as the nun I once was. "And toast."

"Marriage counselors say divorce is easier on kids if conditions improve and parents cooperate with each other. We'll always be a family on some level," Coleman said, trying to ease the sadness of the moment. Both of us sipped coffee from thick porcelain cups. Amid the rush of early morning crowds, the din of activity, the mix of hunger with adrenaline in that popular bistro, it made us feel like we were on a date instead of headed for permanent dissolution.

Upstairs, I was put on the stand to answer if Coleman was a good father.

"Yes."

"You'll have to remain in Cook County to fulfill the shared-custody agreement," the judge said.

I was struck dumb. My mother's words, "Come back home so we can help you," got legally dismissed.

"Believe me, I didn't know you'd be put up there for questioning," my lawyer said afterward. "Your husband must be worried about something."

Once divorced, we worked together for the sake of the boys. In two years, Coleman followed his job to New York. Though the divorce decree specified that I couldn't move from Chicago, it hadn't restricted him. I'd invested in a townhouse and a job. I loved Chicago, but I was stuck.

Coleman's station wagon was filled to the brim. On the rear window a sign read, "New York or Bust!" We'd become better friends after our divorce.

"Be brave," he told our boys. They gave him hugs and I hugged him too. We all hugged each other. We watched his car pull away from the curb, then turn the corner.

Coleman's move to New York jolted me just as the divorce had him. Monthly budget spreadsheet posted on my wall, I faced the world alone with two young sons. It was time to see what I was made of. I did the only thing I knew how to do—worked really hard.

I earned an advanced degree, taught school, paid bills, took the boys on outings, and tried to keep up with homework. I'd never juggled so many things in my life. I was young, focused, and angry again. I stayed healthy and employed.

My worst parental episode was when I hit my boys' legs for not cleaning their rooms. My behavior had nothing to do with them. It was my error. The image of my father striking me spontaneously lit my brain like it had been hovering, waiting for that moment. On the spot I forgave my dad, realizing what a difficult thing it is to be a parent when you haven't come to terms with your own issues. The very ones I loved the most got my remnant impulses, which took over before my good sense had a chance to step in front.

"I'll never do that to you again," I said, tears spilling from my eyes. "If it looks like I might, run to your bedrooms and barricade the doors. You're good as gold and don't deserve this. I am so sorry. I love you. I am so very sorry."

I held them close. I hope they remember the whole thing. We've talked about it. It's never right to strike the vulnerable. Our lives had lost their luster. Kids shouldn't be without their dads. Families shouldn't break apart. What were we supposed to do? American society had no compassionate answer.

A lot of bad things happen to single mothers in the inner city. My car batteries were stolen so often that I lost count of how many. I bought a classic used car from a family member, an incredible Chevy Impala that had only gone to and from church and grocery. An enthusiast recognized a hot vehicle and decided it should be his. One Sunday afternoon not twenty feet from where my boys and I were picnicking, the thief hotwired our car and drove it off my parking space. Future treks to school in the dead of winter meant my boys and I waited on L platforms for trains. One came into view, only to speed by. Another came and sped away. A third one, until finally, trains made up time and stopped for frozen passengers, a daily occurrence for weeks. The mayor lost re-election.

I was held up at gunpoint in front of my kids, ten paces from our front door. I chased that man who took my purse then nonchalantly walked away. He turned and pointed his gun, so I retreated. I had three purses stolen at the school where I taught. Someone cruel broke into our home and took our radio, TV, and favorite records. At a stoplight, I became a victim of a crime commonly referred to as smash-and-grab—teenagers with ball bearings in a sock reduced the passenger window to shards, then reached onto the car seat and snatched my purse and jacket. Once the light changed green, I tried to chase them down with my car, up and down alleys and streets until I realized it was futile. I went to the police station, threw my car keys on the counter, and had a meltdown. I got right back up and took on the city even more, telling myself, *you can do this, you have no choice, you must*. I escaped the convent, survived a divorce, these were mere roadblocks. I knew we'd be all right if I kept jogging, emboldened with endorphins, anger, willpower, and focus. I just had to keep going. I could never give up. Never. Not ever.

Coleman visited a couple times a year, and then one spring he called with an idea. "The boys have you for the entire school year. They need their father as much as their mother. New York has tons of activities. My apartment's only three blocks from Central Park. They'll have so much fun, they won't have time to miss you. Send them to me for the summers."

"How in the world?" I was caught off guard.

"It's real easy. They get on a plane. You'd have three months to be on your own and catch your breath. It'll be good for you, too."

"Can't you fly here and get them?"

"No, you drive them to the airport and they board a plane."

"I'm not putting my kids on a jet by themselves. They're only six and eight years old."

"It's perfectly safe, the airlines handle this all the time. It's a hand-to-hand arrangement. Kids are never without their own private stewardess, who takes them from you and turns them over to me at the other end. We'll have matching documents to prove parentage."

Releasing the boys alone onto a 747 horrified me, but they were excited and I knew they needed their dad. They were introduced to the pilots and assigned a stewardess, who put huge nametags on them. We secured legal release forms, which took them from my hands and transferred them directly into Coleman's. My mother came up, and together, after tight hugs and kisses, we shouted down the ramp, "Have a wonderful summer! We love you!" We watched their plane until it was the tiniest blip in the sky. Two little boys sat together on a plane like Elizabeth and me on a city bus. We were a long way from the family life I'd grown up in. Mother and I drove back to the neighborhood deep in thought.

Coleman's prediction, *It'll be good for you too,* was wrong. I was lonely without my boys every summer. I knew they missed me too, even if he did keep them active every minute of every day. I didn't know who I was supposed to be. It was a cruelty I hardly bore casually, and now I was supposed to recreate a whole new me.

Not knowing specifically which Church rules were responsible for my naïveté and current emotional vulnerability, I threw everything out and started fresh, reinventing myself.

Bookstores became my refuge as I searched out new ways of putting thoughts and actions together. Robert Pirsig's very popular *Zen and the Art of Motorcycle Maintenance* taught me to weigh matters according to their quality and value. Like the taxi driver whose cab was laden with decoration to help him celebrate each day, I too began to relish each moment in my life, proud to shop, cook, clean, work, everything.

I became focused on psychological literature and joined The Human Potential Movement, earning certification after a year's study and leading groups that sat in a circle on the floor, contemplated their navels, and got in touch with authenticity. It was the first time I acknowledged the perpetually tight knot in my gut and eventually got rid of it after three decades, through breathing techniques.

I read Erica Jong's *Fear of Flying*, which supported some secret fantasies. I took her uninhibited writings to heart, deciding to explore the nature of my sexuality so I could have a second chance at love.

The Church had been right about my body being a temple. Sexuality was directly related to my soul. But how, was a complete mystery. I came to realize I had boundaries, because every time I'd be with a man, I felt less than I was before because I wasn't in love. Part of me floated away in the wind, never to be seen again.

I read every Melody Beattie self-help book, beginning with *Codependent No More*, and changed how I perceived my relationships and my *Self*.

"Your opinions count as much as anyone's, including Church hierarchies and scholars," said my one boyfriend, a psychotherapist that I really liked for a year. He left me after deciding I was too strong and independent. Apparently, my opinions didn't really count to him.

I became friends with people of differing spiritual philosophies. When I taught sixth grade, the textbook focused on ancient civilizations and histories of major religions, I learned more about human spirituality than I ever thought I would. Students were fascinated by Hinduism with its 27,000-plus gods and goddesses, the Buddha with his internal quiet and reincarnation attraction, and Jesus with his generous inclusion of everybody. I taught them African tribal dances, and the Jewish dance *hava nagila*. The gentle sides of these religions, held the most attraction for students who were accustomed to sorting things out on the playground with only school norms as a guide.

People's souls naturally hunger for spirituality, I concluded. There's something primal about awareness of our origins. I learned that we need sensitivity in what we feed young children—traditions, rituals, songs, prayers, and lovely myths ought to suffice.

When the summer ended, I broke the speed limit driving to the airport. I had to get reacquainted with my own boys.

The back-and-forth nature of shared custody became constant upheaval. I questioned the practicality of the divorce forever. There wasn't—but there should have been—a better answer. Coleman and I had wasted time fighting each other, but we simply had insurmountable problems. One thing held us together even in our distance—love for our kids. When the four of us got together, it was our best time.

"I'm headed your way for vacation."

"Stay with us," I said.

The spring of our third divorced year, 1980, the boys were eight and ten. Divorce in families seemed to be contagious, possibly a backlash of the Women's Movement, I figured, though I could be wrong. Our little family celebrated Easter with a Sunday brunch. It was delicious—eggs Benedict, pancakes, and French toast slathered in maple syrup. That great restaurant in Lincoln Park made us feel like a normal family amid all the hustle and bustle and animated conversations.

"Coleman, thanks for bringing us here." I smiled more genuinely at him in that moment than I had in our marriage.

"I thought you'd like it. We have to keep family life going.

Boys, go find the bathroom and then look around the restaurant for about ten minutes. Your mother and I have something to talk about. And stay out of trouble." He grinned lightly and gestured for them to scoot.

"What do you want to talk about?" I asked, the old familiar knot retightening in my gut.

"You know I moved to New York to start a new life for myself. I needed a new beginning, and what I've finally come to terms with is that I'm gay." There it was, on the table, at that crowded restaurant.

"How do you know that? Are you sure? Do the boys know?" I asked him, my mind immediately sweeping out the old cluttered spaces, making room for new revelations. I finally felt ready to take it in. His openness allowed me to accept the truth I couldn't face before. Coleman seemed relieved to enlighten me.

"Neither boy said a word to me, they must be overwhelmed. What did you say to them?"

"I said I was gay. They don't fully understand, of course. Basically, I said I liked being with men more than women—that's all they need to know right now. It's just an opening until they get a little older. I'd rather introduce the idea at a young age, so they grow up with some awareness, than wait until they're teenagers and hear it for the first time during that difficult stage of their lives."

"I can't say I'm surprised, Coleman." My mind quickly rifled through the evidence I had linked all those years ago. "But what were the boys' reactions? Were they upset? It's got to be confusing. I can't imagine how they're dealing with it."

"Don't overreact. I didn't tell them much, you can't expect they'd understand something so complicated. Don't make it a problem and it won't be one. You set the tone."

"I don't know what to think right now," I said as I looked around at other customers who ate their meals in peace and harmony, without the slightest clue about us and what we had been through. I kind of wanted to be one of them. I imagine that Coleman did too.

"It'll take you some time to adjust to the idea. I've joined a Catholic group called Dignity—gay Catholic men who have taken a look at themselves and their roles in the Church and have come to realize that it condemns us, pretends we don't exist. Nevertheless, we still feel close to the Church we were raised in. It's taken a long time to admit our sexuality. We want to be part of the Church like everyone else, but without hiding out anymore. We think we have a lot to contribute. We meet once a month at each other's apartments and homes and have discussions about what it all means for us. I'm seen as a leader because of my seminary background. We're trying to get some status and be recognized for who we are. The Church needs to catch up to society and show leadership in this and embrace all the people it serves."

"Don't hold your breath," I said. "What about our boys? That's all I care about. Do they see things they shouldn't? What are their questions? I'm more concerned about how this could hurt them."

"I'm helping them all I can. I also joined a group called Gay Daddies—some of the same men, but they're like me and have kids. It's more of a relaxed group, taking outings and doing fun things, so the boys see others have dads who are gay. Each member has divorced, but the gay factor makes divorce even more confusing for kids. New York is the perfect place for them to sort through it."

What he said sounded so intelligent and well thought out, but I wanted my sons back right then, and there they came, all out of breath, looking fit and fine and lovable and handsome and smart and cultured and adorable. Two happy youngsters. I was so glad to hug them.

"Let's go back to your house so we can talk about this some more," Coleman said.

Things started to make sense. I began to feel closure.

We got up and walked out of the restaurant like a normal little family of four. The sun warmed our faces and regardless of our secret, we took in the crisp, fresh morning air like everybody else. The beautiful lakefront and all the budding green trees and bushes invited us to enjoy. This was our planet too.

The boys seemed happier than I'd seen them in a long time, all of us together.

Back at the townhouse, they ran upstairs to change clothes and then slammed the door on the way out to play. Coleman and I sat down with coffee.

"The boys and I are in family therapy," he said. "It wouldn't hurt for you to do that for yourself or come along with us this summer. You could stay with the boys and me for a few weeks and see what their lives are like in New York. We could get professional help as a family. I spoke with our therapist and she thinks it would be healthy for you to join us."

"Sounds like a good idea." I touched his shoulder and it felt right to do that. It had been so long since we'd had physical contact. He looked at me like a long-lost friend.

"What does your mother think?"

"I've told her, but she's suspected it for many years. She's always known on some level."

"Was it alright with her that you married me?"

"You have to look at it from her perspective. She wanted me to be happy and thought our marriage was a good thing."

"When was the first time the two of you talked about it?"

"Yesterday. She wasn't surprised and has accepted it. She mostly worries about how I'll be treated by society."

"Did she think our marriage would go on forever? Did she think I'd never find out? If you have known for a long time, then why did you marry me?"

"I wanted what every man had. A place in society. Don't feel so let down. We have two wonderful sons. I can't imagine life without them."

The boys were in and out of the house, playing and probably pleased that their parents talked without hostility. As soon as I thought of one question, I could barely wait for the answer before bombarding Coleman with another, but he wasn't willing to ease my anxiety on each and every issue.

"I need to understand more about your mother. Does she know you're telling me? Do you think she has any idea how this has affected me?"

"Get over my mother, this is between us.

"But I want to know what went through her mind."

She was trying to help me, not deceive you. She used to say that of her three sons, I was the most like my dad in temperament and personality. My brothers were interested in math and science, while I was drawn to literature and the arts. We became close because she and I really enjoyed the same things."

"Do you think she gave any thought at all to the fact that I was being lied to?"

"Look, she wanted me to find someone special like both my brothers had. And no, I don't think she considered what it could do to you. She had my best interest at heart. She wanted me to be happy and thought getting married would ensure that. She didn't think of it as a lie. I'm sure that never crossed her mind. She thought of it as a correction. And she always liked you. You fit her definition of what a good wife was. You came from a family that, in many ways, reminded her of her own. She tried to help me figure out how I could have what other people had. I asked her what a woman wanted in a man and she said women like to be romanced. They like men to pay attention to them and want someone to talk to. Sending you a rose every Saturday was my attempt at romance."

"The roses were wonderful."

"Romancing you was perfect for me too, because I loved all the things we were doing as much as you did."

"The things we've done are more wonderful than I could have dreamed. But I've been confused for so long. All those symbols of love didn't make me feel loved, and you didn't treat me right after we were married."

"Couldn't you see that I was trying?"

"But why me, Coleman, why did you choose me? You dated other girls, why didn't you marry one of them?"

"They weren't interested in me as a husband. They enjoyed all the things we did on dates, but after the fun, this one had a headache and that one wanted to go home early. None of them stuck by me like you did."

"But I was so vulnerable. Why ask me to marry you?"

"I thought if I married a good, strong Catholic girl, it would go away."

"But I didn't stay a good, strong Catholic girl. Are you saying that's why our marriage failed?"

"Actually, that had nothing to do with it." He glanced down at his left hand, which used to display a wedding ring. "I've learned that I suppressed my natural tendencies and it was inevitable. It would have come out sooner or later. Our marriage failed because I guess it had to."

Chapter

25

Regrettably, our divorced family life was as complicated as our marriage had been because of the distance. "The boys can continue to live in Chicago with you during the school year and spend each summer with me in New York," Coleman said, ever the energetic dad who planned activities. "Both boys went to baseball camp this summer, played ball and Frisbees, and attended Shakespeare in The Park. They learned how to coordinate inline skates, visited West Point, attended a family reunion in the South, took trips to the ocean, and my brother and I shared a house together on Long Island, where they trapped lobsters in the nearby bay. They're having a blast."

When they returned to Chicago, there was always that adjustment going from one set of rules to another. I wouldn't let them watch *The Brady Bunch* on TV since it bore no resemblance to our lives. Instead they watched *Mash* with me. Things settled down once school began.

Some people were alarmed when they learned the boys lived with their dad. "How can you let that happen? How do you know what's going on? He could be harming them." I couldn't satisfy people's worries, so I didn't try. Those asking the questions weren't of a mind to listen—each question being a statement. I'd done my own research. They didn't know that gay people are like everybody else.

"The boys are happy as clams when they are with their dad, and they've matured beautifully," I told people.

Coleman was a very intelligent person. Like me, he had issues, but he was caring and thoughtful, generous and kind. He shared his energy and humor and never held back his opinions, putting them out front, where others could entangle in good discussions if they dared to have the debate.

The person I eventually chose to confide in was my psychology professor. He'd told a story in class about a young coed who, "When she realized the kind of true love her heart craved most was a myth, she stepped into Lake Michigan," he said, "and just kept walking." He related her hopelessness with such sensitivity that I wanted his perspective on my unusual situation.

"It's the way people are born," he said, "not something they develop into. Just love your sons and live without that worry. It has nothing to do with you." He was way ahead of the general populace.

Of course, I had no intention of not loving my sons. It wouldn't make any difference to me about their eventual sexuality, I decided, though like Sarah, I would have worried about society. I focused on the love. I was relieved to hear someone at the university level say it wasn't a moral issue, because that's exactly how I felt about it. I thought I was a pretty smart person by then, with exposure to things beyond the norm. I was no longer intimidated by Church leaders who had studied the Bible more than I had. I realized my opinion was without historical merit or hierarchical weight, but it was resolute and priceless to me. Simple. It just made sense. Love made sense. And God is Love. If there was one thing I still believed from my lessons in the convent, it was that.

"I experience you as full of rage," my professor said after I shared my parochial school indoctrination, convent experience, and my marriage with its confusing social colluding that had to be part of the picture.

"Rage? How can you tell?"

"It's obvious," he said, and I unclenched my white-knuckle grip on the armchair and laid my hands in my lap.

I denied that rage description for several more years, until three separate people in my human potential sessions told me the very same thing.

"Should I believe what others say about me?" I asked a therapist, "that I'm full of rage?"

"If one or two people gave me such feedback, I'd say it's just their projection. But if three offer the same description, then I'd look into it."

"Look what your experiences have done to you," one boyfriend said over chicken with peanut sauce in a Thai restaurant.

With such a proper upbringing, I started examining every facet of my anger. I turned my life over in my hands, looking closely at every reason why I had a rumbling of anger as a base. The rage had begun as fear. That's what gave it fuel. What kid doesn't have a healthy fear of getting into trouble? It was the convent where I'd felt cornered. It gave birth to resentment, ready to discharge like a hot spring in Iceland. As much as I wanted to be mad at Coleman for what he had hidden from me, I couldn't blame him. He was acting on instinct as much as I was. Marriage seemed the best survival for both of us.

None of my family ever thought he was intentionally devious. He wasn't that type of person. He wanted to fit in too. He was a very good guy and we all knew it. None of us ever stopped loving him.

Sometimes, when Coleman visited Chicago, he'd stay with

us and sleep on our sofa bed, so the boys had the occasional luxury of a fulltime family unit. It was surprisingly harmonious, perhaps a little odd to outsiders, but not to us. We tried to be practical to minimize the scars of divorce.

While in town, Coleman took the boys on daily adventures. One morning, after they left, I noticed his things were spread out all over the living room. As I straightened up, I saw a handwritten notecard on the table and picked it up to read. It was a photo of a man on a pair of skis, poles in hand, wearing only khaki shorts with ski boots, bare-chested. He looked beautifully tan, blond, and handsome. My first thoughts were of how chilly he must have been, and then my throat swelled and burned as I realized what I might be seeing. I opened the note and it began, "Dearest Coleman," and was signed, "Love, Scott." I knew it was private, but there was no question that I'd read it. To this day, I still remember that Scott—whoever he was—felt lonely without Coleman and made arrangements for the two of them to meet and have an opportunity "to be outrageous together." That word "outrageous" described one of the ways Coleman wanted to experience his life. If he was gay—and he said that he was—then that was a state of being that needed celebration. So long as the world was still in denial, then outrageousness was called for, even the in-your-face kind—*we're here, we're queer, get used to it*—if there was ever going to be acknowledgement and eventual respect.

A Native American told Larry King a number of years ago that his tribe celebrates its gay membership. "Gay members are the go-between of the sexes which are always fraught with misunderstandings. They become our counselors, our translators," he said.

So Scott was the person who had won Coleman's heart. I continued to stare at the letter and photograph. Eight years of fruitless yearnings for my husband's love played like a movie through my mind. I realized at that moment that I was never part of Coleman's daydreams. He probably never truly missed me, probably never rushed home to see me, and then I knew, standing there with clarity once more in hand, that it would never have been me. Not ever. We miraculously came together, but lacked the necessary ingredients to fully bond. Suddenly, we were in a new phase of our relationship and we had to make it into something worthwhile. Even when we clashed, our shared desire was to have a successful family. To be excellent parents. To love our kids and give them our best efforts.

At the end of the following summer, I picked up Coleman and the boys from the airport. Coleman would stay a week with us. I saw a little black wired-haired dog accompanying my two cute growing boys—kisses, hugs, squeals, and a dog, jumping, jumping, barking, barking, what a sight. There was Coleman, nice hat, enthusiastic as usual, brief hug, and then, there was Coleman's friend.

"Gretchen, I'd like you to meet Jim. Jim, Gretchen." So we were three adults, two kids, and one bouncy puppy.

"Where's your car?" Coleman asked, picking up bags and leading the way. All but the dog settled in and I drove all six of us home to our little Italian neighborhood on Chicago's Near West Side. The boys ran upstairs and dropped off their gear, then flew out the door, the dog chasing after them. It was their neighborhood.

Coleman and Jim sat down at the kitchen table and I got out some cheese, sausage, chopped up a few apples, and offered wine—which we all needed.

"Let's decide on a good place to eat for dinner," Coleman

said. "We should go to one of the Italian restaurants, Jim, this neighborhood has excellent pasta. The boys love spaghetti. Let's go to Mategrano's right now and make reservations. Gretchen, you and the boys unpack. They'll both need baths after the long flight."

I stood at the front window and watched those two handsome men walk down the sidewalk, not hand in hand, and not ten paces apart. They turned the corner and were out of my line of vision and I just stood there, staring at nothing in particular. My breathing slow and easy, I could hear the dog and kids. It was a pretty afternoon, rather warm, being August. I lingered awhile like that, then opened the door and called to the boys, "Time to clean up, you both need baths." Eight feet bounded up the steps and I took another deep breath. My boys had grown.

"Did you guys have a nice summer? What's your dog's name again? Did you enjoy the plane ride? Are you glad to be home? Are you glad to see me?"

"Yes, Blacky, yes, yes, and yes!" they answered all my questions.

I was grateful our townhouse had two floors, two baths, and three bedrooms. The men slept downstairs on the sofa bed. Though Coleman's name wasn't on the mortgage, he helped pay for our house every month with his child support, which he began even before we went to court. And he never missed a payment.

The boys had their rooms upstairs with mine. Coleman was more thoughtful toward Jim, I noticed, than he'd ever been with me. I felt a twinge of jealousy over that. But he wasn't the Scott from the photograph. I asked about Coleman's relationships later.

"Is Jim your lifelong partner? Is he the one you've been searching for?"

"The gay life is very fickle. Some men jump from one partner to another because it's hard to commit since we're not allowed to marry. Promiscuity is the result. In New York it's particularly difficult to find enduring love. Jim is a good friend, but I doubt he's the one for me. I've never envisioned living permanently with a man, to be completely honest. I always felt a regular marriage was in my future, like ours. But that seems out of the question now. Who really knows for sure?"

Coleman seemed proud to have finally unraveled the threads of his life. He said the people most threatened by homosexuals were those most afraid of their own tendencies, or those confounded by ancient Biblical text. I thought he probably knew what he was talking about. He must have felt so isolated in his seminary, even if he didn't understand why.

I believed his reasoning and since it was his life he was talking about, he was the expert. It was sad to me—we were two lonely souls, once hoping for lasting marriage, now realizing our search was likely endless. Neither of us planned to walk into open water like the young coed, but coming to terms with the possibility we'd never find someone to share the rest of our lives with was heavy for us both. Coleman was as good as it ever got for me. I wish we could have stayed together like our sons needed us to.

I stopped looking for lasting love with a partner. I already had what I needed. I was free to speak my mind. I had my sons. They were the family I'd dreamt of. Ever since, I've concluded that I could turn my compassion inward. Now I could love and appreciate myself. I could give myself the acceptance I craved.

"I miss the continuity that our marriage offered," Coleman said.

So did I. He wasn't asking to return to the marriage, but he told his sons later that it represented the best part of his life.

What had felt boring to him at the time had represented stability—another human yearning sometimes at odds with personal needs. I must confess I felt exactly the same.

Coleman came up with a new, even bigger plan and asked that the boys spend a year in New York with him. "I live across the street from the Metropolitan Opera. They can audition for the Children's Choir," he said.

They were in several operas at the Met and City Operas, under the tutelage of a patient, musically talented Mrs. Hohner. They earned paychecks and have the stubs tucked away with their resumes. They sang in Italian, they wore operatic costumes and makeup they scrubbed off each night. They sang the music of Mozart, Brahms, Puccini, and Verdi.

"I had no idea our boys could sing so well."

"We're not talking operatic talent. They sing on tune and loudly, and they always show up—prerequisites for the Children's Choir."

My sons were miracle children. Not many offspring have an ex-nun and an ex-seminarian as parents. It seemed incredible that they were even born. With such an unusual origin, it didn't sound at all extraordinary that they would enjoy a childhood beyond the norm, as Coleman offered, this man of dreams, this dad who hoped to share his love of life with his kids.

"Let the boys stay an additional year," Coleman said. "After school, they can come do their homework and wait for me to get off work."

"But New York is too far away. I couldn't bear such a separation." Within a month, I missed them so profoundly I became the traveling parent. I got a leave of absence from work, packed lots of clothes, and drove to New York. Friends thought I was going out East to reunite with Coleman. I considered it for the sake of our boys, envisioning myself as the wife who served Sunday dinner to my family with a special someone dropping by unexpectedly. But I couldn't have a family with secrets. I had to confront our problems honestly. That was my only choice.

Coleman tried talking me into reuniting. "Here's a therapist who wrote that children growing up without benefit of both parents become depressed," he said, showing me a news clipping. "We need to find a way to prevent that."

"That was one article from one psychologist with one opinion," I said, but I was alarmed by what I read too.

The first day I arrived, Coleman came with a longtime acquaintance to the apartment I'd rented.

"Look, Dorothy, my bride is here!"

I loved that he was happy to see me, but I was delighted that the boys stayed with me because I couldn't get enough of them. Coleman lived just blocks away. We traipsed back and forth for six months. Sometimes the four of us met for breakfast, lunch, or early suppers before Coleman went to work. Coleman made our weekly schedules, and we parceled the warmth of family life the best we could, becoming closer than we'd ever been— walks in Central Park, boys on skates or bikes, plays, movies, games, all with heartfelt conversations.

Within a week, I found a lady who tightened up my resume and gave me pointers about finding work in New York City and I pounded the pavement for weeks. I retired my fashionable strap heels because the very day I secured a position, a shoe strap broke. I saved them as a reminder of how hard I looked for that job.

My boss was Catholic, so we felt that common bond of experience, except that he attended church and hadn't known the dark side of the religion.

"You're like my daughter, going through life the hard way," he said, like I'd planned it.

"How am I like your daughter?"

"She doesn't attend church either. She gave it up. She said it wasn't relevant to her life," he said as if to knock some sense into me since he could no longer influence her. "I told her that I hoped one day she'd see the value of her religion. It puts order into our lives. No need to go it alone." I let his words remind me of the Mother General's warnings. Her words occupied a similar and permanent spot in a corner of my mind where they could wrestle with me every time I had to make an important decision. It was a tiresome intrusion.

On the evening of my birthday I celebrated in New York. I walked up to the Met and watched David on the stage in the first act of *La Forza del Destino*, then over to the City Opera across the Plaza to watch Greg in the third act of *Carmen*. During the second act, both boys secretly left their respective opera houses, ran to their dad's apartment and got their stray black cat, ran it down Broadway to our twelfth floor room at the Hotel Beacon, then ran back for their third acts. I had no idea until I got home, when the cat answered the door.

The boys beamed with pride. "Happy Birthday, Mom. Say hello to Manhattan."

I looked down quizzically at the cat and she returned my confusion. I petted her head and she purred at my touch. I knew then that she'd be a good listener and a loyal companion. What a sweet gift from my thoughtful kids.

When all of that came to an end a couple years later, they'd kept as souvenirs: a plastic red carnation from *Carmen's* flower wagon, a piece of the gingerbread house from *Hansel and Gre-*

tel, and a button off Pavarotti's vest he wore in *La Bohème*.

"I can't afford New York. The taxes on my house just went from $200 to $2000. I have to move back or I'll face foreclosure." I quit my job, packed up, rented a U-Haul, removed the boys from their schools and their dad, and returned to Chicago. Within the year, our townhouse sold and we moved back to my hometown.

"That's wonderful," Coleman said. "The boys will have the benefits of your wonderful family."

"You mean the family you wanted to get away from?" I got out of the marriage to find a second chance at love and now I was on my own. Coleman moved us from my hometown to escape my family, now he wished we'd never left.

"We may never have divorced had we remained there," he said.

"What do you mean?"

"In a smaller community where people have strong connections, have social standing, and social expectations, where everything centers on the family, schools, church, and cooperation, that's a support system that could have held us together, avoiding the freedoms we've allowed ourselves in the anonymity we found in a big city. We would have felt the pressure to conform, unlike here, where individuality is celebrated."

"You're probably right." I wished we'd never left.

Church affiliation was important in a smaller city, but we weren't accustomed to that. I chose to keep a safe distance, since each time I attended, I experienced a rush of anger and an urgent need to question every well-intentioned word. A visiting priest in the parish asked my sons and some other boys out for pizza, and deep inside, I knew to steer clear, even before accusations began to surface. In high school, one girlfriend had told me, "You don't want to know," when I questioned her about a mysterious priest, who showed up every so often and went into a small room with a teenager. Some people knew stuff. Not specifically, but generally. Corporate denial. Now that I had boys, I stepped in to protect them.

On Sunday mornings, when other people went to church, we'd go someplace for pancakes. The phrase "broken home" came into our vocabulary then, judgments and suspicions, and it relegated us to a lesser status. I was tagged a free spirit. We fought to keep our hard-earned self-esteem intact, shocked that not attending church would turn us into an enemy. When asked which parish we belonged to, I'd answer that we didn't belong to any and that would end conversation. Otherwise perfectly good people, decided I was unworthy. The big Church condemned us as "fallen away." I'd given up the religion of my youth and that couldn't be tolerated.

My mother was never critical, understanding that mine had been an unusual journey and she remained forever loving.

People were upset that my boys didn't know traditional prayers. I didn't want my sons in church. "It's not like it used to be when we were kids," family said when I told them I couldn't expose my kids to things I didn't trust.

"I want to move back to New York with Dad," David said, when I tried marriage for a second time. I didn't blame him.

"I want to stay here with you," Greg said. So we were more split-up than ever. We were a family trying to manage our unconventional situation.

"I'm a candidate for NASA's Journalist-in-Space 1986 project," Coleman wrote to me. He had turned in his full application with recommendations from numerous former bosses, who encouraged that endeavor and gave high praise for his outstanding journalism. But on a day in late May of that year, I got a call from Coleman's friend Dorothy. She and her husband Felix, a famous duo of architects, the Candela's, had been our neighbors in Chicago. They had renovated five houses and then moved to New York where Coleman reconnected with them there. On Sunday mornings, Coleman and the boys had breakfast with them.

"You'll never find as good a person as Coleman," Felix had said, and was right.

"I just drove Coleman to Bellevue Hospital," Dorothy said to me on the phone. "I wanted you to know. He called this morning, barely able to breathe. He's very weak."

"What's wrong with him?"

"We don't want to be alarmists, but it is serious, it could be pneumonia. He can't eat and has lost weight and he hasn't been to work for weeks."

"I didn't know it had been weeks."

"He couldn't get his words out this morning. It took all his energy just to ask for help. When I got to his apartment, it took an hour to get him down six flights of stairs and to my car."

"Oh, Dorothy! You're scaring me." I was nearly out of breath too at this point. I felt like oxygen was leaking from my pores before it could reach my lungs.

"I know. I've never seen him like this. Bellevue's a good place, he has no insurance, but they'll take him. He just can't stay there long, only until he's better. I tried to tell him his was not the age to quit a good job and begin freelancing, but he wouldn't listen to me."

I feared the worst. How would I help him now? Everybody knew that with a particular diagnosis, a person had two years to live, and the end was quite bad. I didn't have the resources to quit my job and move out there. A lot of people had reached a panic level. Those suspected of a gay lifestyle were feared like a disease. People, compassionate by nature and probably more spiritual than most of us, came forward to help those stricken. But a whole host of problems were manifesting. The medical and pharmaceutical communities desperately tried to manage a new contagion, treat the symptoms, and counsel patients.

Coleman should have had wealth and prestige for all of his talents. Something kept him from rising to the top of his field. In Paris, he had translated French to English perfectly, they'd told him. Yet he wasn't hired. And they needed someone. He was passed over numerous times in the news business. Becoming a bureau chief would have suited him well, but he was blocked from working up that ladder to reach a goal. Precious few truly reach their potential. But Coleman had obvious abilities, was in the field of his choosing, in the right places at the right times, and yet, he wasn't getting the rewards that he should have. And friends knew it, colleagues knew it, I knew it and he knew it. I have to wonder if sexual preferences hampered other people from promoting him. I'm sure he thought of that. I'm sure it sat at the back of his mind each and every time he lost out on a promotion. He was way more competent than sending out press releases at the Illinois Arts Council. He knew he was the strongest choice for a position, and yet, he was repeatedly turned down. It didn't make any sense. What other conclusion would he have reached other than that he was quietly sabotaged? Even if that weren't completely true, he knew it was somewhere in the mix. He was AP's second recommendation for a journalist into orbit. "Why was I second?" he asked me. There was a lot of pain in that. Although Coleman recognized his strengths and weaknesses accurately, I think he was acutely aware that people had inefficiencies—and by that I mean societal colluding, societal prejudices —which prevented him from getting to perform at his optimal level. His ancestry won notoriety for generations. He carried the very same genetic traits. Like the richest heaviest cream, he should have risen to the top. I saw his pain behind every disappointment. And now I realize how much I hurt him with what he called my lack of support. He wanted to create a legacy for himself. I realize how difficult, how tormented, the isolation of being gay on planet earth was. How heavy a cross had God intended for His creatures when he created a fanciful twist of nature? None whatsoever. It's no twist. It is nature. Gay. Straight. Equal footing. Someone misguidedly once said to me, "He was a loser." Oh no. No, he wasn't. Never a loser. He did lose his life. Yes. That happened. But he was startlingly amazing. He was brilliantly alive. He was a wonderful human being.

Coleman's immune system was compromised and any simple infection could shut down his health. It was several weeks before he got back on his feet, but he took very expensive and very potent medications with a list of things to avoid—people with colds, fevers, crowds, and entanglements. For a man with his unbridled enthusiasm, it would change who he was and how he lived his life. He had to remain alert for situations that could jeopardize his health and put him back in Bellevue. Any little microbe could prove fatal.

Coleman always viewed the world as his oyster. It was here for his pleasure. He lived with the memories of traditions from his Southern past. His was to have been a gentler philosophical life. Now he was isolated in a back wing of a hospital, which was as frightening as the illness. Exposed, a gay man would lose his job, parents, siblings, friends, history, health, and now his life. Press coverage made a valiant attempt to balance the news, while some religions claimed AIDS was proof that God punished homosexuality.

Our boys were in high school. How would I explain society's reaction toward the illness to them? How could I tell them that churches said their dad deserved to die? We stood alone.

I had a difficult phone conversation with David. He lived with his dad, so the contagion factor threatened. We didn't know then what we do now. He helped Coleman every day. Everything had to be sterilized or bleached. Schools, hospitals, the workplace, family units, neighborhoods were all in an upheaval. I tried to stay current about the illness and direct things from a distance, but David did the work. Greg missed his dad and Coleman wanted to see him, so that young boy flew alone on a plane to New York. It was frightening on every level. Eventually, I told David he'd have to move back. At sixteen years of age, he needed protection. It would leave Coleman completely alone in his sixth floor apartment. The decision was way too big for our little family.

I got a phone call from the Albright family in New York, "Think it over, but we want David to come live with us and finish high school with his friends. We'll resolve problems as they come up. We love him and want him with us. He only has one more year of high school. He should stay with his friends. New York has been his home and he wants to be with his dad." When our days could not get much bleaker, here was a family giving unconditional, unselfish love and compassion. It was good to know that such people existed.

Greg had to let go of his one and only brother, and his beloved dad. Barely a teen, he too was in a tender stage of life. We talked in whispers about the illness, privately and fearfully.

302 Ring Around the Rosary

Communities were overreacting, so there was no hope for us. Not until Elizabeth Taylor spoke up for her friends and Princess Diana reached out to AIDS patients in hospital wards, did the rest of us follow their lead and calm down. But not the gay community. They couldn't calm down. They were dying.

Coleman was in the initial stages of having the virus and he tried to prevent it from becoming full-blown, but his illness came before groundbreaking and affordable medications. He wouldn't be one of the lucky ones.

A little over two years after being diagnosed, Coleman went back into the hospital to an isolated area. He died quietly on May 22, 1989. David, who had visited his dad every single day after school was not with him that one night. He was heartbroken. And when the hospital called him, he called me, and I went downstairs and woke Greg.

Coleman was gone. It was the saddest night we ever experienced. He and I floundered in our marriage, then floundered some more in our search. Our family loss is a wound that keeps reopening to this day. His sons only had him for a brief part of their lives. Within the month, Coleman was buried and Greg and I went to the service on the grassy hillside. Both boys were dearly loved by their dad, and they gave him their affection in return. David, who'd suffered with his dad for two years, cared for him, listened to him, and loved him, was too grief-stricken to attend.

"Couldn't you at least say the Our Father?" Sarah asked the officiating priest on the grassy knoll.

Evidently, being gay didn't warrant Mass or much more than a couple of Biblical phrases and sprinkling of holy water, but at least there was that. All of her prayers to help her son ended in disappointment with the Church, for not giving him what he needed, for not respecting him once he had passed. My tears welled up as I witnessed Sarah bury her precious son.

She and I corresponded once or twice, in an effort to make peace afterward. I apologized for any hurt I'd caused. One of her letters to me included a clipping from the *Chicago Tribune* about how lonely a woman felt in a marriage where her husband was gay.

"Is this why you wouldn't talk to me about what was wrong?" she wrote. I drove north to see her twice. We tried to only speak about the boys, not the marriage or Coleman—too painful, bitter, and difficult. Visiting was hard on both of us.

Coleman had so many good friends, some so fond of him that to blame me for the divorce that caused him pain, was part of their relationship. He and I ran out of the luxury that time could have given us to understand one another better. I loved Coleman too, more than any of them, but our partnership evolved under the weight of things too big. Friends miss him because he brought energy and excitement to ordinary things. My sons and I miss him because he was ours.

I don't remember anything in fairytales about the prince dying. It didn't seem fair, didn't seem like part of the story. I still have the Cinderella picture book from my youth, copyright 1950. It was published two years after my kindergarten debut on Mrs. Woodward's stage. I saw that dear woman in a nursing home a few years ago. She hadn't changed, still had her sweet, crinkly eyes, charming smile, lilting voice, and she said she remembered me. I quietly sang the Cinderella song from her operetta. She created a new one every year. I asked if she'd saved them. "Yes, they're in a box somewhere in my house."

My Cinderella book has changed. Like me, its edges have softened from the passage of time. No pages are missing. Elizabeth repaired its binding for me. I can still get flecks of gold on my finger when I rub along the decorative highlights that shine when the book gets tipped in the light.

"Is there a God?" both boys asked me one Christmas Eve under our tree.

"Yes, I think so," I said quietly. "I don't know for sure, but I think maybe there is. I don't know. Probably. I hope so. There's a lot of natural evidence."

I left the Catholic Church that I loved, not because I wanted to, but because I had to. I keep an eye on it, hoping that with credible changes, it will flourish, like any church that offers people nourishment.

After Coleman's death, I began to pray again for the courage to accept the things I couldn't control. On my knees next to my bed, my head buried in my hands, I've asked for understanding and strength to live my life honestly. I lost my religion then defined my own purpose. I try to control situations, my environment, and anything pertaining to social adjustment. I have friends, but I don't look for entanglements. Mostly, I keep a grip on my health, my home, and my bills. Though I lost out on having the kind of a marriage that would take my family the distance, surrounding us with security, and giving us the same holiday celebrations to match my family of origin, I try to focus on keeping a light heart and to find laughter wherever possible. I hang onto hope that there is a heaven. In the moments when I think there isn't, sadness nearly consumes me. And then I'm fine. I'd love to see my mom and dad again. Coleman and I could delight in our two grown sons. We were not a storybook family, but a dear family nonetheless. I was not a princess, but I never needed a crown.

Epilogue

I attended my convent's reunion in early 1990's. There were twenty-one girls in my class. Not all of them returned for the celebration. But of those who did, only five or six had remained in the convent. Nearly all were Academy girls. About thirty percent. The rest of us were in street clothes. Had I only known I wasn't the only misfit.

Coleman died May 22, 1989.

I never found a man to love completely.

As a single mother and grandmother, I have a full life and amazing experiences to remember.

My two sons are successful in their careers.

About the Author

Gretchen Grossman spent five years as a nun in a Catholic convent, which dramatically changed the course of her life. She's a mother, grandmother, and a retired teacher.

You can contact Gretchen at **info@gretchengrossman.com**.

To view photos, visit **http://www.gretchengrossman.com**.

Acknowledgements

Alice Peck has been my literary sculptor for five years. Initially, I sent her the equivalent of three books. She curtailed my need to tell absolutely everything that ever happened to me, and defined my story. She organized my ideas, gave me tips on how to write better, how to engage a reader, how to move the story along, and how to find my voice. She asked questions to help me dig a little deeper, to understand why I made certain life choices. She supported my efforts toward publishing with suggestions, information, links, names, and websites. Alice's talents and her artistry is sensitive and remarkable. She's a writer's dream of an editor, and very likely my guardian angel.

Valerie Romack worked with me online, a week at a time, back and forth, she answered every silly and important question. She literally mapped out the story on a spreadsheet. She taught me the importance of enriching my story with personal opinions. She is a very talented editor. Her insights were startling to me.

I consider myself very fortunate to have Duane Stapp use his sensibilities for the cover. His keen artistic eye gave a professional flair to the flat collage I sent him. He designed the interior and got it ready for publication. He can do anything. It would never have gotten done without him.

Additional Thanks

A coffee buddy, Duane McCoskey, set up my 21st century marketing strategy. Several friends read my earliest version and gave me valuable feedback and support. Helen Miller and Laura Bickers were my discerning eyes, reading the final version of the book looking for every kind of flub. Laura heard my worries and outlined my prologue and epilogue. She wondered, "What would this story have been like had Coleman written it?" "Much different, better," I said. My special thanks to: Donna Harris, Karen McCoskey, Levora Siefert, Carole Sarafian, Mary Lou Huhne, Sharon Ray, Yvonne Keck, Mary Greene, and my two longtime Chicago friends, Marie Gunther, Marie from the story, and Karen Kozica Cichon, Karen from the story. Other names in the book have been changed.

A final thank you to a man I serendipitously shared breakfast with in Caffe' BACI, on Michigan Avenue in Chicago. Were it not for him, I would never have begun my writing. "Madam, you have the next bestseller," said the Catholic university professor. Well, I couldn't deny myself that challenge. "I just have a unique story," I said. I thought I had an obligation to write something down. Thank you, Ahmed. You helped me settle things and find peace.

WITHDRAWN

Made in the USA
San Bernardino, CA
30 May 2014